TWO BILLION EYES

Also by Ying Zhu

Chinese Cinema During the Era of Reform:
The Ingenuity of the System (2003)

Television in Post-Reform China:
Serial Dramas, Confucian Leadership
and the Global Television Market (2008)

TWO BILLION EYES

The Story of China Central Television

Ying Zhu

Requests for permission to reproduce selections from this book should be mailed to:
Permissions Department, The New Press, 38 Greene Street, New York, NY 10013.

Published in the United States by The New Press, New York, 2012
Distributed by Perseus Distribution

LIBRARY OF CONGRESS CATALOGING-IN-PUBLICATION DATA

Zhu, Ying, 1965–
   Two billion eyes : the story of China Central Television / Ying Zhu.
      p.   cm.
   Includes bibliographical references and index.
   ISBN 978-1-59558-464-9 (hc. : alk. paper)   1. Zhong yang dian shi tai (Beijing, China)
2. Television broadcasting—China.   3. Television broadcasting policy—China.   I. Title.
PN1992.3.C6Z484 2012
384.55'4550951—dc23   2012010091

Now in its twentieth year, The New Press publishes books that promote and enrich public discussion
and understanding of the issues vital to our democracy and to a more equitable world. These
books are made possible by the enthusiasm of our readers; the support of a committed group of
donors, large and small; the collaboration of our many partners in the independent media and the
not-for-profit sector; booksellers, who often hand-sell New Press books; librarians; and above all by
our authors.

www.thenewpress.com

Composition by dix!
This book was set in Minion

Printed in the United States of America

10 9 8 7 6 5 4 3 2 1

To my family

CONTENTS

ACKNOWLEDGMENTS

When approached to write a book on China Central Television, I thought the idea intriguing but challenging. Access would be one formidable obstacle. To this end, several prominent individuals who wish to remain anonymous came to my aid. My first thank-you goes to them. Further along, Professor Lu Xinyu of Fudan University, Professor Lei Jianjun of Tsinghua University, and Professor Huang Shixian of Beijing Film Academy provided a road map as I navigated the complex terrain of CCTV. Initial field research for the book was done in China in the summer of 2008, courtesy of an American Council of Learned Societies Fellowship, which was jointly funded by the National Endowment for the Humanities. I wish to mention that an NEH fellowship in 2006 made it possible for me to initiate my research on Chinese television, which eventually led to this book. Frances Hisgen, my then nine-year-old daughter, was a loyal companion during our chaotic six-month sojourn in Beijing. Her intellectual curiosity and moral compass kept me on my toes. A PSC-CUNY Research Award provided funding for my additional trips to Beijing, on one of which I was joined by John Jirik, a fellow traveler who accompanied me to a couple of interviews and who graciously shared with me his solo interview with Jiang Heping. I wish to thank all the CCTV practitioners with whom I had the pleasure of engaging in candid dialogue about China and Chinese media. My hearty appreciation goes to Jason Ng, my editor at The New Press, who initiated this book and provided thoughtful feedback and thorough editing. Together with Jason's enthusiasm and dedication, I am grateful for the patience and faith of Marc Favreau, The New Press's editorial director, who tolerated a prolonged process as I struggled to bring the book to its completion. Sarah Fan's efficiency during the production process prevented further delay. Julie McCarroll, the publicity director at The New Press, has been instrumental in bringing this book to wide attention. The book benefited from Bruce Robinson's editorial and intellectual inputs during the early stage of writing and from Michael Keane's efficiency for "tidying up" during the final stage of writing. Both Bruce and Michael generously shared with me their ideas, phrases, and passages, some of which I shamelessly and seamlessly blended into this book. I thank Stanley Rosen and Stephanie Donald for being my cheerleaders on various fronts. My brief acknowledgment here does not pretend to do justice to all the individuals whose contributions made this book possible.

TWO BILLION EYES

INTRODUCTION

Just before 2:30 P.M. local time on May 12, 2008, an earthquake measuring 8 on the Richter scale hit Sichuan Province. I was alone in my Beijing apartment that afternoon and felt a slight shake. To confirm that I wasn't imagining things, I called a friend to ask if she felt anything—I wasn't. In another day and age, my next response might have been to head to the street and await instructions, but today, information comes much faster online, and it was there that I read the initial announcements about the earthquake. Another friend phoned to check in and tell me to tune in to China Central Television, which was reporting on the disaster with a rolling ticker. In fact, CCTV began to broadcast news of the earthquake via rolling tickers within minutes of the quake, and by 3 P.M. it had reporters on the air with updates. By 3:20 P.M., the CCTV News Channel had prepared a special program, *Exclusive Reports on Sichuan*.

The swift media response was striking. In the past the Chinese media had generally shied away from instant coverage of natural disasters. Domestic disasters of any sort were considered too hot to handle without instruction from the state and could harm the national image. Disaster reporting had gradually become less of a taboo from the 1990s forward, yet up until the Sichuan earthquake, CCTV did not aim to be the fastest; instead it vowed to be "the most correct" in its coverage of such events. The network's flagship News Channel, CCTV's version of CNN, was established in May 2003 in response to complaints about the Chinese media's cover-up of the SARS epidemic. The News Channel started to offer a state-sanctioned release of SARS-related news bulletins, including information concerning prevention and treatment of SARS. Although envisioned partly as a platform for live coverage, the News Channel's reporting on SARS was tentative and measured, following strict government guidelines, and in the years after, it continued the trend by confining its live reports mainly to planned events rather than breaking news. But things were dramatically different this time. Instead of waiting for guidance from above on how to report the earthquake, Chinese media from across the country, including CCTV's News Channel, took advantage of the scale of the disaster—this would be much harder to hide than an outbreak of a mysterious disease—and allowed journalistic logic to prevail over party logic.

The speed and initial frankness of Chinese media reports from Sichuan were unprecedented, surprising everyone both at home and around the world. This surprise was especially keen in light of the fact that during the run-up to the Olympics, which opened a few months later in Beijing, the Chinese media had been tightly controlled and packaged by the government. The earthquake coverage was instantly recognized as a milestone in Chinese journalism and disaster reporting, and for a moment, the Chinese media appeared to break free of their assumed propaganda role.

In the immediate chaos of the quake, the Propaganda Department of the Communist Party of China (CCP) either recycled outdated control orders or was too rushed to issue detailed instructions on appropriate news coverage. Leaked reports suggested that the Propaganda Department was initially shocked and disoriented, and it was only hours later that an order was issued to Chinese news organizations not to send reporters to the scene, but instead to use only information released by either CCTV or the Xinhua News Agency, the official press agency of the state.[1] Because of this pronouncement, for the next three to four days CCTV and Xinhua faced little competition from other news organizations and CCTV's news crews were free to act according to their professional ambitions and the commercial demands of their trade. Here at last was a chance to raise the network's global profile, the epochal opportunity every globe-trotting media organization dreamed of, akin to the first Gulf War for CNN and the Iraq War (and later the Arab Spring) for Al Jazeera. It was a chance, too, of course, to restore the credibility of Chinese television news at home and to further media reform. And it appeared to have worked spectacularly: according to research published in 2008, 1.03 billion people tuned in to CCTV's saturation quake coverage between May 12 and May 21. On May 18, CCTV's share of the viewing audience peaked at 47.38 percent.[2]

In this initial phase, the Chinese media coverage was open and free, looking much like Western media coverage. Indeed, Western media outlets themselves made extensive use of Chinese reports, and journalists everywhere applauded those responsible. The Sichuan earthquake revealed a Chinese media ready and able to work to international standards, when free to follow their own instincts.

It was a crowning achievement for a network frequently dismissed as propaganda by those abroad and suffering much derision by its own citizens—"Hee-Hee-TV," as Chinese netizens call it. Since its founding in 1958, CCTV has sought to become the respected source for Chinese news and culture but has been encumbered—some would say hobbled—by a secondary mission: mouthpiece of the state. Then, as reform since the 1980s ushered in a market economy, the network must also seek to maximize its profit share by producing and scheduling programs of popular appeal, which introduces the notion of "public interest." These triple goals, at times competing and at others compatible, are at the core of what make CCTV so intriguing.

What's the Point? Why CCTV?

In a world vastly influenced by what social scientists refer to as a "globalized climate," we have extensively mapped and analyzed our own media as contributors to global social change. We have even started to recognize the growing importance of foreign media. But one of the most powerful media systems operating in the world today, China Central Television, remains little known; it continues to be largely opaque to international observers and equally mysterious for many Chinese. It is seen as a symbol of a repressive authoritarian system by Westerners and a sign of paternalistic control by Chinese people at home.

Over the past three decades, China has traded Mao for markets, opened most of its closed doors, and transformed with startling speed from third world straggler to superpower-in-training. After Mao's death in 1976, Deng Xiaoping rose to power and initiated a series of radical economic reforms that effectively brought an end to the country's revolutionary era. China was reopened to foreign trade and investment, and the socialist economy of mainly state-owned enterprises and state-directed production was converted in stages to a capitalist economy of mainly private enterprises operating in commercial markets. Furious economic development followed and continues apace, unaccompanied by political reform. Deng coined this "socialism with Chinese characteristics."

Books have been written about how popular culture, including television, is powerfully involved in this radical post-Mao reformation, but few deal extensively with CCTV, China's only national television network. Yet in just two decades CCTV has grown from a primitive channel of state-funded polemic drudgery to an aspiring player in China's newly commercialized media industries—at the behest of the state, of course.

CCTV engages the world's biggest audience as a critical instrument of state control, driving popular consciousness of news and events and managing messages in popular entertainment. CCTV's national monopoly is facilitated by China's four-tier television structure, which has TV stations set up at the national, provincial, county, and city levels. Both national and local regulators operate their own TV stations and serve audiences within their own administrative boundaries. The central government oversees CCTV via two interlocking systems, the ideological system of the party's Propaganda Department, which provides mostly guidelines and thought directives, and the administrative system of the State Administration of Radio, Film, and Television (SARFT), which performs the actual daily oversight, including censorship of sensitive content. Under a "must carry" rule, provincial, regional, and county-based stations are required to carry CCTV's programs, guaranteeing the network's nationwide coverage. CCTV is also granted exclusive coverage rights to major national and international events, and the CCP regularly leaks exclusive information to CCTV, making it the go-to source for insight on the party.

CCTV began to experiment with television advertisements in 1979, following the state's marketization directive. By now the network is financed entirely as a commercial operation, with much greater operational autonomy than before. But the state continues to exercise ideological and personnel oversight, and the network must turn over part of its revenue to SARFT. This means that the regulatory authority is economically "affiliated" with the broadcasters that it regulates. Thus, instead of the classical antagonism between the party line (ideology) and the bottom line (economy), the state and the media practitioners have mostly moved forward hand in hand in their common pursuit of profit. This alliance has functioned to advance mainstream television shows that are both ideologically inoffensive and commercially successful, with CCTV often required to deliver both at once.

CCTV faces growing competition at home from major provincial television operators less enthusiastically subservient to the state (notably in Hunan, Shanghai, and Guangdong) and from foreign channels and programming. Indeed, most provincial broadcasters have managed to extend their regional reach via independent satellite and cable distribution deals with other provincial broadcasters. Meanwhile, CCTV is up against—if only indirectly at the moment due to protective state policies—programming from global players such as Time Warner's CNN, News Corporation's Fox News, the BBC, and Al Jazeera, none of which is encumbered with the same burden of political water carrying. The problems and issues that CCTV faces at home, and those that it might introduce to the global media environment, are of imminent relevance to the media watchers in the United States and elsewhere.

If CCTV is unique among media operators for its direct connection to a superpower state, its global expansion comes at a moment when the extent of *indirect* connections between commerce and politics in the world's leading media operations is under close scrutiny. In the United States, for instance, media outlets have consolidated into a few major conglomerates. As noted media scholar Robert McChesney charges, these behemoths, beholden to shareholders and myriad interests, are conservative by nature, with too much invested in the status quo to risk upsetting consumers and regulators.[3] While the control mechanism varies, issues of free and balanced media coverage apply to media in both developed and developing nations and regions. As the popular faith in the structural and professional superiority of Western media practice faces crisis, what might be the ramifications of an entry into the global media system of a state-controlled commercial enterprise such as CCTV?

After three decades of economic reform, political reform has not yet come to China, but political evolution has. Still autocratic in form, China's polity has become a "deliberative autocracy" in practice—"deliberative" because changes in the society accrued from China's rapid development and its reengagement with the outside world have produced a quasi-public sphere that compels the state to actively cultivate and incorporate public opinion into a more overtly deliberative policy-making process. With no regular means of popular participation in Chinese politics, CCTV now sits at the intersection of official discourse and popular discourse, constituting a critical site of negotiation between the two.

The state continues to manage CCTV as an agent of ideological control, but the game has changed. Mao began his revolution with rhetorical paeans to the masses. The masses of Mao's time were poor, unsophisticated, shut off from the world, and entirely at the mercy of a hyperbureaucratic, authoritarian state. That image has been shattered in post-Mao China by the twin detonation of economic development and globalization. China's masses, CCTV's audience, are now better off, better educated, and much more aware of their own world and the world outside China. No longer helpless, isolated masses, they are now critical masses—"critical" to the tenure of a one-party state that is no longer in a position to easily put down a popular rebellion by force; "critical" in the sense that they see rampant official corruption, a deteriorating environment, and grave class disparities and expect the government to act; and "critical" in the sense of constituting *potential* publics—networks of passively associated audiences and information consumers who may, in a moment, achieve a critical mass of shared outrage or excitement over some event that transforms passive association into active participation in anything from an online debate to a street-level demonstration or an extended political movement. The taxicab labor strike in Chongqing in November 2008, the village protests in the aftermath of the Sichuan earthquake over unsafe school buildings that caused the needless deaths of thousands of students, and the widespread anti-Western media campaign over the slippery reportage of Tibetan riots in spring 2008 are three cases in point. This conception of China's newly critical masses as constitutive of a quasi-public sphere, the idea that a newly dual-purposed CCTV could operate as a central conduit through which the state speaks to the public and the public speaks back, and the proposition that this is a central dynamic of China's changing state-society relationship are a few of the themes that this book seeks to explore in the hope that this can contribute to our understanding of media and society in China.

As China reforms itself and emerges as a nouveau superpower, it is defining a new approach to politics, power, and national development, a hybrid model that combines an authoritarian state with a market economy, which defies the notion that capitalism is naturally linked to a democratic political system. China has cherry-picked among market mechanisms, Confucian ideals, and socialist principles to pursue a hybrid course of development that has so far kept the one-party state entrenched and the masses mostly pleased with their improving living conditions and the invigorating spectacle of China's rise in the world. According to policy makers and proud citizens alike, China is going its own way, not bending to external pressure, and leading the world by its innovative example. Even George Soros, the anticommunism crusader, marveled at China's spectacular economic performance. In a comment regarding the political gridlock in America, Soros said, "Today China has not only a more vigorous economy, but actually a better functioning government than the United States."[4] On external matters, though, Soros implored the Chinese state to look beyond its own interests and to "accept responsibility for world order and the interests of other people as well."[5] Nevertheless, the spectacle of China's rising via a hybrid "Chinese model," one comprised of seemingly contradictory forces (communism vs. capitalism, Confucianism vs. individualism, tradition vs. modernity), is a point of national pride.

China's national TV network, CCTV, is an example of this hybrid experiment, a reflection of the untested path China is taking on its way to global superpowerdom. This book considers how, as a state-controlled yet commercially operated entity, CCTV has become the very archetype of the Chinese model. The ultimate goal of this book is to bring media to the center of our thinking about China's ongoing transformation. Thus, CCTV is one place we can turn to as we attempt to make sense, at least from the perspective of media and society, of China's transformation and its global ramifications.

From the perspective of the state, as Mark Leonard observes, "soft power" has been one of the hottest buzzwords in China. Soft power is the capability to persuade others to desire what you desire. It depends neither on economic carrots nor on political sticks, but rather on the attractiveness of your culture and ideas, your legitimacy in the eyes of others, and your ability to set the rules in international organizations.[6] To this end, China is busy cultivating a benevolent image via PR campaigns utilizing modern communication strategies.[7] Known media personalities now function as top advisers to governing bodies of the Chinese state's communication and media policy. This soft-power strategy of converting the skeptical not via force but via attractive ideas applies to both domestic and international viewers. Perceived openness and transparency are keys to successful soft power.

Despite the growing popularity of the Internet, television continues to lead the way in delivering these messages—and, increasingly, in receiving feedback from the public as well. Television penetration is effectively 100 percent; channels have proliferated to the point that urban viewers typically have access to thirty to fifty channels,[8] and viewers watch an average of three hours per day.[9] Although educated elites have increasingly turned to the Internet for information, CCTV is still the main source of news and information for most mainland Chinese. With its new commercial imperative in place, CCTV is a servant of popular taste and collective judgment about the network's credibility and appeal competes with a vast array of alternative sources of information and entertainment. It is in this context that CCTV could function as a site of exchange between official and public discourse. The burden of political, financial, and professional water carrying inevitably falls upon the people who work at CCTV.

The CCTV Practitioners

Beijing's Chaoyang District is the archetype of China 2.0, a place where media, money, communications, and politics blend seamlessly. More than 150 foreign embassies and the branch headquarters of two-thirds of the world's top five hundred companies crowd into this busy central business district. The "central" applies not only to its place within Beijing: this is, in many ways, the central business district of China as a whole in the twenty-first century.

The landscape of wide streets, busy ring roads, and bustling subway stations fills with noisy activity: people and cars provide an ever-present urban soundscape to match the rapid development. Here is where iconic architectural structures compete for attention amid Beijing's equally famed pollution. Chaoyang's constructions include the National Theatre for the Performing Arts, affectionately called the "Egg"; the National Stadium, known as the "Bird's Nest"; and the new CCTV building, humorously referred to by locals as *da kucha*, "the big underpants," for its curious twin 230-meter-tall towers connected in the air by an 80-meter-long stretch of administrative offices. The stunning Rem Koolhaas–designed tower is meant to project a vision of Chinese soft power for the coming century, one that is an intentional departure from the old CCTV—a monolithic institutional construction erected in the 1990s in the western district of Beijing responsible for the best and worst media campaigns of the past thirty years.

Despite the cutting-edge new building, CCTV is *still* the mouthpiece of the CCP, a political institution with roots in Marxist-Leninism, albeit with a modern capitalist twist. Today's CCTV is a mix of new and old ideas, youth and experience, and modern management and classical bureaucracy, as well as innovation and inertia. Several generations of talents work together, offering expertise in propaganda and public relations as well as programs of enlightenment, entertainment, and some serious journalism.

It is these practitioners at CCTV who make it possible for the once exclusively party organ to perform a civic function. The CCTV practitioners perform their jobs with purpose, conviction, and skill, all in the name of professionalism. The choices they make on a daily basis have a cumulative effect on how CCTV functions. To understand it, one must go directly inside: this book is thus also about those who work at CCTV. It is an account of experiences, reflections, and outlooks told by them. It is a story of their frustrations, aspirations, satisfactions, defeats, and all of what matters to them.

It is true that CCTV is still heavily controlled by the state and that it suffers from a severe reputation problem, an issue acknowledged by all of the CCTV employees I interviewed. A few go so far as to speak of the network and their colleagues with disdain, claiming that they don't watch CCTV programming at all and that they find news from foreign outlets or the Internet more reliable. Speaking of the Internet, jokes ridiculing CCTV are rampant in online circulation, so much so that people actually cheered when the new CCTV building caught on fire in 2009. Photos and videos were gleefully shared online, with the hilarious punch line being that CCTV could not even mention the fire in its own daily news reports.

Will CCTV ever be able to shake off its legacy as a propaganda machine, even as its practitioners strive to function as a true conduit of "negotiation" in the newly emerged civic exchange between the state and the society? The most pressing issue at CCTV that I detected over the course of my interviews was how the network planned on balancing the commercial, the political, and the professional imperatives of running a state media organization. The pressures of generating revenue alongside conforming politically are frequently at odds with media practitioners' sense of duty associated with watchdog journalism and cultural enlightenment. How do these CCTV employees cope with both the daily and long-term struggles of these seemingly Sisyphean tasks?

"Thick description" is the late cultural anthropologist Clifford Geertz's term for the kind of historical, social, and personal contexts that make unfamiliar societies and behavior meaningful to outsiders. It is achieved by both traditional research and living among one's subjects for an extended period. This book organizes its narrative around a "thick description" of CCTV. To this end, it goes right to the people whose work directly and indirectly shapes the course of CCTV. Through extensive interviews, the book reveals the personal stories behind CCTV's storytellers themselves. The first round of interviews in 2008 was done at a time when the Olympics and the Sichuan earthquake swarmed around me. The second round was conducted in the summer of 2009, when I went back to Beijing for field research. The interviews purposefully linked the transformation of CCTV to China's gathering weight in the world, to all things positive and negative that Western readers might enjoy fretting about, and to CCTV's place in China's domestic media structure and its potential global presence.

I hope this look at CCTV's inner workings sheds new light on China's rapidly evolving state and its relationship with the Chinese society. While no formal means of popular participation in national Chinese politics exists yet, there is nonetheless an emerging dynamic of informal negotiation carried out between the citizenry and its handlers and, crucially, within CCTV among various power dynamics. CCTV provides a window through which the evolution of China's state-society relations can be glimpsed. The book treats CCTV not only as a media institution but also as a quasi-institutional conduit of civil discourse performed by its boundary-breaking practitioners in an emerging model of state-society relations. On the path toward experimenting with and perfecting a hybrid model of state-run and commercially independent media practice, recriminations and misgivings as well as achievement and worthy speculations abound. This is the story of CCTV.

1

TELEVISION AS CULTURAL CONTROL IN CHINA

As the story goes, on July 16, 1985, a morning phone call summoned Yang Weiguang, vice president of the Central People's Broadcasting Station, to the office of the deputy head of the Ministry of Radio, Film, and Television (MRFT, the precursor to SARFT), Hao Pingnan.[1] Hao informed Yang that he would be reassigned as vice president and deputy editor in chief of China Central Television. Yang was incredulous. Leaving twenty-four years of service at the national radio station for uncharted territory at the age of forty-nine would be no small challenge. The next morning, he anxiously pulled the MRFT chief aside, pleading to stay on at the radio station. His wish was not granted—Yang was dispatched to CCTV to lead its News Division. Just six years later, in December 1991, he was appointed president and tasked with overseeing the first decade of CCTV's transformation from state-funded proselytizer to commercial broadcaster.

Despite arriving at CCTV trailing a professional provenance of decidedly doctrinaire training and experience, Yang would eventually prove to be an innovator. A graduate in 1961 of the first journalism department in China at Renmin (People's) University,[2] Yang immediately took a position at the national radio station. Among twenty-eight graduates that year, he was one of seven who were allowed to stay in Beijing. In those early years leading up to the Cultural Revolution, his peasant family background no doubt helped him secure a steady position at Central People's Broadcasting Station, where he worked until his reassignment to the national television station. From central training, to central radio, and on to central television, he imbibed and embodied journalism according to Mao, making him a safe choice to lead CCTV when the party embarked on its radical media reform.

Yang Weiguang left his CCTV post in February 1999, three years past the typical retirement age of sixty. Today, many seasoned CCTV employees still consider the ten years of Yang's management CCTV's best days. When I talked to people in the spring of 2008, fond memories about Yang abounded. He oversaw a period of unsurpassed productivity and innovation, and numerous programs, such as the enterprising current affairs programs *Focus* and *Oriental Horizon* and the newsmagazine *News Probe*, were introduced in an effort to break CCTV's staid image. Documentary filmmaker Xia Jun, a CCTV producer under Yang, reminisced about how Yang skillfully navigated the competing interests at the station: "Yang was one of a kind, someone who cares only about building a top-rate media enterprise. Yang was motivated by his desire to advance CCTV. This, together with his superb individual quality, wisdom, dynamism, and his ability to motivate other people for the good of CCTV, was what made his time the golden era of CCTV." Yang's decade at CCTV was unquestionably the network's high point in terms of party approval, market position, and public stature. And though he was no longer the president of CCTV, Yang remained a formidable force in the industry and continued to be consulted on policy issues. At the time of our interview in the summer of 2008, he still held the title of honorary chairman of the Chinese TV Artist Association, a trade union formed in May 1985.

But if he'd had his way in 1985, none of this would have come to pass. Indeed, Yang loved his radio days, so much so that he was reluctant to leave: "I had worked in radio for a long time, working my way up from a journalist to editor, division chief, director, and then president. Radio was my world. Television was relatively new at the time and did not have the same cachet as radio. All the talents were in radio."

Interviewing Yang triggered my own reflections on the changes taking place in Chinese society and brought up my own memories of growing up listening to radio back in a time when television was still mostly just fantasy.

Radio had diligently served the CCP and the party-state since its origins during the revolution in Yan'an Province in the early 1940s. During Mao's era, radio connected China's rural masses to the state through a pervasive system of wired loudspeakers installed in schools, on army bases, and in other public spaces. These were part of the fabric of my generation's childhood. Growing up in a large apartment complex that belonged to my parents' work unit, I woke up every morning at 6 A.M. to the news and revolutionary songs on China National Radio blasted over loudspeakers mounted under a roof corner of each apartment building. In addition to delivering party directives and revolutionary songs and music, radio programs via loudspeakers set the daily rhythm for us. The company's loudspeakers further inserted announcements about open-air movies, special performances, and holiday schedules, and information about last-minute meetings, which meant that parents would be frequently away from home to study new party directives, leaving us latchkey kids to entertain ourselves. Not much room for "tiger moms."

The mission of radio during Mao's era was simple and effective: propagate the party line and its ideology of mass mobilization, class struggle, thought reform, and continuous revolution—essentially, promote every aspect of the greatest social engineering show on earth, designed literally to change people's minds about how to live and co-exist. No doubt, the ubiquity of radio transmission aided considerably in the conversion of the masses to their patriotic role.

From the late 1950s, as China launched its Great Leap Forward, a range of other media, from newspapers to posters to live theater and film, thrived, as did television, which debuted in 1958 when Beijing Television was founded. From 1958 to the late 1970s, Beijing TV served the party by advocating continuous political movements from the Anti-Rightist Campaign of 1958 to the Great Leap Forward campaign of 1959, and finally to the 1966–76 Cultural Revolution. Beijing TV was renamed China Central Television in 1978, the year China ushered in an era of economic reform.

Even with an established national television station, up until well into the 1970s, TV was still not a popular medium. China lagged behind in the adoption of television sets because of the enormous poverty among its mostly rural population, which was exacerbated by the economic disaster of the Great Leap Forward (1958–61) and the chaos inflicted on cultural production during the Cultural Revolution. Television development only really took off in the 1980s following a series of decisions to boost the production of television sets and expand the number of channels and broadcast hours. It wouldn't be until the early 1990s when television finally eclipsed radio as the most important mass medium in China.[3] When it did, the party's leaders had a number of ways to utilize this new tool. Yang's move from radio to television was a natural progression despite his initial misgivings: it echoed the impetus for reform, modernization, and nation building of the new China under Deng Xiaoping. This was probably what the ministry had in mind when he was reassigned—Yang would be the person to carry the central mouthpiece function from one medium to the next.

The Development of an Interventionist Cultural-Media Policy

Every government has its own ideas about the role of media in society and how best to regulate it in order to achieve a proper balance of economic, social, and cultural forces. In the West, cultural policy ostensibly aims to promote the broadest possible "marketplace of ideas" and facilitate the national ideal of an informed and intelligent public as the foundation of democratic government. This basic ideal has been a constant in American cultural policy. While such democratic rationales for cultural policy underwite Western liberalism, actual cultural production is not free of policy or, for that matter, government intervention.

Cultural policy in the People's Republic has been interventionist for several decades—the constant being the subservience of art to politics. However, the goals and methods of cultural (and media) policy have changed in tandem with distinct periods in China's political development. PRC cultural policy is founded on principles formulated by Mao in his "Talks on Literature and Art," delivered in the caves of Yan'an (headquarters of the revolution) in 1942, which called for a "didactic, propagandistic art for the masses."[4] Richard Kraus notes that "the new state created a set of institutions that hired more artists in more organizations, but produced less art with less variety."[5] And as George Semsel suggests, this notion is rooted in a longer tradition: "Chinese aesthetics places emphasis on the unity of beauty and kindness—relating the appreciation of the beautiful with moral and ethical conduct. For centuries the ideas that 'literature expresses ideology' and 'art contains morality and ethics' dominated the ancient theories of literature and art. The establishment of film as a tool for political education probably resulted from the culture that formed when changes in Chinese society took the political standard as its essence."[6]

This is not to establish a hoary philosophical ideal—Chinese aesthetics—as an inalterable stamp on the soul of the nation, but rather to acknowledge a greater relative emphasis, compared to Western traditions of art as critical vanguard, on the responsibility of art in the normalization of society: in other words, art teaches moral lessons rather than testing boundaries. The subservience of the media to politics remains part of China's official ideology, wherein regulating art and entertainment to conform to and strengthen the moral and ethical fabric is the norm.

Today, cultural policy in the post-Mao reform era might have moved away from overtly didactic propaganda, but the notion that literature and art must serve the people endures as a first principle, reinforced by successive Chinese leaders, from Deng Xiaoping to Jiang Zemin, Hu Jintao, and, very likely, the upcoming new leader Xi Jinping. In January 2012, a new round of crackdowns on racy entertainment programs on prime-time Chinese television prompted Western media analysts to speculate about China's tightening cultural control. The cycle of tightening and loosening is nothing new in China; as the

Chinese put it, "For every measure from the top, there are strategies to side-step it."

In *Marketing Dictatorship*, Anne-Marie Brady describes the evolution of Chinese propaganda theory in the 1980s and early 1990s, which proceeded through fits and starts until it was settled, along with broader questions about China's developmental course following Deng Xiaoping's "southern tour."[7] With the party leadership still unsettled in the wake of 1989's Tiananmen protests and with some conservatives visibly doubting the reform agenda, Deng went on the road in the spring of 1992 to sell his market reform agenda, which was at the time under attack by archconservatives. Traveling from the southern province of Guangdong to Shanghai, he made a series of speeches reasserting the necessity of the "open door" policy and economic liberalism. Then president Jiang Zemin eventually fell in behind Deng's vision, and the reform era rolled forward, including transformations to the party's approach to media and communications, which moved from a Leninist model that functioned as a "tool of mass propaganda and agitation" to a more "public relations" style that was suited to "ruling by popular consent."[8]

In 2000 Jiang embarked on a southern tour of his own, during which he added his own enumerated theory to the party platform, the Three Represents. The Three Represents are less significant for their particular content, which is hazy party-speak, and more for their titular emphasis on representation, which suggests a government awareness of the changing basis of its legitimacy, thus indicating a shift toward a model of gradually increasing dependence on popular approval.

> The Party's greatest political strength is that we have maintained close ties with the masses, and the greatest danger since assuming political power has lain in the possibility of being estranged from them. Whether the line, principles and policies the Party formulates conform to the fundamental interests of the overwhelming majority of the people must be taken as the highest criterion for judging them, and *whether the people are satisfied with and agree with* them must be taken as their basis and goal. Our cadres must maintain the work style and the way of thinking of "from the masses, to the masses." They must be concerned about the people's hardships, *listen to their opinions* and protect their interests.[9]

The Three Represents were eventually replaced by the Harmonious Society, introduced by the new administration, led by Hu Jintao, during the 2005 National People's Congress. Hu's new guiding model was a concerted effort to shift China's focus from economic growth to a more traditional emphasis on societal balance and harmony across all fronts, including art, literature, culture, media, and education.[10] After Hu and other party leaders, including the former propaganda czar Li Changchun, met with 450 media chiefs at the Great Hall of the People in October 2006 to reinforce the "harmonious society message,"[11] Chinese television responded by embedding its programs with themes promoting sage leadership, a more egalitarian distribution of income, community harmony, and state benevolence.

The domestically targeted "Harmonious Society" slogan has in recent years been coupled with "going out" (*zou chuqu*) and the promotion of China's soft power globally. The attention now accorded to soft power is intended to repair the country's tarnished international image, which remains, for the most part, negative.[12] To raise China's global profile and improve its image abroad, a new Office of Public Diplomacy has been established under the Foreign Ministry. Meanwhile the State Council Information Office coordinated with China's media organizations to "go out" and establish a global foothold. Reportedly the Chinese government invested US$8.7 billion in 2009–10[13] in China's four major state-run media organizations: China Central Television, China Radio International, Xinhua News Agency, and the *China Daily* newspaper. The investment was intended to give the major party organs a design makeover and expansion of capabilities to lessen the appearance of propaganda—so long as one didn't know where the four were getting their money. Xinhua TV now operates a twenty-four-hour News Channel imitative of Al Jazeera, and CCTV News is poised to compete with CNN and the BBC, broadcasting in five languages with a global audience of about 125 million.[14]

Transparency and the Right to Know: The Earthquake Coverage

In the initial days following the Sichuan earthquake, the government's investment in "going out" seemed to be paying off. After recovering from its initial shock, the party seized the opportunity opened up by the global outpouring of sympathy and the extraordinary performance of Chinese media professionals to actively work on reconstructing its image, which was tarnished at the time by the negative international media coverage regarding its treatment of Tibetan protesters in the run-up to the Olympics. The Hu Jintao administration made a practical and diplomatic decision to accept foreign assistance, and, in pointed contrast to the foreign media exclusion from Tibet, allowed reporting in Sichuan by both foreign and domestic journalists almost without restrictions. As a result, state-run media like CCTV no longer enjoyed the exclusive access they had had for the previous four days. More than 550 journalists, including 300 foreigners from 114 overseas news outlets, swarmed into the area.

Following this lead, CCP propaganda chief Li Changchun called CCTV president Zhao Huayong on May 14. While speaking highly of CCTV's live coverage, he also made several detailed requests about how to improve the coverage going forward. On May 17, Li visited CCTV to give further instruction and encouragement: "Your work won great appreciation from the Party and the State Council, setting up a great example for the whole nation and winning praise from the international community. You have proved to be politically trustworthy, professionally capable, highly disciplined, and hard working." [15] Whether it was intentional or not, from the night of Li's visit onward, the character of CCTV's coverage began to subtly change. From the free-flowing, broad-ranging reports of its early quake coverage, CCTV now began to focus more narrowly on stories about "heroes" and the achievements of official disaster-relief efforts at all levels; the *National News Bulletin* aired an item called "Heroes in the Disaster," and other similar programs would follow across the network. On the first and second of June, Li visited reporters in Sichuan and actively encouraged this focus, and CCTV easily reverted to its customary mouthpiece mode.

Perhaps the most tragic aspect of the earthquake was its timing in the middle of the afternoon, when many schoolchildren were still in class. School buildings proved particularly vulnerable, collapsing like houses of multiton playing cards on top of thousands of students. Inadequate building codes, poor enforcement of the standards, and outright corruption were blamed in criticisms that ran rampant on the Internet but appeared nowhere on CCTV. Concerned netizens voiced their opinions on a number of issues, including the distribution of relief funds and conflicts of interests between local officials and relief workers, and they urgently called for an investigation into why so many schools collapsed. Although the state eventually acknowledged that a rush to build new schools during the country's economic boom might have led to shoddy construction that resulted in the deaths of thousands of students during the earthquake, Internet complaints and appeals for punitive measures were carefully filtered out. CCTV, for its part, avoided covering the topic of school-building collapse from the angle of corruption, as images of death and anger over shoddy school construction were censored from its news coverage.

Despite the criticism from domestic netizens on its muted coverage of school-building collapses, CCTV's earthquake reporting did help to repair both its own image and the government's in the run-up to the Olympics. CCTV's coverage appeared to open a window onto the workings and advantages of China's powerful central leadership, showing the swift coordination of relief efforts bringing together the political leadership, the army, and the whole society in a way that would hardly be possible in Western democracies. The international community applauded the effort and the appearance of increased openness. To the world outside, CCTV's quake coverage succeeded as a demonstration of soft power. Some Chinese media watchers, meanwhile, commented on their leaders' more professional manner in front of the camera, suggesting that Chinese leaders were coming to understand the idea of "governing with the news," a concept from American political scientist Timothy Cook's book of the same name. Cook argues that the American news media depend so heavily on government press releases for their political reporting that they are effectively servants of a government-authorized version of the news, all without the necessity of a propaganda department telling them what to do. That isn't quite what happened with the earthquake story, but the international reception of the quake coverage surely did alert China's leaders to the possibility that a more flexible kind of media oversight might increase the country's soft power.

The Chinese government and media had learned their lessons from the disastrous SARS cover-up of 2003, which caused citizens to turn away from the state-run media in anger and seek out alternative and overseas news sources: too much information management (that is, censorship) could turn a natural disaster into a credibility crisis. CCTV's first SARS report did not come until more than three months after the first confirmed cases in November 2002, and the media blackout was finally broken only after a whistle-blower's report was leaked and translated to *Time* magazine's website in April. A flood of new reporting on SARS followed, but very little of it was critical of the government's handling of the epidemic. Out of forty-five CCTV reports on SARS, only three contained any faultfinding commentary, and in each case the criticism was leveled at private citizens—conniving individuals who tried to exploit and profit from needlessly frightened villagers. As quoted by Zhang Xiaoling, CCTV's pro-government SARS coverage led Propaganda Department head Liu Yunshan to declare, "CCTV is a team capable of fighting in the war against SARS; it is an excellent team of journalists, a reliable team of the party."[16]

Since then, Chinese policy makers have learned their lessons and are now more proactive in exerting their voices—and, by extension, allowing the media to exert their own—in disaster coverage. Handbooks have since been written mandating that public officers should reach out to journalists "as soon as possible and provide them with rich enough and updated information" so as to "prevent journalists from looking for other sources."[17] This focus on effective communication has become a mantra for the CCP. Communication experts have replaced engineers of the previous generation as China's new leadership. According to a report, "seventeen out of the 31 provincial secretary-generals have previously worked at the party's information office."[18] Transparency and proactive news reporting helped the CCP to exert its own voice in domestic and international affairs in the post-SARS years. In 2005, when asked by American journalists to explain the surge of friendly news coverage about China, a Chinese official replied bluntly, "Because we are now the ones who write the news."[19]

Indeed, as the government learned from the SARS incident that providing some sort of information is better than providing none at all, the Sichuan earthquake supports the notion that a torrent of transparent and open coverage—so long as it does not question the government's legitimacy—may be best of all. CCTV was able to lead public opinion through the earthquake most effectively when the controls were off. During its quake coverage, twenty-three domestic satellite channels merged with CCTV's News Channel, making the channel and its website important platforms for useful public information. Globally, twenty-eight TV networks in 113 countries and regions used CCTV's footage. CCTV, Xinhua News Agency, and Sichuan TV became the primary sources of information for global media companies including the BBC and CNN. According to then CCTV president Zhao Huayong, public opinion on the Internet was at first "rebellious, independent and irrational,"[20] but when it became apparent in the early going that the state media were presenting a transparent account, public opinion was at least temporarily guided back to supporting the party and the government.

In fact, before the earthquake, while it was still smarting from the SARS cover-up, the state affirmed the people's "right to know" at its Seventeenth Congress in 2007 and set to work on new "Open Government Information Regulations." With these new regulations, policy makers appeared to tip the regulatory bias a little in the direction of "supervision by public opinion," adding alongside the state's "tongue and throat" a set of market-driven ears, a suggestion that the government should ideally gauge public opinion first and adjust its agenda accordingly. The shift was rewarded almost immediately. The relatively free press of the earthquake did not produce instability or turmoil; instead, it appeared to promote national cohesion and mutual understanding between state and society. CCTV's continuous coverage of the earthquake actually became part of the emergency response, facilitating the efficient transmission of information helpful to the state's mass mobilization effort.

Since the Open Government Information Regulations went into effect, China's state media have eagerly tried to consolidate their gains. Not satisfied with the regulations' generalities, journalists campaigned to add tools to ensure compliance by local governments and rules to standardize the information release process. They argued, tactfully, that policies supporting the people's "right to know" would benefit the state by projecting the image of a respectable press and a responsible state to the international community and by giving the state a more credible voice with which to guide public opinion. The Sichuan earthquake raised public expectations of the media, lending media a new card in their never-ending negotiations with the state about where their boundaries lie.

The Challenges of Broadcasting in China

Major disturbances like the Sichuan earthquake and the SARS epidemic crystallize just what kinds of challenges the Chinese government faces in its quest to control the message and its citizens while also maintaining credibility globally and at home. As the country has opened up to outside trade and influences, media reform has played out against the need to maintain national security and the aspirations among progressive forces to change global perceptions of China. In the late 1990s the term "cultural security" arose to describe China's own insecurity about its impending opening to the world, as dictated by China's joining the World Trade Organization and the unstoppable forces of globalization. After many years of isolation, joining the WTO provided the opportunity for China to be at the center of the world, albeit primarily in the trade sphere, abandoning the markets of culture to its Western competitors.[21] To rectify the perceived weakness of Chinese culture at home and abroad, at the annual plenum of the party's Central Committee in October 2011, Hu Jintao gave a speech addressing the need for bolstering China's cultural influence. "The overall strength of Chinese culture and its international influence is not commensurate with China's international status," Hu reminded his fellow party members. "The international culture of the West is strong while we are weak." Hu reasserted the party's control on culture and ideological affairs in fending off Western culture pollution. The battle against Western popular culture is equated with building Chinese cultural security.

With *Avatar* dominating the Chinese screen and Lady Gaga a popular icon among Chinese youth, a prevailing sense of anxiety among Chinese cultural guardians echoes Hu's assertion in his speech that "the West is try-ing to dominate China by spreading its culture and ideology; China must strengthen its cultural production to defend against the assault." Pitting Chi-nese culture against Western culture, Hu declared that an escalating culture war between the two sides had begun. A version of the speech was published in the party magazine *Seeking Truth*, wherein Hu continued to urge in cold war–like terms that Chinese cultural policy makers ought to "clearly see that international hostile forces are intensifying the strategic plot of westernizing and dividing China." Not surprisingly, in 2012 a sweeping new policy wiped scores of "Western-influenced" entertainment shows off Chinese prime-time television. To those who lived through China's Cultural Revolution or the antispiritual campaigns of the 1980s, Hu's militant rhetoric and the new rules on Chinese prime-time television that immediately followed are reminiscent of the various cultural cleansing movements of earlier CCP eras.

This domestic culture war, played out on the battlefields of the Chinese media, is never ending, with regular ebbs and flows and shifting national di-rectives. From the mid-1990s to the mid-2000s, the TV industry underwent significant structural change: from a planned economy model to a quasi-market system co-existing with public service and commercial broadcasting. CCTV now has the added directive of running a commercial enterprise, resulting in a mission that is an odd "mix of Party logic and market logic,"[22] which often, at first glance, strikes observers as an untenable and unsustain-able contradiction in terms.

CCTV was subsidized by the state from 1958 to 1978, regardless of how big or small the tab was. The subsidy began to wane once commercials were introduced in 1979. With advertising providing a revenue source, the state began to fix the size of the budget it allocated to CCTV in 1984, leaving the network to take care of any additional expenses. The regular state subsidy gradually diminished from CN¥45 million* in 1991 to CN¥34 million in 1996 and was dropped altogether in 1997.[23]

Prior to 1997, TV stations were allowed to negotiate with their respective government broadcasting bureaus, be they state, provincial, municipal, or county level, to set up the terms and amount of their state subsidy and what amount of any profit they would be expected to remit to their bureau. After remittance, stations retained the remaining revenues. Contract terms varied by case, depending on each station's bargaining power. As the state stopped

---

* As of May 2012, the equivalent of CN¥1 is US$0.16.

funding CCTV, the network, like many other former state-owned enterprises, scrambled to become self-reliant, and did so quite successfully, quickly turning a profit and contributing to SARFT a percentage of its annual revenue. CCTV remitted to SARFT CN¥1.3 billion from 1991 to 1997, almost twice the total taxes of CN¥720 million the network paid to the state.[24]

Since the early 1990s, TV stations have been important economic contributors to local government revenue and their broadcasting bureaus. This is particularly evident in affluent regions. A 1997 study of ten provincial and municipal TV stations revealed that the amount of money contributed by these stations to their corresponding governments was ten times the financial subsidy received from the government. Meanwhile, the proportion of advertising revenue in stations' total annual income increased from 85 percent in 1995 to 92 percent in 2000.[25]

Though CCTV now had to support itself in a competitive marketplace, courting audiences and advertisers in active competition with each other, its fundamental task—the party mouthpiece function—remained. CCTV's position was unique, though: the radiant sun at the center of the media galaxy, it retained its protected status as China's monopoly national television broadcaster.

The hierarchial structure of China's television system means that television stations, broadcasting bureaus, and governments at the same administrative level are closely linked in economic and political exchange. While TV stations depend on national or local government and broadcasting bureaus' policy protections to monopolize regional markets, government and the bureaus count on television stations to propound their political influence and provide financial support. Local cooperation has been a crucial determining factor in CCTV's attempts to achieve national coverage. In order to secure local support, MRFT, and later SARFT, released several policy documents, demanding that local terrestrial, cable, and retransmitting stations carry CCTV-1's programs in full, including commercials. SARFT emphasized that guaranteeing CCTV-1's national coverage is a political mission, an "undeniable" obligation and responsibility of local broadcasting bureaus and television stations.

Meanwhile, provincial channels have been competing with CCTV-1's terrestrial channel for ad revenue. In the 1990s, although MRFT persistently reiterated the "must carry" policy, many local stations ignored these directives. Local stations' open violation of the "must carry" policy and the central government's demand to secure CCTV-1's "full transmission and effective coverage" triggered a major change in China's TV networks in the late 1990s. MRFT launched a campaign to recentralize what it saw as a "chaotic" and "disordered" four-tier TV network by administrative means. In 1996, it ordered the closing down of unapproved TV outlets across the country. Following this, it merged county-level cable, terrestrial, and educational television and radio stations and city and provincial cable and terrestrial TV stations and tightened control over program sources, requesting that county TV stations allocate most of their airtime to transmit central and provincial TV stations' programs.

But because it is *the* national broadcaster, CCTV's special status comes with the same strings attached that all television operators have to deal with in China, perhaps even more so: interfacing with the CCP and the various departments in charge of regulating what goes on air. In practical terms, cultural policy in China follows directives issued by the party's Propaganda Department, which is embedded at all layers of government, from the national level all the way down to the local. These party propaganda departments, along with the party committees within media institutions, act as censors and set the policy and propaganda tone according to the directives of the Ministry of Central Propaganda. The local Propaganda Department operates mainly behind the scenes and in broad strokes, except for editorial content (news and information), which it manages very closely via secret weekly instructions to the media. In the past the Propaganda Department also actively directed the variety, quantity, and content of cultural products. In the reform era, however, self-censorship by media professionals has been the principal mode of control.

Day-to-day supervision of CCTV falls to SARFT, which coordinates and evaluates the network's key propaganda efforts, regulates its signal coverage, controls its senior appointments, and decides on its organizational structure and all of its programming. Meanwhile, the Ministry of Central Propaganda under the CCP manages the broad propaganda mission and provides ideological guidance. These bodies exist to "strengthen the structural management of the media through specialized government agencies."[26] The structure of these two is replicated at the network level: CCTV's internal leadership is comprised of a party committee and a senior management team. The former is responsible for ideological control, while the latter is in charge of the station's daily operation. The memberships of these two groups closely overlap, though the party committee ultimately trumps the management team.

Formally, the state controls broadcasting through administrative regulations, which include administrative statutes promulgated directly by the State Council and department rules enacted by SARFT.[27] Both administrative statutes and department rules are law, but neither requires a cumbersome legislative process. Instead, new statutes and rules are negotiated internally among affected departments before being submitted to the state's legislative department to be recorded. This special, nonlegislative process of establishing media law reflects an intention to keep the media leash short. At the next level, and more immediately, SARFT and its local bureaus manage television via internal normative documents. These normative documents do not need to be recorded by the State Council, and their legal status is variable—courts may treat them as established law or something less in any particular case.

Between May 1994 and February 1995, following party orders, the MRFT undertook a comprehensive analysis of broadcasting in China, culminating in a *Report to Further Strengthen and Improve Radio, Film and TV Work*. The report established "guiding notions, objectives, tasks, strategies and important areas" of television development for the next five years. The guiding notion of the report, "accepted in principle" by the CCP in February 1995, was to follow Deng Xiaoping's theory on developing "socialism with Chinese characteristics." The report distilled this admonition into four major objectives for the media: retain correct opinion guidance, improve program quality, enhance the government's oversight, and promote technological development.

Speaking at a national broadcasting and film working conference in 1995, Li Tieying, a member of the Central Committee of the CCP, revealed a key consideration in cultural policy going forward. The party anticipated increasing social tension in response to problems associated with economic reform, problems such as inflation and cuts in China's social safety net and housing systems. Li emphasized the imperative of leading people with correct opinion, thus providing a positive environment for reform, development, and stability, and letting "the whole Party and entire people of the country recognize the socialist market economic system and understand its basic elements," should be the "top priority" for broadcasters.[28] The deeper the economic reform became, Li indicated, the more crucial this public relations project would be. Out of economic reform and development had grown this new force to reckon with: public opinion.

Public opinion is the explicit focus of the first 1995 MRFT report objective—retain correct opinion guidance—but it is an implicit concern of all four objectives. The second MRFT objective was to improve the quality and quantity of radio and TV programs. The MRFT defined "quality" as content that would "promote the main melody and advocate diversity."[29] The "main melody," according to President Jiang Zemin, was "patriotism, socialism and collectivism," a song to "reflect the spirits of the era and nation, unite people's hearts, encourage progress and propel social development and advancement." For more cynical observers, however, the main melody is a code for more politically correct stories about history. "Diversity," meanwhile, implies that "under correct ideological guidance," cultural products should be "richer," more "colorful," and "creative" [30] in order to attract viewers. Buried in the earnest rhetoric was recognition that commercial cultural products, especially television programming, had to be popular. In the face of a tide of East Asian popular culture, including an increasingly dominant Korean pop culture, this was a great challenge.

The third MRFT report objective spoke to strengthening the government's macro-control over broadcasting and establishing legal frameworks as "a long-term important job" for regulators. [31] With the channels for public opinion increasing, and with the media growing into their commercial responsibilities, cultural management was an increasingly complex and subtle undertaking. The then head of MRFT, Sun Jiazheng, noted, "A critical question for MRFT and the Party is how to correctly manage the relations between TV and radio's other functions and their main function, propaganda, and how to effectively deploy macro-control while avoiding and defeating the commercialization of spiritual products." [32]

Finally, the MRFT report recognized that both production values and media platforms would have to be technologically competitive. "Science and technology," Sun said, "are the foundation for the survival and development of broadcasting," so China must "gradually reduce the technological gap with developed and newly industrialized countries." [33] In sum, the 1995 MRFT report was a comprehensive reformulation of the cultural control regime for a new era. Couched in rhetoric that spins the commercialization of China's cultural industries as a natural evolution of the party's leadership, it nevertheless heralded the unavoidable admission of two new "parties"—market forces and public opinion—to a conversation that the party had hitherto conducted almost exclusively on its own terms.

Of course, markets and public opinion have no formal authority, and unlike in the broader economy, reform in the cultural industries does not include privatization. All broadcast media are still owned by the state, and China's legal reforms have so far set few limits on the state's power over the media. While the party-state must now attend to markets and their systems of rules, it still exercises what often amounts to ad hoc control over the media. Party leaders and senior government officials' speeches and written comments, as well as internal documents issued by the Propaganda Department, are more routinely used and have a more profound impact on media operations and development than statutes, laws, and normative documents.

This rule by directive practice is built into the Chinese system of governance, and it is a primary reason why rule of law is such a difficult proposition in China. The state government establishes laws, but because the party appara- tus ranks above the state government, party directives trump everything else. For the media this amounts to an informal regulatory practice that results in frequent, disruptive regulatory fiddling. For media professionals it creates a climate of constant uncertainty and self-censorship.

What emerged as the "guiding theoretical principle for broader and more advanced media development" [34] in the mid-1990s was the concept of *chanye- hua*, or "industrialization," a term that suggests the change of emphasis from propaganda to profit making. Notionally, this change of emphasis would seem to weaken the party-state's ideological oversight. In fact, the new in- dustrial focus did encourage some media elites and critics to press for greater media autonomy. Not surprisingly, this impulse soon alarmed the regulators. In 1996 the MRFT issued a new report, *Several Important Problems and Opin- ions about Our Country's Present Broadcasting Development*,[35] repudiating the *chanyehua* concept and warning against full financial independence for TV stations. Advertising, it argued, should only fill the gap between government funding and operational costs and should not be exploited for profit. The MRFT also emphasized, "TV and radio stations are the Party and govern- ment's publicity apparatus and public opinion battlefield; [they] are public interest serving institutions and must be completely held in the hands of the Party and government." The key term here is "public interest serving institu- tions," or *shiye*. The now blurred line between the interests of the state and those of the society is evidence of the party recognizing its citizens' aspira- tions for reform, at least among progressives in the party. In addition, the report warned that pushing electronic media into the market would inevita- bly push TV and radio stations to pursue economic interests to the utmost, violating their function as the party's and government's "mouthpiece" and leading to the inevitable emergence of foreign, joint, collective, and private ownership of stations, especially in economically underdeveloped regions, where lack of funding meant vulnerability to commercial competition and aggressive courtship from Western media. The report concluded that govern- ment subsidies should continue to provide major funding for the broadcast media.[36]

On August 11, 1997, the State Council promulgated the *Regulations Gov- erning the Administration of Radio and Television*, confirming that the media's main roles were "to serve the people, to serve socialism and insist on correct public opinion guidance." [37] It also stipulated that television and radio stations could be set up only by national or local administrative departments of the state and prohibited joint ventures with foreign media firms. At a subsequent news conference, MRFT officials reiterated that the media must "meet the spiritual and cultural needs of ordinary people" and "enhance socialist material and spiritual civilization."[38]

If all this wasn't enough, at the Fifteenth National Congress in 1997, Xu Guangchun, vice minister of the Ministry of Central Propaganda, laid down the "four no changes" in media reform: "no change in [radio and television's] nature as the Party, Government, and people's mouthpiece and the Party's important public opinion apparatus and battlefield"; "no change in [radio and television's] glorious duty of serving the Party's national work"; "no change in [radio and television's] responsibilities of persisting in correct public opinion guidance, creating a good public sphere, and providing strong public support for reform, liberalization, economic, and social development"; and "no change in the leadership of the Party over broadcasting." "Except for these," Xu summed up, "all other areas . . . can be reformed."[39] These directives were reiterated in 2011 as the party-state reined in programs that were deemed to have deviated from its propaganda and control mandate. Meanwhile, economic logic continues to encourage entertainment programs of popular appeal, which will inevitably exert pressure for censors to loosen their grips. These contradictory mission statements and swings—from forays into market reform to retreats to conservatism, from initiatives to commercialize to those attacking it—have been typical of media regulation in the post-Mao era, and they have contributed to the on-the-job training of a new generation of media professionals thoroughly steeped in the fine art of intuiting what their overseers want. It may involve self-censorship, the primary mechanism of cultural control in contemporary China, or at times out-and-out censorship. Whatever the case may be, it is up to people like Yang Weiguang to interpret and execute the will of their bosses. Who that might be—the CCP, the censors, or even their audience—well, figuring that out was part of Yang's job.

2

A VIEW FROM THE TOP: MANAGING THE COMMERCIAL REVOLUTION AT CCTV

I visited Yang Weiguang three times in the summer of 2008, meeting at the Heaven, Earth and Human Media Corporation, a company he established in west Beijing, a ten-minute drive from CCTV's headquarters. Inside Yang's office three scrolls of calligraphy adorn the walls: "Purple Air Comes from the East," implying good fortune coming from the East; a professional message on the northern wall proclaiming "Quality Program First"; and an axiom from the Tang poet Wang Zhihuan, "You can enjoy a grander sight by climbing to a greater height." I imagined that any visiting party officials would have wholeheartedly approved of the calculated mixture of patriotism and office management motivation. I was in the presence of someone who was very aware of creating proper first impressions.

Yang comes from an earlier generation of journalists, who operated on a short propaganda tether, and throughout his career he seems not to have challenged whether journalism should try to be something more than the party's instrument: the party sets the rules, and that's that. When I asked him how he gauges what is permissible or not, he simply replied, "The basic principle for me is to operate according to the law and value of news. My professional principle was in line with the direction of China's democratic and legal reforms." And when the party changed the rules, putting him in charge of CCTV during its first decade as a commercial broadcaster, he was ready, in effect, to change himself. Yang quickly adapted to juggling politics, commerce, and the constantly shifting regulatory climate, an example, perhaps, as David Lampton would describe it, of Yang's adherence to "an intrinsically productive set of cultural values."[1] Yet, in many ways, his eight years (1991–99) as head of CCTV were among the most dynamic in the network's history, owing partially to the context of the times, but also to Yang's shrewd management, especially in his efforts to nudge CCTV toward the path of commercialization and to increase the quality of the news reporting.

Commercialization

As state subsidies to CCTV dropped during the early 1990s, Yang made the radical decision to expand ad revenues by attaching commercials to the *National News Bulletin*, the prime-time news program carried by all stations in the country. It was a risky proposition because, though television commercials during programs of light entertainment were well established by then, the flagship prime-time network news program was the program most scrutinized and controlled by his bosses at SARFT, and attaching commercials to it might attract criticism about commercializing and thus trivializing serious news programs. Yang was aware of how sensitive the situation was.

"The division in charge of commercial spots within CCTV approached me in 1993, asking if I dared to run commercials right after *National News Bulletin*, as the golden time slot would bring in lucrative ad revenue. I gave it some thought and told them to go ahead, but keep it small. We started out conservatively, running a thirty-second spot. Word got around to the minister of SARFT, Ai Zhisheng, that I was adding commercials to *News Bulletin*. Ai rang me up and demanded an explanation. I quickly corrected the rumor, assuring Ai that I was only adding a thirty-second ad *after* the news program. That eased his concern."

Yang sat back, chuckling to himself; his eyes glistened playfully. "But you know what? Had Ai received the accurate information from the beginning about inserting ads after the news, he might have had time to develop an objection to it. The rumor, which might have been spread to him intentionally to sabotage my effort, actually did us a favor since I was able to counter with my unexpected correction, which caught him totally off guard."

Yang was quite happy with what he was able to pull off. "The thirty-second spot was stretched into sixty seconds six months later. We then started to run into problems, not because people find commercial interruptions offensive but because companies began to lobby for more airtime to run more ads. Given the allocation for just a single commercial, we decided to do an auction, awarding the time slot to the highest bidder. Eighty-two companies joined the bidding, and two wine companies ended up being the finalists, and they bid up the price against each other. It was the war between the Confuciuses—as one company was named Confucius Family Wine and the other Confucius Banquet Wine. In the end, Family Wine secured the contract for the first year, bringing us over CN¥30 million. Banquet Wine secured the contract for the second year, bringing in CN¥66.66 million. Given the high demand for commercial time, I eventually allowed the addition of a one-minute commercial spot before the *National News Bulletin* and expanded the commercial slot after to three to four minutes." With commercialization entrenched by the mid-1990s, Yang's opening up of the party news program for commercial gains did not raise many eyebrows among the party leadership. In 1995, prime-time commercial spots brought CCTV CN¥1.06 billion. In 1996, the total jumped to CN¥2.3 billion. The total ad revenue in 1998, the year before Yang stepped down, amounted to CN¥2.8 billion.

Yang's maverick actions in auctioning commercial spots for the tight-lipped evening *National News Bulletin* may have created a windfall for CCTV that everyone in hindsight applauded, but at the time he was risking party censure by mixing news with commerce. But Yang skillfully navigated the straits, and it wasn't until after he stepped down in 1999 that CCTV's un-abated march toward commercialization would be questioned.

In February 1999, Zhao Huayong was appointed to replace Yang as the head of CCTV. Unlike Yang, Zhao was the consummate insider, having worked in various divisions inside CCTV since 1975. At the end of his admin-istration, Zhao's legacy would be defined by further commercialization and aggressive institutional reform built on the platform of "specialty channels, individualized columns, and quality high end programs,"[2] but the year after his new appointment, media commercialization hit an unexpected (though it would prove to be only temporary) roadblock with a changing of the guard at SARFT. In June 2000, Xu Guangchun, the conservative former vice min-ister of propaganda, assumed leadership at SARFT. Five months previously, in a speech to the National TV and Radio Propaganda Working Conference, Xu had openly criticized *chanyehua* (industrialization) and *qiyehua* (enter-prising) in the news media and reemphasized the role of the media as party instruments.

Both *chanyehua* and *qiyehua* point toward commercialization. For the media, *chanyehua* entails a change of emphasis from pushing propaganda to generating profit. Simultaneously, it encourages a consolidation of media industries. *Qiye* translates as "enterprise" (the root of "entrepreneur") and is associated with personnel and wage systems determined not by govern-ment bureaucracies but by the market. The transformation of media units from nonbusiness, not-for-profit state institutions into modern enterprises means profit becomes a key consideration—at least on par with their political function. The newly "liberated" media enterprises enjoy greater autonomy in making decisions about personnel and wages, as well as business and invest-ment strategies.

Xu feared that the industrialization of the media sector and the fragmentation of the state media business model would inevitably change the nature of news media as the party's mouthpiece. He worried that it would sacrifice the news media's public guidance and educational functions and warned that substituting markets for party directives would "divide the Party from the people and divide the Party's will from the people's wish." With these concerns in mind, Xu and the Propaganda Ministry ordered strict control over investment, particularly money from nonmedia business interests in the electronic media. Xu acknowledged that such nonmedia investors "may not want to control our news media and practice 'westernization' and 'disintegration'" but worried that they "might undermine the Party's leadership of the news media."[3]

The slowdown of media reform in the early 2000s was further influenced by domestic and international events. Domestically, a crackdown on the Falun Gong movement in late 1999 contributed directly to the CCP's determination to reinforce ideological and political control in 2000, which led to the departure of a number of talented individuals from CCTV, including the disenchanted iconoclast Xia Jun, CCTV's renowned producer of the popular newsmagazine program *News Probe* and the director of 1989's groundbreaking documentary *River Elegy*. Marketization in the broader economy had seen the government retreating from social safety-net systems, increasing social unrest. Internationally, the party was concerned about the implications of elections in the United States, Russia, and Taiwan, especially the prospective victory of the pro-independence Democratic Progressive Party in Taiwan.

Meanwhile, the government was campaigning heavily for WTO membership, sending out conflicting signals on media commercialization via *chanyehua*. In 1999, the Propaganda Ministry released an internal document, MCP (98) No. 1, initiating support and planning for broadcast industry conglomeration.[4] This became the basis of the important Document No. 17, jointly issued by the Propaganda Ministry, SARFT, and the General Administration of Press and Publication, in 2001. In anticipation of China's accession to the World Trade Organization in December 2001 and the increased exposure to international media competition that WTO rules would bring, Document No. 17 urged the construction of cross-media and cross-regional media conglomerates better suited to competition in a more globalized marketplace. It also identified broadcast digitalization, cable network development, and channel specialization as additional steps toward a more competitive industry.

The challenge was evident: consolidate or perish. Realizing that the party might have no significant media mouthpieces to control if it didn't take its foot off the ideological brakes, party conservatives began to change their views on *chanyehua*, or media industrialization. Cultural policy priorities were shifting away from propaganda and toward business, technological development, and entertainment and artistic content. Xu softened his own position when he outlined the next five-year Broadcasting Development Plan in 2000, calling for the building of "top standard, top teamed, top equipped, and top managed broadcasting and film aircraft carriers" (big broadcast media conglomerates) in order to expand China's influence around the world and enhance its voice in the international public sphere.[5] Xu's speech amounted to an early public voicing of an emerging, post-WTO cultural policy objective: building China's soft power. The following year, responding to President Jiang Zemin's call to "let China's voice broadcast to the world," SARFT launched a "going out" project. The project was to first establish Chinese television and radio channels overseas in five years and then to provide, in ten years, multi-language, regionalized broadcasting and coverage. China's media would play in the same global pond as CNN, the BBC, and other big Western media firms. Specific "going out" strategies included broadcasting CCTV-4 (the Chinese-language International Channel) and CCTV-9 (the English-language International Channel, renamed the Documentary Channel on January 1, 2011) in important regions around the world. Taking up the cause, the newly anointed president Zhao Huayong of CCTV launched the English Channel on September 25, 2000, and French, Spanish, and Portuguese channels soon followed.

After beginning his reign at SARFT as a critic of media industrialization, Xu Guangchun became a leading architect and cheerleader for the new cultural industries strategy by 2002. At a National Working Conference, Xu even excoriated senior broadcasting officials for not having "business sense" and demanded that they be more visionary about developing new markets like interactive TV and video on demand.[6] In November 2002, in a speech that was widely interpreted as an official endorsement, Jiang Zemin said that the industrialization of broadcasting needed continued development.[7] Media industrialization was thus publicly endorsed, indeed encouraged, by the state.

At a National Broadcasting and Film Working Conference in January 2003, regulators proposed to separate the institutional (state interests) aspect of media industry from its enterprise (commercial interests) operation. In late 2003, the party issued its "Opinions on Experimental Works of the Cultural System's Institutional Reform," a document establishing a regulatory distinction between cultural production serving the "public good" and cultural production for commercial interests. In Chinese policy circles, this was the ongoing conundrum of public institutions versus commercial industries.

In the broadcast sector, separate market-oriented and public service systems were established. TV and radio stations were directed to take profit-seeking units and spin them off into separate companies managed primarily according to market imperatives. Those units that remained were recategorized as parts of the public service system and continued to serve the traditional mouthpiece and propaganda functions, wholly owned and closely managed by the government. For the most part, these are the "editorial," or news and information, divisions of broadcast operations. What is left unattended in this trade-off is the interest of the public, which is characteristically and conveniently lumped together with the interest of the state. The public service system Chinese regulators envisioned does not resemble at all the public broadcasting systems in the United States and the United Kingdom, which maintain political impartiality.

SARFT followed up with its "Opinions on Improving Broadcasting and Film Industry Development" at the end of 2003, signaling another step toward liberalization of television channel ownership. It converts television, including CCTV, from a state monopoly to a mixed-ownership system, provided that the majority stake is still owned by the state. The non-news, market-oriented units that were spun off by broadcasters could now be listed on domestic or overseas stock markets, in which qualified foreign companies could take minority stakes.[8] In an interview given to the *Wall Street Journal*, Zhu Hong, spokesman for SARFT, explained that China was pursuing broadcast deregulation "in light of the principle of separating [the state's] ownership from operation," and the decision to exempt news production and ownership from deregulation was to "serve public interests," "deliver the Party and State's voices to Chinese households," and "convey China's voices to the world."[9] In practice, though, the lines between ownership and operation and between public-oriented and market-driven sectors have remained blurry and still constitute the central conundrum of contemporary media practice in China.

Reforms at CCTV reflected practices and changes that had been implemented more broadly throughout the television sector. On February 16, 2003, Zhao Huayong announced that, with the exception of the News Channel, all CCTV channels were to be judged as commercial specialist channels, meaning the success or failure of individual programs would be measured on the basis of advertising revenue. March 2003 saw the introduction of a survival-of-the-fittest policy: programs receiving two consecutive performance warnings or three within a single year were to be dropped.

Hiring Practices

Hiring practices also underwent liberalizing reforms under Zhao, but most of these changes, including a shift toward "contract" labor, began during Yang's time. Employment practices at CCTV prior to the early 1990s followed the general practice in China's state-run enterprises, which put family and political background and connections ahead of professional credentials. SARFT enforced a similar practice at CCTV, and it meant that the first generation of CCTV employees was mostly former army officers and people with the right family pedigrees. This became a headache to Yang, whose attempt to introduce new program formats and expand CCTV programming needed capable raw talent: "More often than not, we had no say in who would be allocated a permanent position at CCTV. We had to accept whoever was handed to us."

Unable to find the talent he wanted in-house, he looked outside the network. Without the authority to hire new permanent employees, a prerogative reserved to SARFT, he adopted a new practice, contractual employment. He recounted, "To bypass the permanent recruitment system, I started to hire talents on temporary contracts." And in order to lure top-notch talent away from their steady jobs, he offered higher pay (though the base pay was low, employees would make up for it by earning a percentage of any additional ad revenue their programs brought in) and more flexibility in project choices than regular employees at CCTV received. Yang's experiment was a rousing success at expanding CCTV's human capital. "The drawback for these employees was obviously the risk of being fired if you did not perform well. But many talented people were attracted to the higher pay. People with real talent were not afraid of losing jobs, so we managed to lure many good people into working for CCTV. In fact, the most capable CCTV people currently at work all came from the era when the contractual labor system opened up space for them. I learned that for recruiting and retaining talented people for CCTV, the two essential things are attractive pay packages and allowing them room for creativity and innovation."

Some of China's leading television talents were recruited through this system, including Bai Yansong and Cui Yongyuan from the Central People's Radio. Jing Yidan, by now a seasoned anchorwoman with a number of high-profile programs to her credit, was a radio announcer in the northern province of Heilongjiang before coming to CCTV. She interned at the *Evening News* while getting her graduate degree at the Beijing Broadcasting Institute. Impressed by her work ethic and photogenic look, Yang decided to keep her at CCTV via the contractual system. Yang provided a platform for Jing and other talented people from all sectors of the media to flex their creative muscles at CCTV. The talents recruited returned the favor by producing innovative and commercially successful programs. The quality programs they produced contributed directly to CCTV's rapid revenue growth.

The contractual labor system was not Yang's innovation. China's labor system had been made more flexible in 1992–93 with the dismantling of "iron rice bowl" jobs, which guaranteed lifelong employment and benefits. Employment and wages began to be linked to performance and profits. It didn't work quite that way at CCTV, however, which because of its special mouthpiece function required that SARFT continue ideological oversight of regular employment. But Yang's "network contractual employment system" skirted SARFT's oversight by contracting with independent production units that hired their own talent and paid their own expenses, including wages and bonuses. In practice, this resembled the "unit-producer" system of classic Hollywood, and it meant, for instance, that among more than one hundred people working on *Oriental Horizon*, only seven were permanent employees on CCTV's official payroll.

The contractual system brought in talent that would otherwise never get their feet inside CCTV, bypassing the rigid state quota on the size of CCTV's regular staff. Normally, the recruiting pool for new regular employees came from college graduates selected and assigned to CCTV by the state. Yang utilized, with audacity, the secondment option, which meant temporarily borrowing talent from a different institution, a variation of signing a temporary contract. This way, people could retain their old permanent post by taking an unpaid leave of absence. At times an entire CCTV production crew would be comprised of temporary staff poached from somewhere else. Yang put them on CCTV's contractual payroll and usually managed, over time, to convert them into permanent staff.

CCTV paid a base salary of only CN¥$280 per month for these contract employees, roughly equal to the wage of a janitor at the time. No health coverage was provided, nor was opportunity for promotion or other incentives enjoyed by the network's regular employees. But Yang allowed production units to keep the commercial income from the programs they produced and use it to cover expenses, wages, and bonuses. It meant that contracted temporary employees could make a lot more money from successful productions than many of the seasoned CCTV employees with higher regular wages. "With talented people on board, we were able to do quality programming that brought a stream of ad revenues. Our ad revenue witnessed a steady growth, from CN¥100 million in 1990 to CN¥4.5 billion in 1997. After a little over CN¥400 million in tax and some amount obligated to SARFT, we were allowed to keep the rest for program development and employee bonuses." With such incentives, it's not surprising how the fluid contractual labor system worked hand in hand with commercialization.

Reforms Under Zhao

Zhao Huayong pushed for further commercialization by applying the contractual employment system to all employees in 2004, essentially dismantling the network's permanent employment system, allowing CCTV to lay off 1,654 workers. Those remaining were transferred to the new subsidiary, CCTV Labor Services Allocation Company, which became their legal employer for allocating social insurance benefits. By the end of July 2004 there were more than 2,600 registered employees at the company, a flexible workforce that Zhao and his managers could adjust as the situation called for. Zhao then implemented a competitive contract system for all programs, which limited bidding for new contracts to producers who had worked for CCTV for at least three years in the past. These measures helped consolidate resources and ignite growth. A dramatic surge in advertising revenue followed, reaching CN¥5.3 billion in 2004, almost a third of all television spending in China at the time.[10]

More reforms came in 2005 when Zhao and his management team ushered in a new "screen-test certificate" system to standardize employment procedures for on-air talent. Newly introduced fines and penalties were levied on those who brought negative publicity to the network, while employees who brought positive recognition to the network would be rewarded. The system of penalties and incentives helped to rein in corruption and power abuse, as it curbed commercial kickbacks, excessive product tie-ins, and illegal moonlighting among celebrity hosts. The image-building effort was intended to solidify CCTV's reputation as a national broadcaster with social and cultural integrity as CCTV continued to meet challenges from local stations.

CCTV has faced growing competition both at home and abroad since the mid-1990s. By 2003, more than thirty overseas media companies had been allowed into China under various arrangements. Meanwhile, domestic broadcasters, especially provincial satellite stations, which cooperated with local cable stations to achieve national or near-national coverage, have also eroded CCTV's dominance. A new round of even fiercer competition started after SARFT licensed additional channels for nationwide satellite broadcasting, with more than fifty by the end of 2005, including the News Channel of Shenzhen Television, Southern Television's Cantonese Channel, Hunan Satellite Television's (HSTV) Golden Eagle Cartoon Channel, Beijing TV's Cartoon Channel, and Shanghai Television's Cartoon Channel.

The provincial stations and their innovative, more Western practices have often pushed CCTV to follow suit. For instance, HSTV separated its advertising and other noneditorial businesses from the news operation and floated the company on the Shenzhen stock exchange in 1999.[11] Since then, HSTV has established itself as one of China's prime entertainment channels. Others have more recently carved out their own niches in the market. Hainan Satellite Television has transformed itself into one of China's leading travel channels; Anhui Satellite Television has a strong reputation for television dramas; Guizhou Satellite Television has largely taken over the "western China" brand following the demise of CCTV's own specialized channel. Meanwhile Guangdong and Zhejiang Satellite Television have worked on a collaborative strategy exploiting their combined strengths in entertainment and economic news broadcasting. At the same time, Hong Kong–based Phoenix has established itself as a leading international Chinese-language channel. The success of provincial and local satellite television stations gradually poached a larger and larger share of CCTV's once captive audience, forcing CCTV to scrap its more moribund practices even faster and move more aggressively toward reform.

Further changes were made to content innovation, personnel management, and administrative and organizational practices. Program adjustments were driven by SARFT's schedule for digitization and the rollout of pay TV. These imperatives drove the proliferation and branding of new specialized channels in the CCTV spectrum—for instance, CCTV-2 devotes itself to financial news in an attempt to brand itself as the Chinese Bloomberg or CNBC. Management and organizational restructuring, on the other hand, were part of the redefinition effort in making CCTV a commercial entity. Organizational restructuring aimed to address the cumbersome administrative and organizational aspects of running what is essentially a state bureaucracy. Operational efficiency, economy, and standardization were emphasized; redundant casual personnel were eliminated; and, as mentioned previously, the universal contract employment system was introduced. Greater autonomy was offered—and expected—and a system of rewards and penalties was introduced to incentivize channels and production units toward financial responsibility. The introduction of a competitive contract employment system for program producers aimed to improve creative efficiency and quality by curbing internal clientelism and favoritism, as the existing management structure at CCTV enabled the formation of "mini-fiefdoms" within the organization, often producing complacency, unaccountability, favoritism, and overall mismanagement. By increasing competition among program producers, organization reforms stimulated innovation and creativity. Overall, the transition to a modern corporate system enabled CCTV to adopt more flexible personnel and wage systems.

Zhao had laid the foundation for the genesis of these reforms in February 2003 when he indicated that all channels were to become relatively autonomous business operations that would follow market forces and maximize profits. CCTV continued its market-oriented operation throughout the latter part of the 2000s, following the general direction laid out by the party at the sixteenth plenum of the CCP in 2006, in which the party indicated the need for further structural reform of the cultural industries. In many ways this was the party catching up with changes that were already afoot in the Chinese cultural industries. It nonetheless presented an opportunity for CCTV as the network strived to expand globally and maintain its dominance domestically.

To some, the drive toward commercialization, especially under Zhao, has been pursued overzealously, affecting the morale of CCTV's employees. My conversation with a number of seasoned CCTV practitioners in July 2009 suggests that the desire is strong for a more balanced approach for both enlightenment and profit. A number of people, including some of the leading hosts and producers, voiced their concerns, and indeed indignation, about CCTV's relentless pursuit of profits at the expense of cultural value. A debate was raging, in early 2008, concerning CCTV's dual identity as a commercial entity and a state-controlled national network with a cultural mandate. A number of those I spoke with pined for the days of Yang, who seemed to effortlessly traverse the world of markets, the party, and the newsroom.

Programming

A consummate "party businessman" at CCTV, Yang combined the party-line devotion of his radio days with an innate entrepreneurial sense. With new room to move, he originated programs that pulled in audiences with more topical and frank content than they had ever seen before on Chinese television. Yang pioneered profitably controversial programming and at the same time modeled the kind of boundary-testing self-censorship that would become the norm. In 1993, for instance, CCTV produced a twelve-episode documentary about Mao Zedong at around the time that Mao's legacy was coming under revision in the popular and official discourse. Frightened, none of CCTV's midlevel bureaucrats normally charged with prescreening new productions would touch the potentially explosive series when it was sent to the MRFT and the Propaganda Department for evaluation. Frustrated, Yang took a gamble and brought the documentary directly to Bo Yibo, a Politburo member and vice chairman of the party's Central Advisory Commission, and the father of Bo Xilai, a champion of the antimarket Chinese New Left ideology whose promising political career came to an abrupt halt in March 2012 amid a corruption scandal.[12] Bo, who along with Deng Xiaoping and many others had been purged from the party leadership by Mao during the Cultural Revolution, endorsed the documentary after watching only one episode, and it was broadcast nationwide on December 26, 1993, Mao's centenary birthday.

Having succeeded once, CCTV followed with a twelve-episode documentary on Deng Xiaoping. This time, Yang bypassed the midlevel regulators altogether and submitted the documentary to Zheng Qinghong, then director of the General Office of the CCP Central Committee, who would go on to be elected vice president in 2003. In 1996, with Zheng's blessing, the documentary on Deng was approved for broadcast. It began its run on New Year's Day 1997, a month and a half before Deng passed away. The fortuitous scheduling turned out to shield the series from the lengthy revision process that might otherwise have been required to make it conform to the official eulogy. Instead, the official eulogy and appraisal of Deng's legacy turned to the documentary for cues. The documentary was rebroadcast on CCTV and all local stations before and after Deng's state funeral.

Epic-scale historical dramas and TV adaptations of Chinese classical novels also became cash cows for CCTV during Yang's reign. A history buff and a drama lover, Yang headed an organization ponderously called the Committee for Significant Revolutionary Historical Film and TV. He orchestrated the production of many TV dramas adapted from classical Chinese novels, such as *Romance of the Three Kingdoms* and *Water Margins*. Other historical dramas made under his reign include *The Battle over the Fate of China*.

Yang reminded me that *Romance of the Three Kingdoms* earned CN¥1.8 million for the three minutes of commercial time during each episode. The serial also succeeded as an export, becoming popular in Hong Kong, Taiwan, Japan, and the Chinese diaspora overseas. It even helped to revive Hong Kong's failing Asia TV, which purchased the rights to showcase the drama in the territory. Asia TV's viewership in Hong Kong leapt to first place when it aired *Kingdoms*, beating its rival Hong Kong Cable TV (TVB). Legend has it that TVB chief Sir Runrun Shaw chastised his staff for not having the foresight to purchase *Kingdoms*. After this initial misstep, TVB was eager to buy whatever was in the CCTV drama pipeline and bid up the price for the next classic, *Water Margins*, paying US$12,000 per episode for the exclusive rights in Hong Kong, beating Asia TV, which offered US$9,000.

Yang's love for TV drama extended to domestic comedies, a genre he helped to cultivate after retiring from his CCTV post. A comedy he championed was *Home with Children*, a hugely popular domestic comedy in the vein of *Growing Pains*. A standard half-hour series, *Home* dealt with real-life issues in a blended family. The premise of the show, which features doting, if often exasperated, parents and their children from previous marriages, is atypical for most Chinese households, which are regulated by the one-child policy. Cultural clashes and power dynamics among multiple kids living under one roof, a sight that has become decidedly rare for urban viewers, provide compelling comedic elements as well as cultural commentary. "The comedy is about building a harmonious family and about respecting children and nurturing their independence and self-confidence. I followed the development of the show every step of the way, frequently stayed up well after midnight to discuss story lines with the production team. I read and approved every single script. Getting this closely involved in a show was impossible when I was the head of CCTV. By the time I started to do *Home*, I had been granted permission from the central government to form a company specializing in making TV dramas, including sitcoms. *Home* was one of our initial products."

This was a curious project for a history buff to take on, so I asked Yang why he decided to focus on children's programming. Were there commercial incentives?

"It's a call of duty," Yang said. "The central government urged media to develop programs that would enrich child education in the early 2000s. I was the president of the TV Association at the time and led the efforts in developing quality children's programs. I came up with the idea of a family sitcom that would be both popular and educational. We started in 2005, and now we have produced 376 episodes and counting. We also developed a cartoon version of the same show, and it took us three years to develop the animated series." I sat bemused as this reliable party hand, who had once begged not to be reassigned from his radio post, ticked off *Home*'s various multimedia ventures. "We made several spin-offs, including *Home with Parents*, *Home with Aliens*; both continue to be popular with kids. We have licensed the *Home* brand for comic-book publishing and Internet gaming, making the *Home* franchise a Disney-style operation. And we had *Home* incorporated into middle school education and as part of the Chinese-language learning tool for international students at Beijing University."

I attested to the effectiveness of the show in teaching Chinese language, as my then nine-year-old daughter had gotten more out of watching the show than she did attending a local Chinese school during our six-month sojourn in Beijing in 2008.

"With the one-child policy, people either overindulge kids or push them to excel. Both extremes are detrimental to children's development. *Home* attempts to change the culture of child rearing in contemporary China. We want to promote a new educational approach, which shows that knowledge and wisdom can be passed along in a happy and relaxed way. We did plenty of homework during the preparation stage, inviting community leaders, school principals, and the chairs of local women's federations to discuss stories and plots. Our efforts paid off."

This is not Yang's first taste of programming success, of course. His legacy at CCTV rests on his creation of newsmagazine-type programs—think *60 Minutes*—that were once alien to Chinese television. *Oriental Horizon*, a current affairs program, debuted on May 1, 1993, and a similar show, *Focus*, came out on April 1, 1994. Both were designed as more lively and accessible formats for presenting news and information than the traditional news broadcast. For *Oriental Horizon*, News Division head Sun Yusheng and Yang gambled by hiring several well-known, politically courageous print journalists, including Bai Yansong, Shui Junyi, Fang Hongjin, and Cui Yongyuan, despite the fact that none of them had any previous television experience. But integrity won out, and the show was a hit.

"The Propaganda Ministry issued a directive in 1992, encouraging media organizations to pay attention to social issues of public concern. I gathered a group of talented young people in 1993 to experiment with a new program, *Oriental Horizon*. I vetoed the initial title they came up with, 'New Sun,' in fear that it might make some people uneasy, as Mao was considered the Sun. We did not want to leave the impression that we thought Mao had become the old Sun. Despite a new title, the program was still a risky one, as we intended to report political corruption and the seedier sides of society. To play it safe, I initially chose to run the program at 7 A.M. with a return at 1 P.M. both lousy time slots with few viewers. The production team complained, but I explained to them that less attention meant less political risk. If problems emerged, we would have the opportunity to make changes. A year after its debut, *Oriental Horizon* became the darling of both the policy makers and the public. The show also converted audiences from listening to morning news on radio to watching morning news on TV. Later, more established divisions ended up begging me to have a 6 A.M. time slot." Yang chuckled, momentarily lost in his own memory.

Oriental Horizon quickly became so popular that it did indeed change the viewing habits of people who seldom watched television in the morning. Even reruns were spectacularly successful. *Oriental Horizon* was thus described in official Chinese media reports as a "silent revolution in daytime TV programming." [13]

Horizon originally comprised four segments: "Celebrity Talks" featured interviews with prominent Chinese; "MTV" introduced new pop songs; "Everyday Life" told stories about common people; and "Focus Time" discussed hot topics. The show quickly became a powerful force in shaping public opinion. According to the producers of the "Everyday Life" segment, the show succeeded because it treats individuals, big or small, with respect by encouraging people "to speak truthfully and honestly." [14] Instead of hard-edged investigative reports, the segment is styled with more of a talk-show approach, with a host, invited guests, a live audience, and conversations among all three. Covered topics are diverse, purposely mundane, and widely resonant, for example, whether keeping birds is a good hobby, if children should be brought up by their grandparents, and job-hunting tips for workers laid off from China's shrinking state enterprises. Guests and audience members air differences, share experiences, and offer advice. Through identification with guests and audience members, viewers feel that they are participating in the conversation, a process as important as the issues discussed.

Mini-documentaries about the daily lives of ordinary people in the "Everyday Life" segment resonated particularly well with viewers. [15] Featured characters have included a street cleaner, a migrant worker, a student taking care of his physically disabled mother, a teahouse attendant, and an independent artist. The "Focus Time" segment has garnered a reputation for creative editorial content and for reacting quickly to breaking news. [16]

Janice Xu characterizes three distinct roles assumed by *Oriental*'s reporters: the "advocate" of state objectives, the "voice of the victim," and the "social commentator." [17] "Advocate" stories show viewers such events as farmers electing their own village chiefs or Chinese law enforcement agencies both acting against violent crime and carrying out relief work. Reporters monitor malfunctioning or ineffective state agencies and thus help facilitate efficient functioning of government. Because corruption and mismanagement are exposed, people know the government is aware of the problems and those responsible will be held accountable.

"Voice of the victim" stories similarly expose illegal or immoral practices by local governments, factories, hospitals, department stores, etc. Here, television reporters take on the watchdog role, providing a measure of accountability. They speak for the victims whose rights or interests are being violated and act as mediators between individuals and institutions. The stories often involve power abuse or consumer fraud, with the victims presented as deserving sympathy and protection. Chinese audiences are thrilled to see real-life authorities being challenged, even if the authorities involved are mostly low-level.

Commentary pieces identify social phenomena that deserve public attention. Reporters comment, analyze, and sometimes warn viewers about a problem or a new trend in society, for example, how increasing commercialism in publishing has led to "poor taste" books that may negatively affect young children. A November 25, 1995, segment called "Whose Thinking Needs a Sharp Turn?" pictures a female reporter alongside a collection of children's books from different publishers with titles such as "A Sharp Turn of Thinking."[18] A group of schoolchildren appear in a shot. The camera then briefly shows pictures of half-naked women featured in the book's cartoon illustrations. The reporter turns to the camera and remarks, "There are questions like these in the books: 'What is the first thing for a girl to consider if she gets pregnant?' The answer is: 'Whether to get married.' 'Where is the place that adults play and occasionally sleep?' The answer is: 'A bed.'" The reporter looks angry. "Looking at these questions, it is hard for us to understand where the publishers want the children's minds to turn." In such instances, media professionals assume the roles of educator and counselor for the public. They select stories for moral impact and for illustrating society's declining moral standard and lapsed judgment.

By carefully vetting story topics, *Oriental Horizon* balances the dual purposes of meeting the government's propaganda goals and maintaining ratings. For instance, the reports about major criminal cases and police investigations are aired only when there is an ongoing government crackdown against crime. Ultimately, *Horizon*, like many subsequent magazine-type news programs, adheres to the paternalistic public service discourse that portrays the state as embodying the will of the masses. In turn, the state is genuinely more attentive now to gauging and responding to matters of public concern. As the state seeks to enhance its image as representative of people's concerns, television also identifies and voices some of their concerns back to the state. In this sense CCTV journalists become watchdogs.

In the mid-1990s, CCTV set out to develop more programs modeled on

Oriental Horizon. Yang recounted, "As *Oriental Horizon* stabilized as a morning show, I rewarded the team with a new program for the prime-time slot,
after the *National News Bulletin*. The new program they came up with is the
now well-known *Focus*. Initially they wanted to call it *Perspective on News*.
I thought the name a bit pretentious, as if to stake out the viewpoint of individual journalists instead of the central government. So we settled on *Focus*.
The short program became a must watch for policy makers, including Vice
Premier Li Peng and Premier Zhu Rongji. *Newsweek* in the U.S. commented
that it did not expect this sort of watchdog program on Chinese national TV."

In contrast to *Horizon*, which endears itself to audiences mainly by documenting the "real lives" of ordinary people, *Focus* emphasizes investigative,
edgy "exposé" stories. According to Yang, *Focus* was developed specifically in
response to a Propaganda Department call for the media to actively explore
issues of public concern and to "provide correct guidance to public opinion"
by framing stories according to the official line. The party wanted a program
that would be "innovative and democratic in form" to achieve greater propaganda effectiveness.[19]

A prime-time and condensed version of *Horizon*, *Focus* soon established a
dedicated audience for revelations about corrupt individuals and businesses
as well as issues such as pollution and unresponsive bureaucracies. For a long
time, *Focus* ranked second only to *National News Bulletin* and attracted 300
million viewers. People across the social spectrum bombarded CCTV with
telephone calls, letters, faxes, and e-mails, expressing their opinions and suggesting stories.

At its height, *Focus* also drew the attention of top party and government
officials. Former party leader Jiang Zemin, former premiers Li Peng and Zhu
Rongji, and the current party leader Hu Jintao all made phone calls to relevant
state agencies to solve problems exposed by the program. In 2000, a story on
the cause of seasonal sandstorms in Beijing prompted the central government
to allocate some CN¥8 billion over the next five years to plant trees and move
factories away from Beijing and its suburbs. Zhu Rongji is said to have never
missed a single episode of *Focus*. Supposedly, he endorsed the program for
functioning as part of the central government's work. According to Li Xiaoping, a journalist for *Focus*, Zhu started official meetings early so participants
could watch *Focus* together. He would then begin each session asking his colleagues how they could resolve problems aired on the show. *Focus*'s influence
at the highest echelons, though radically diminished, continues even today,
with Hu Jintao reportedly a faithful viewer.[20]

Endorsed by the top leadership, *Focus* provided a platform for the public to vent anger against authorities. With more frequent and sharper attacks on corruption and wrongdoing than other current affairs programs such as *Oriental Horizon, Focus* was one of the few programs that managed to retain the trust of both the viewing public and the party.

Focus soon became a household name. Li said that stories they did the night before frequently became the topic of conversation everywhere the next morning, in restaurants and on the street. "If you walked down the street in those days, you'd inevitably hear people talking about the bad guys exposed on *Focus*," Li said. "There was a sense of excitement, a mission. Everybody on the production team was on a high, as if we were all on drugs."

A few years later, though, *Focus*'s repeated exposure of domestic problems started to raise eyebrows among policy makers concerned about maintaining stability and social order. Thus, in his speech at the 1995 Radio and TV Current Affairs Program Conference, Sun Jiazheng, then head of the MRFT, urged *Focus* producers to exercise caution.[21] Sun also reiterated the party Central Committee's position on maintaining the authority and unity of the party and the nation. Yang Weiguang reprised the party's message in a similar speech to a number of his employees in 1996. Yang criticized producers who failed to provide balanced reports: "It appears that some departments have not been communicating timely and widely enough the central government's intentions and propaganda specifications. Some programs that are not in accordance with the propaganda specifications are still being made and broadcast."[22] Though on the face of it, it appeared Yang was capitulating to his party bosses—he'd even been quoted as saying, "If a state TV station reports problems here and there every day, how can it be called the tongue and throat of the Party?"[23]—Li credits him for having an innate sense of what the absolute limits of permissibility were and knowing when to pull back.

Focus was thus restricted to two critical reports a week at most. As noted by Zhang Xiaoling, local stations and programs were warned away from edgy topics altogether, leaving them to *Focus* alone: "The practice of putting hot topics in every program must be stopped. They are to be done by *Focus* only."[24] Going forward, *Focus* would exercise greater caution in topic selection and in the timing and intensity of its criticism.

A strict editorial control system has been in place at *Focus* ever since. Journalists are required to submit topics to the producer, who takes a first cut and then passes them on to the head of the News Center, a division within CCTV, for a further approval. As Zhang Xiaoling noted, "the final decision rests with the president of the TV station."[25] Choosing their topics, journalists and producers avoided reporting any problem that could not be solved quickly under existing conditions. Topics and their presentation are also tailored to "avoid triggering instability at home and providing subjects to be attacked from abroad."[26] Journalists' changing professional aspirations notwithstanding, many critical reports were censored. Some reports were scratched before the journalists managed to return to TV stations from field investigations. These rules would gradually neuter *Focus* and other challenging news programming at CCTV. As TV news ratings and relevance decreased, the Internet and a new breed of edgy commercial urban daily newspapers have become the "new mainstream" for public discourse.[27]

Even before the mid-1990s crackdown, *Focus* could not critique major state policies or directly report top-level policy-making processes. Criticism was limited to policy implementation by local officials. When reporting on the wrongdoing of local officials, *Focus* had to provide perpetrators a chance to correct their mistakes and errors in order to convey an image of the party as self-cleansing.[28]

Since 1998, any problems exposed on a *Focus* segment have required follow-up segments to prove that the "negative reports achieve positive effects."[29] Typically now, whenever *Focus* reveals a social ill or some instance of injustice, it also shows how the party leadership becomes involved, ameliorating the ills and making sure that wrongdoers are punished. A similar ethic is carried over to narrative programming and movies—bad guys are always caught and problems resolved in PRC films and television dramas. Even Hong Kong's film industry, which built its contemporary reputation largely on the strength of its gritty, energetic, morally ambiguous crime genre, has had to edit films for the mainland market by replacing questionable endings with ones where criminals are caught and punished. For instance, producers shot two endings for the 2002 Hong Kong police and mafia thriller *Infernal Affairs I* (which was eventually remade by Martin Scorsese as *The Departed*). Hong Kong audiences were treated to an ambiguous ending with no clear indication as to the fate of the criminal, while mainland viewers saw justice done and the criminal taken away in handcuffs.

After 1998, *Focus* and other investigative news programs featured positive reports highlighting the achievements of the party and the government, exactly what television news had done before *Focus*, and the opposite of how that program earned its reputation and its fervid audience. In a stark instance of disconnect between commercial and political imperatives, *Focus* lost its focus and soon thereafter its huge audience share. Viewer numbers began a steady decline starting in 1995.[30] From an audience share in the 40 percent range, *Focus* dropped into the low teens by late 2003.

In 2004, under the pressure of ratings, which had become the driving force under Zhao Huayong's reign at CCTV, *Focus* announced that it would go back to producing stories with more edge. In 2009, riding the wave of news revival under CCTV's new president, Jiao Li, *Focus* promised to recapture its watch-dog role. By then, though, PRC audiences had the Internet, social media, and other alternative sources of news and information. *Focus* would have to be an especially rabid watchdog to get even the slightest attention back from more sophisticated audiences.

When asked why *Focus* has lost its appeal in recent years, Yang Weiguang denied that the show was failing because of censorship. He said the problem was perhaps with the way the stories were told. Insisting that official oversight is more relaxed now than when he was at CCTV, he openly questioned the direction of *Focus* today.

"The issue is not on how far one can go to expose problems. The key is to locate a right reporting angle to get to the problems that concern both the state and the public. Are the problems reported common concerns to the majority of the Chinese? Have continued efforts been made to solving the problems? Or are we deliberately blowing things out of proportion in our reporting? It is not acceptable to pursue hot topics for the sake of the hot topics themselves. What do we hope to achieve while addressing problems? Sensationalism is not the way to go about addressing issues. I am not clear about the current status of the program. But *Focus* functioned fine when I left CCTV."

With *Focus*'s recent fall from relevance, sometimes one forgets just how refreshing its in-depth coverage of hot-button issues and its critical view of the government and government officials were. The early and mid-nineties were a sort of renaissance at CCTV, relatively speaking, that is, since even then television practitioners still had to contend with nosy censors. But Yang was able to oversee the creation of a slew of other new acclaimed programs such as the now canceled talk show *Tell It Like It Is*, which was hugely popular during the first several years of its run. The new programs provided unprec-edented forums for the public to vent grievances against government abuse and corruption.

"*Tell It Like It Is* aimed to provide a forum for the public to voice their opinions on social issues," Yang said. "At first, SARFT and the Propaganda Ministry were worried about what this program might lead to. But the audi-ences loved it, praising us for allowing a platform for their voices to be heard and emotions felt. We then followed with the creation of *News Probe*, an in-depth news investigative program. By then, one thing left unaddressed was the speed and efficiency of news reporting, also the issue of reporting news live."

Yang started to talk about his early obsession with doing live reports, a step he saw as essential for CCTV to become a network of global caliber. "At the time we did not have proper equipment for live reporting. To prepare for reporting the Hong Kong handover the following year, we spent CN¥$800 million in 1996 to purchase the most advanced digital equipment at the time. We conducted seventy-two hours of live broadcast during the handover in 1997. These days, our live reporting can now match the international standard. The open and live report of the Sichuan earthquake is the most recent example."

As Yang mentioned, the Sichuan earthquake may have been CCTV's finest moment in recent history, but it was possible only due to the foresight Yang and other managers at CCTV had in the decades leading up to it. A turning point of sorts was the station's reporting during the 1997 Hong Kong handover, an event that introduced the network to the value of live, saturation coverage.

Hong Kong Handover

Events become "live" when they are transmitted in real time and "real" settings, and covering live events requires sophisticated technology, an expert crew, and skilled presenters. Even in the early years, Yang had already begun to envision CCTV's transformation into a flagship global media outlet equal to the likes of CNN, the BBC, and Japan's NHK. As he related to me, "Cultivating the network's ability to do live broadcasts was essential to CCTV's great leap forward." In his biography, Yang proudly recounts how CCTV experimented with live broadcasting in 1992 at the Barcelona Olympics. Less than a year into his tenure as the president of CCTV, Yang took a group of CCTV reporters and technicians to Barcelona. With limited resources, the CCTV broadcast team could not afford to rent a studio on location—they couldn't even afford to rent a vehicle. Instead, CCTV shared a production suite with Hong Kong Cable TV (TVB), utilizing TVB's equipment and live feeds, only dubbing in CCTV's own commentary on the events. Still, the limited budget did not prevent CCTV from broadcasting 250 total hours of coverage, trumping the U.S. (200 hours), Japanese (200 hours), and Korean (180 hours) networks' Olympics coverage.

Five years after its tentative entry into "live" broadcasts, CCTV debuted as a full-fledged live broadcaster on the eve of the Hong Kong handover, June 30, 1997. The Hong Kong handover ceremony was the single most significant event in the history of Chinese television to that point. With little prior experience in live broadcasts of major events, CCTV pulled it off by sheer willpower, with, of course, heavy backing from the Chinese state. This time around, CCTV rented 485 square meters in the Press and Broadcasting Center in Hong Kong to build its studio, which was the largest production center among the seven hundred world media organizations that descended upon Hong Kong to capture the moment. Recognizing that "the whole world is watching," British and Chinese negotiators struggled up until the last minute to hammer out the most minute details of the handover, and the international media reported on these negotiations with liberal amounts of speculation about Hong Kong's future under Communist rule. Even the G8 leaders, who were gathered in Denver, Colorado, for their economic summit, were compelled to comment on the handover. Among other things, CCTV's coverage of this historical event was to show the world that Hong Kong would be maintaining its unique system under China's "one country, two systems" framework.

CCTV invested millions in new equipment for the handover coverage. According to the network's official account, preparation started a year in advance, when the network organized a Hong Kong Return Coverage Leadership Group headed by Yang Weiguang. Thanks to its size and its success in its first decade as a commercial broadcaster, CCTV was able to spend more than CN¥800 million of its own funds to purchase the most advanced satellite and broadcasting equipment then available for the handover. Yang Weiguang emphasized during our interview in 2008 that both financial and human resources were critical to the handover coverage, but CCTV would never have been in a position to invest such large sums in technology if it had to wait for the state to approve a budget and make funds available.

CCTV set up an Office of Hong Kong Return Coverage in March 1997, about four months in advance of the event. Coverage of the handover involved more than 1,660 people, including 289 people sent to Hong Kong and 100 more in twenty-three crews sent to eight cities in China and fifteen cities in foreign countries. Before the main crew was dispatched to Hong Kong, they were gathered together to study Deng Xiaoping's speeches on the "one country, two systems" principle under which Hong Kong would be assimilated, as well as party requirements and regulations specifically concerning the handover coverage. In addition, Hong Kong representatives in the National People's Congress and the Political Consultative Conference (a political advisory body) were notified to accept interviews with CCTV, the *People's Daily* newspaper, and the Xinhua News Agency. With its news net arranged and mobilized, CCTV set up for "live coverage" according to the official script for the handover.

CCTV's marathon coverage began with highly charged anchors in the Beijing studio introducing the network's game plan, followed by reporters in Hong Kong, other cities in China, and abroad introducing the "local" activities to be covered at those sites. CCTV also announced that it would mix its "live coverage" with prerecorded documentaries, interviews, and MTV-style videos selected through a nationwide competition. With a few glitches here and there, about one-quarter of the seventy-two-hour nonstop telecast was broadcast in simultaneous live transmission. As Yang told me, CCTV aimed to provide the "most comprehensive and live" coverage of the "celebratory activities."

For both foreign and domestic media, the progress of People's Liberation Army trucks and troops crossing the border at Shenzhen into Hong Kong made for the most compelling images of Hong Kong's new reality. Befitting the city's apolitical, business-first culture, and in contrast to the patriotic fanfare on CCTV, Hong Kong people who went out to see the troops' arrival generally treated them as a tourist attraction—from what I remember, there was a lot of posing for pictures with the green-clad PLA troops and with departing British troops. Anyone wearing a uniform of either authority became a photo opportunity.

CCTV sent Shui Junyi, a star news personality known for his ability to conduct interviews in English, his knowledge of international affairs, and his "star" quality, to anchor the broadcast from Hong Kong. In the Beijing headquarters, four regular evening news anchors rotated to host the seventy-two-hour "nonstop live broadcast." Dignified, assuring, and authoritative, Shui occupied the center of the live broadcast. His presence brought the Hong Kong scene closer to audiences at home in China.

All the major media outlets fought for camera angles at key border crossing points, vying to capture the best images of the PLA troops as they advanced through the heavy rain early in the morning of July 1. CCTV used the visuals of armored vehicles crossing over to Hong Kong as a defining moment of Chinese national pride. Media from the United States, Canada, Australia, and Taiwan depicted the same images as filled with ominous portents. While the BBC and ITV of Britain positioned legions of cameras and reporters at East Tamar to catch Prince Charles and Chris Patten (the outgoing British governor of Hong Kong) boarding the royal yacht and bidding an emotional farewell to the people of Hong Kong, the lone CCTV camera positioned at the same spot showed their departure in silence under the dark of night.

CCTV shaped the event as an unprecedented celebration for Chinese around the globe. A countdown clock on Tiananmen Square synchronized all the celebratory activities, and CCTV's Beijing anchors coordinated reports from around the world, while its anchors in Hong Kong coordinated local activities. The arrangement reflected and subtly enforced the centralized structure of the Chinese political system. As "junior partners" of the state's organizers, CCTV, the *People's Daily* newspaper, and the Xinhua News Agency all participated in orchestrating the "live spectacle," mixing news, entertainment, and propaganda.

Contemporary party propaganda is very much about celebrating Chineseness. In the postrevolutionary, postideological reform era, the one-party state authorizes its rule in part by featuring itself as the keeper of China's cultural heritage—the greatness, colorfulness, and multiplicity of Chinese tradition and ethnicity. Along these lines, CCTV's Hong Kong coverage tapped into a reservoir of cultural images and symbols. On the evening of June 30, CCTV news included live coverage of a traditional Chinese folk dance and drum performance, Yang-ge, performing under yet another fireworks display in Beijing. In one of many specially prepared videos, one hundred pop stars joined in singing a commemorative song, "1997, Eternal Love." In another video, while pop stars sang "going home, going home," iconic images of the Great Wall, the Yellow River, the Forbidden City, a rising rocket, and the China Bank skyscraper in Hong Kong filled the screen. The chorus continued, "The descendants of the dragon; / Leaning on the Yellow River and Yangtze River; / After one hundred years of suffering, / China is prospering, Hong Kong is returning home."

Deng Xiaoping, who had died earlier in the year, featured heavily in the broadcast. As President Jiang Zemin arrived in Hong Kong and delivered a speech, CCTV interspersed its coverage with close-ups of Deng's widow, who was said to have come despite her obvious frailty to fulfill Deng's wish of setting foot in Hong Kong after its return to China. In a staged "live report" from bordering Shenzhen, a group of students gathered in front of a huge portrait of Deng. One student thanked Deng "from the bottom of our hearts" for "bringing Hong Kong back to the embrace of the motherland." Finally, in a twelve-part documentary series, Deng was eulogized as an icon of national unity and the sentimental hero, in particular, of Hong Kong's reunification. The central, oft-repeated image of the series was his handwritten note: "I am a son of the Chinese people. I am deeply in love with my country and my people."

Hong Kong has a history, of course, but it is a history that is particularly open to creative narration and interpretation, which is to say, use as propaganda. It can be a story of enlightened colonial governance at its best: Hong

Kong's growth from undeveloped territory into one of the great cities of the world came entirely under British rule. It can be a story of foreign aggression and Chinese victimization: the agreements that put Hong Kong under British rule were "Unequal Treaties" negotiated after a series of "Opium Wars" and other conflicts in which the Western imperialist powers and Japan used superior military force to wrest concessions from the collapsing Qing dynasty in the late nineteenth and early twentieth centuries. Its success, likewise, can be a story of imported capitalism and good government or of native industriousness and Confucian values, of creative potential unleashed or of an opportunistic and alienating but hyperproductive get-it-while-you-can mentality.

China and CCTV actively sought to control and shape the narratives involved. In a fundamental semantic distinction, the outgoing British colonial government termed the historic event a "handover," while the PRC called it "*huigui*," or "reunification." The distinction reflects the different versions of official history that the two sides wished to authenticate, and while the British and other Western media on hand were not obligated to support the British version, most nonetheless adopted the "handover"* rubric, connoting a gracious departure after a job well done, with no more critical consideration than if they had been directed by state propagandists. On the Chinese side, CCTV's narration of Hong Kong's "reunification" began with the story of past humiliation and ended with the reunification as a moment of national rebirth and righteous triumph. David Lampton writes that "regime legitimacy in China currently rests on two pillars—rapid economic growth and vigorous defense of nationalistic values."[31] Reunification was partly an economic boost for China, but much more important was the tremendous opportunity to cultivate nationalistic pride and popular support for the government. In one of its prerecorded pieces, CCTV featured a Chinese diplomat who had participated in the negotiations with Britain over the future of Hong Kong and who had lived in Macao and Hong Kong as a boy. As Pan, Lee, Chan, and So recount in their excellent article "Hyping and Repairing the News Paradigm in the Age of Global Media Spectacles," "The camera focused on his dying father, a historian, in a hospital bed, with the diplomat's voice on the sound track: 'The return of Hong Kong has been my father's lifelong wish. Now that people of my generation have won back Hong Kong, we can face history, our ancestors and offspring.'"[32] In another prerecorded piece, as Pan, Lee, Chan, and So recount, villagers on the Hong Kong side cross the border to congratulate a

---

* My adoption of the term "handover" succumbs to the common usage but not to the ideological connotation.

family on the mainland side who have moved into a new house. Explaining his family tree, the seventy-year-old owner of the new house tells his grandchildren "never to forget that you are Chinese."

As much as anything, though, it was two things—the weather and the arriving PLA troops—that excited news broadcasters on both sides to wax ideologically, and even, about the rain, theologically. CCTV commentators read the rain and fog that fell on June 30 and July 1 as an act of heaven to "wash away 150 years of humiliation." To the British media, however, God was "mingling rain with tears" over the loss of the empire. Then, as PLA troops crossed into Hong Kong territory, CCTV's reporter on location exclaimed, "The PLA vehicle is moving! It's getting close . . . it has now crossed the border! The mighty and civilized PLA have now entered Hong Kong!" Meanwhile, over at CBS, Bob Simon declared, "For folks here, the PLA means Tiananmen Square."

Naturally, CCTV's coverage gave no hint that any protests marred the handover. Its commentators and reporters treated protests, primarily by pro-democracy groups, as minor annoyances. In its eyes—and the eyes of China itself—nothing would spoil the event, and CCTV led the way in dictating how the story would be remembered by citizens across the country. However, as future incidents such as the SARS epidemic and the Olympics protests would show, it would be hard to always maintain total control of the story, especially as viewers grew savvier.

3

MAKING THE NEWS

Journalism is one of the areas where you find the greatest number of people who are anxious, dissatisfied, rebellious, or cynically resigned.
—Pierre Bourdieu, French sociologist

The end of the last decade turned out to be quite eventful for CCTV and for its then president Zhao Huayong. After the spectacular success of the Beijing Olympics in summer 2008, a major fire at the nearly completed Mandarin Oriental Hotel, part of the new CCTV tower complex, in February 2009 threw the network into turmoil. Since its groundbreaking in 2004, the building had been a subject of popular jests—though one could argue that citizens resented less the building itself than what it stood for: CCTV and the Chinese Communist Party—and once the fire broke out, schadenfreude spread throughout the city and online. After the blaze, CCTV sought to distance itself from the accident, portraying it as the result of an unauthorized fireworks display organized by a few executives acting in an unofficial capacity. The state investigation later revealed substandard insulation materials, which contributed to the fire. Zhao, by then sixty-one, should have already been retired according to Chinese regulations, but he had originally chosen to linger on and oversee the completion of the new CCTV building. He consequently spent his last months cleaning up the mess of the CCTV fire and the subsequent fallout. Zhao received an administrative demotion and a "severe warning" from the party and stepped down on May 16, 2009.

Upon Zhao's departure, CCTV welcomed the arrival of its new czar, Jiao Li, previously a vice minister at the Propaganda Ministry. Jiao came from Liaoning, a northeastern province where he was in charge of the provincial Propaganda Department. Jiao's arrival precipitated yet another round of reforms, this time pushing the network back to its roots in news reporting.

Following the strategy he had employed in Liaoning, Jiao set out to revamp CCTV's news broadcasts and to make news operations CCTV's anchor.

On May 27, 2009, just ten days after Jiao took over, CCTV announced that its around-the-clock News Channel, which for six years had been available only to premium cable subscribers, would now be free to air and be included with channels provided in basic television service. The change, which was warmly received by News Channel personnel, allowed many Chinese viewers access to News Channel for the first time, boosting the channel's domestic audience share. News Channel would be revamped and would now broadcast live throughout the day, as opposed to airing prerecorded segments during certain hours. Other changes included strengthening news commentary by establishing an international news commentary program and increasing the ratio of international news to domestic news. Meanwhile, to reverse the trend of more popular programming on CCTV-1 under Zhao Huayong, Jiao Li increased the number of news programs on CCTV's flagship channel beginning on August 17, 2009. As a result, the current affairs talk show *Xiao Cui Talks* was relocated from the News Channel to the flagship CCTV-1 channel, a move roughly akin to NBCUniversal promoting one of its MSNBC shows to air on NBC.

The recentering of news at CCTV reflected the network's realization that the domestic and international reputation of CCTV, for better or for worse, rested on its news programs. Indeed, as experiences like the Sichuan earthquake and the SARS scandal have proven, news programs are a useful tool for the party-state to influence public opinion, both domestically and globally. The influence and impact of news programs at CNN, the BBC, and Al Jazeera are invoked as models for CCTV to establish its own imprint on the global media landscape.

The Journalist's Burden

CCTV's reputation as the official (if not always accurate) news source for the country began with Yang's arrival in 1985: "Given that I was in charge of news programs at the radio station, I naturally started out by evaluating news operations here. I noted how slow and irrelevant the majority of the news items and programs at CCTV were. For instance, one news program used three minutes to do a story about a minuscule village enterprise that nobody cared about. Instances like this were numerous. What a waste of resources."

Though the party heads in the Propaganda Ministry were enthusiastic about Yang's desire to reshape the antiquated news reporting at CCTV, his colleagues were less so. "Resistance came from all fronts," Yang said. "At the time, CCTV only reported news from the previous day. I asked why and was told that speed did not matter as TV had both image and sound and could easily beat newspaper and radio in its appeal even if it was outdated news. I said, well, wouldn't it be more attractive to deliver better-looking *and* more timely news? I told them that we needed to beat other media in news delivery. So we started to broadcast same-day major news on *National News Bulletin*. We managed to factor in last-minute news items for the seven o'clock news, an unprecedented move at the time. People were resistant because they resented having to stay at work right up until the start of the program. But the results turned out to be rewarding."

Yang also exercised control on news values. "I shortened the average length of news items and mandated we increase the news value in each story, as long news stories without substance kill audiences. The imposed timeliness and time limit dramatically raised CCTV's reputation. Organizations started to schedule their meetings around the availability of CCTV journalists. Major events had to have CCTV's presence—soon no one even cared if journalists from the *People's Daily* were absent."

Wearing his competitive edge on his sleeve, Yang aimed his reforms at competing with radio and newspapers for better and more timely stories. Yang pointed out the irony that the first thing he did upon arrival at CCTV was to find ways to beat his first love, radio. In fact, during his time at the Central People's Broadcasting Station, he had focused his energy on how to sustain radio's attraction amid the potential challenge from television. Yang was unsentimental in swiftly shifting his loyalties, as any good manager in the CCP system should be. Yang would prove to be a daring reformer with an instinct for pushing right up against the boundaries without crossing them.

"Do you remember the *Challenger* story?" Yang asked me. "In 1986, as the U.S. *Challenger* spacecraft suddenly exploded, knowing that this would be the headline news all over the world, and that CCTV would look foolish if it failed to capture the news, I decided to run it as the lead story for that night's news broadcast." The news of the explosion on the *National News Bulletin* on January 28, 1986, broke the ground for CCTV's stiff domestic affairs–oriented evening news program.

"I ran the story out of my professional instinct for news value and did not seek preapproval from my boss. It turned out okay and I was not chastised. There were several similar instances of fait accompli where I took some measured steps to test the limits. In September 1986, the State Council proposed to establish China's first bankruptcy law. It was a controversial proposition, and when the proposal was sent to the Standing Committee of the People's Congress for debate, reporters from CCTV's Special Topics Division suggested that we record the entire session and then do a story about the debate. It would be rather refreshing if the proposal was rejected by the People's Congress, which would suggest to the world that the People's Congress was not merely a rubber stamp for the State Council. Previously, significant policy deliberations were simply reported outcomes as brief news items by CCTV and thus the public was left unaware. I decided that it was worth a try to at least make the program. As it turned out, the Congress rejected the bankruptcy law and we made it into a program."

Yang sent a copy of the program to several key persons at the central government to gauge their reactions. After the head of the Standing Committee of the National Congress, Peng Zheng, endorsed it, CCTV broadcast the piece and was widely praised for promoting transparency in policy making and bringing policy makers closer to the public.

Throughout Yang's time at CCTV, his instincts served him well. "While reporting the fifth conference of the Sixth People's Congress in 1987, the new Standing Committee of the Politburo announced that it would hold a news conference with international and domestic news media. But the person in charge of the news conference forewarned the domestic media that the conference would be only five minutes long and that members of the Standing Committee led by Zhao Ziyang would not answer questions. I told my reporting team to be prepared for a longer conference than planned, as it would be impossible for the international journalists not to fire questions, and obviously the committee members would have no choice other than answering them. But I had faith in our central leaders' readiness in conducting an impromptu Q and A session. I told my team to bring extra videotape for recording and set up both steady and mobile cameras in case the leaders answered questions while walking. CCTV's live report of the news conference was a hit, beating reports filed by News Studio, which had to abort reporting halfway when its reporters used up its tapes." Yang told me he was especially pleased with the results. "It instantly changed the pathetic state of Chinese people getting domestic news from international sources. Chinese people should be granted the right to know, though we do need to get permission from SARFT and the Propaganda Ministry for running sensitive stories."

Journalistic Responsibilities

Though CCTV's journalists and workers are often depicted as mindless government lackeys who broadcast stale propaganda, the sense of pride found
in Yang's voice as a journalist serving and shaping the people and public
opinion has a long tradition in Chinese culture. An early-twentieth-century
intellectual, Liang Qichao (1879–1929), is considered to be the "doyen of
modern Chinese journalism."[1] Liang and other "enlightenment scholars" of
the May Fourth Movement and the broader New Cultural Movement, including Sun Yat-sen and Chen Duxiu, sought to modernize China and to save it
from foreign imperialists by trading its "feudal" traditions for science and
democracy—ideals that had raised the Western powers to predominance.
In the late Qing and early Republican eras, when China's titanic struggle
with modernization began, Liang and his fellow New Cultural intellectuals
emphasized communication between the authorities and the people via the
enlightened newsmen, thus spawning a new breed of journalists as enlightenment intellectuals. Liang Qichao put forth that the press should perform two
major functions: communicating information and ideas to the public and
supervising and mobilizing public opinion in order to influence government,
a philosophy much closer to the Western notion of journalistic functions than
what Mao later envisioned.[2] The journalists of Liang's time used the print
media to encourage a dialogue between traditional and modern conceptions
of society and politics and between imported and local ideals and concepts.
Chinese journalists have since been regarded as intellectuals.

Different from the Chinese tradition that systematically produced intellectuals as a class of civil servant advisers and administrators qualified
through a rigorous imperial examination system, the modern, informal mix
of professional credentials, public acknowledgment, and self-identification is
not far from Western ideas about what makes an intellectual. However, in
China, "intellectual" still carries a more definite sense both of class distinction
and of social responsibility—something like the Western notion of "noblesse
oblige," but with public *guidance* added to the public *service* remit. In contrast
to Mao's stated ideal of a two-way flow of information and opinion between
those who lead and those who follow (which never really worked that way),
Chinese intellectuals now assume the role of mediators between the party and
the public.

Chinese journalists now serve, as one journalist joked to me, a "trinity" of
masters: the party-state, the market, and an increasingly lively public. They
remain officially tied to the party-state, but they are now equally disciplined

by the market. Yet the professional "calling" that they are instinctively drawn to is a public service. If a new professional ethic lends Chinese journalists a sense at least of aspirational independence from the party-state, it is not entirely free of the authoritarian impulses of its propagandist tradition. As Yu Haiqing notes, *News Probe* specifies four guidelines for its investigative journalists: they should have a spirit of questioning, a perspective of equality, a sense of balance, and an attitude of equilibrium.[3] Yu points out that while the first three guidelines have counterparts in Western journalism, the fourth, the attitude of equilibrium, is uniquely Chinese. Equality and balance refer to qualities—objectivity, impartiality, fairness, thoroughness, accuracy— generally understood as crucial for journalists, but "equilibrium" is something else. Equilibrium, in the Chinese lexicon, is about promoting unity, order, and a fundamental faith in the national project. The impression should be that while there are many problems, there are also solutions, ameliorative factors, and a net balance of positive developments—no reason to panic. Maintaining social equilibrium is, of course, also the primary aim of the party's current propaganda mission, except that the party regards cultivating specific faith in its own leadership as the first priority. Given this shared impulse to promote social equilibrium, the distance between what Chinese journalists would do independently as a matter of professional conscience and what the party-state directs the news media to do might not be very great in actual practice, but the party is in no way ready to put that theory to the test. The government continues to tightly regulate the Chinese news media, even though based on what I heard from journalists it probably wouldn't have to: many regarded the upholding of traditional moral standards, social order, and a collective cultural identity as their primary mission.

News Probe and Zhang Jie's "Enlightenment" Turn

In 1996, after the success of *Oriental Horizon* and *Focus*, CCTV-1 launched another newsmagazine program, *News Probe*, in the network's evening slot, with Xia Jun as producer and the now renowned anchorman Bai Yansong as host. Backed by Yang Weiguang, who saw the program as a potential third flagship after *Horizon* and *Focus*, *News Probe* had designs on being China's *60 Minutes*. As recounted by Sun Yusheng, he and his colleagues in the News Division first encountered *60 Minutes* in 1993, with limited understanding of the program content due to the language barrier. Sun was finally able to comprehend the program in its entirety when, in 1994, he received from his friend Zhang Bubing, who later became *News Probe*'s first producer, a subtitled episode about a car insurance scandal. Sun was engrossed by the investigative-style approach of the program and thought it was more suspenseful than fictional TV.[4]

Sun put together a production team that included Xia Jun, Liu Chun (who later left CCTV to head Phoenix's China operation), and Zhang Jie, who was working on *Oriental Horizon*. I had a chance to speak with Zhang Jie about the early days at *News Probe*. A man of slight build, Zhang looked and sounded careworn when I spoke with him. His colleagues later told me that anxiety is the default mode of CCTV newspeople. But when I spoke to him, he was feeling particularly daunted by a new round of program restructuring at CCTV that had him understaffed, over-censored, and still under the gun to deliver ratings. Though distressed, he talked nonstop, more like a poet than a producer, and with a genuine desire to connect. As Zhang Jie recounted, "We started preparation in 1996. The new program would be an extension of *Focus* but would touch more of the gray rather than black-and-white areas. It was to surpass *Focus* in doing stories with depth and with objectivity. *News Probe* also relied on a team of expert consultants, which helped to ensure quality."

The show started off well, winning popular and professional praise, but it still needed to define itself. "It was not easy for *News Probe* to emulate the edgy style of *Focus*," Zhang recalled. "At the time, *Focus* was already raising eyebrows among a certain segment of the population who equated watchdog-style programs with negative depictions of society." After an exceptional period of official tolerance and encouragement, the censorship restrictions began to tighten up again. As a result, *News Probe* was forced to back away from the edgy investigative journalism that had made its reputation, and audiences booed its retreat.

Muckraking, watchdog-style journalism captured the imagination of a new generation of Chinese journalists in the late 1990s, with *News Probe* leading the charge on television. These reports had quickly garnered great public currency, but now that the official sanction was being withdrawn, that currency dissipated. Li Datong, a veteran journalist who was purged from the top post at the journal *Freezing Point* over exposés of official corruption published under his leadership, was pessimistic about journalists' ability to act independently from the state: "Investigative journalism has been in a clear cycle of weakening over the last two years. Very rarely can you see investigative reports that make a deep impact. . . . CCTV's *News Probe* is now effectively barred from investigative reporting, so this excellent television program has been reduced to nothing."[5]

In defense of the show's less edgy turn, Zhang said that *News Probe* was making a transition from exposé stories, mostly of particular instances of official corruption, to "enlightenment" stories, mostly of broadly defined social ills with no particular villains. "Enlightenment" is used as a term of art by some Chinese journalists these days. It paradoxically fits well alongside the state's renewed insistence on "correct opinion guidance" in the media while also being in line with the progressive intellectual tradition of the May Fourth Movement, which is how journalists like to imagine themselves: as independent intellectuals and champions of the public's right to know.

In line with the intellectual tradition, Liang Qichao's notion that the press should supervise and mobilize public opinion in order to influence government obviously didn't fit the propaganda paradigm of the PRC's revolutionary era,[6] but in the reform era journalists are channeling Liang anew, and the current regime recognize public opinion as a force to be solicited in a carefully guided dialogue between state and society. Zhang Jie's view of journalism at CCTV is not very different from Liang's earlier ideal. Today's Chinese journalists, including Zhang, have incorporated Western ideas into their professional lexicon, becoming serious about pursuing journalism as a profession, with ethics and procedural standards of its own, wholly independent of the state. Meanwhile, as the party works to adapt its propaganda to changing conditions, it has allowed the news media more room to investigate and criticize, understanding that in a more open environment the popular appeal and credibility of the news media is up for judgment at all times. Journalists constantly test the limits of this leeway, trying to negotiate the boundaries of the permissible further and further out. Stanley Rosen, for instance, recounts how *Beijing Youth Daily* covered controversial social issues while casting them in the conventional rhetoric of "nationalism" and "patriotism." The debates surrounding the issues nevertheless helped to stimulate public reflection on citizenship and democracy.[7]

State directives putting the media and cultural industries on a competitive commercial basis and encouraging media expansion, innovation, and professionalism inherently put some mental distance between media professionals and the state that they work for. Professionalism has become a point of pride, and it makes media workers conscious of serving public interests that are not always synonymous with party directives. In my talks with frontline CCTV personnel, I heard over and over acknowledgment of the party's ideological preeminence, but this was almost always paired with a sense of duty to question authority on behalf of audiences. CCTV professionals, journalists in particular, are conscious of struggling against both political and commercial limits in order to serve the public interest.

At the turn of the millennium, media scholar Chin-Chuan Lee called for new research perspectives that take into consideration "the role of China's journalism in the growing interpenetrating web of the local, the national and the global to maintain a dynamic equilibrium between universal principles (human rights, freedom of expression) and national narratives (sovereignty)."[8] The contested reception among the scholars of China studies immediately after Lu Xiaobo's Nobel Peace Price in October 2010 is the most recent case of the struggle between such universal principles and the ongoing narrative of China's national stability. In less academic terms, Lee was suggesting, back in 2000, that Chinese journalists were doing less state-directed transmission and more balancing—mediating among different interests, sources, and ideas. Still tied to their official mouthpiece function and conscious too of carrying forward the intellectual tradition of guiding public opinion (which is not identical to the state's interest in "correct opinion guidance"), the latest generation of Chinese journalists have added a new task to their job description, positioning themselves more explicitly as "mediators," to borrow Yu's term, between the state, business, and other institutional interests, and society.[9] *News Probe* is a perfect place to observe Chinese journalists trying to mediate "a dynamic equilibrium" between competing forces and discourses.[10]

"Some charged *Focus* with being anti-party and anti-socialist China and called for the show to be canceled," Zhang recalled. "To avoid that criticism *News Probe* adopted a calmer approach, seeking to address long-term social issues from an analytical perspective. Nineteen ninety-six and ninety-seven was a time when China started to experiment with housing reform, urban reform, state-owned enterprise reform, et cetera. Those were closely watched yet nonexplosive issues. In short, we tried to avoid explosive stories. Hard-edged stories would not have been aired anyway. So we adopted this analytical approach, more like scholarly research into the issues. Xia Jun was the one who proposed the model. He was called on to take over the program when a bunch of us from the hard-core *Focus* background failed to come up with a softer approach. Xia was a thinker and an avid reader, also a scholar with a cool and analytical head. So we did stories on public transportation reform, medical reform, and so on and so forth. These types of programs put high demands on producers and team members, as we all had to be semi-experts before we could comfortably comment on these issues. The learning curve was huge and we coped. The group of experts we gathered helped. So we produced some quite influential stories. But our analytical approach made the program less exciting. Some commented that the program was unnecessarily ponderous and too complicated."

Zhang continued, "So we later came up with a three-stage development strategy. In the first stage we would do stories that just deal with surface issues. In the second stage we would do investigative stories that unveiled the power struggles behind the surface issues, which borders watchdog journalism. And in the third stage we would have our top product, which exposes the inside stories and reveals the dark elements of the society. We anticipated that it would take us three years to reach that top stage. Interestingly, in 1998, the third year, our program did several real heavyweight investigative stories. And by that time, the audiences had grown mature and come to terms with investigative journalism. So it took us three years to reach the 'probing' part of *News Probe*. Real investigative research that unveiled corruption did not appear until 1998, though the official ideology still did not endorse the media's exposé function at the time. Both the bureau in charge of ideology and·the relevant government offices were resistant to these types of stories."

With such issues resolved, *News Probe* took a renewed stab at investigative reporting with a story in October 1998 about fraud on an irrigation project in Yuncheng, a city in Shanxi Province. The effort pleased audiences and reinvigorated the practitioners. A more significant *News Probe* milestone came two years later. As Zhang related to me, "At a media conference in 2000, critics pointed out that our program was too ambitious and inclusive in its coverage. Indeed, prior to that, we had covered topics ranging from major flooding to condom distribution in colleges, assisted suicide, et cetera. It would be good for us to settle on a group of core topics so that audiences knew what to expect. So we explored two options. One was to focus on events that made national news, which would make our program a national archive of some sort. But after several months of experimentation, this option did not work out because some of the major events took a long time to unfold and we did not have the capacity to actually perform the role of investigators. Instead, our journalists chiefly assisted investigations carried out by the Central Committee for Discipline Inspection and judicial institutions, which reduced the relevance and uniqueness of our reporting. The second option we explored was to focus on unveiling truth, or unearthing the real event behind what it appeared to be. When we threw out the slogan of 'unveil one truth per episode,' media experts expressed skepticism, reminding us that investigating the truth was frequently beyond the capacity of the media and that truth is relative, depending on one's angle and perspective. So we modified our goal to 'probing the truth,' which became the official motto for the program in December 2000 at a promotional event. The program thus took shape as an independent investigating entity. In our concept, truth stands for facts concealed by power, special interests, and prejudice, and is sometimes limited by our social circle and collective conscious."[11]

"So you made a promise to seek truth?" I asked.

"We are not promising to find the truth but to take the audience with us as we embark on a journey of truth probing," Zhang said. "We would not be so presumptuous as to say we are providing the truth but rather simply telling you what we consider as the truth based on objective laws and regulations. The motto was similar to the name of the then popular talk show *Tell It Like It Is*. *Tell* had become part of the popular lexicon at the time, which suggested that the public had accepted media's new role."

So around 2000, *News Probe* found its identity and established practices that continue to guide its production. Story selection follows three guidelines: the topic must be newsworthy, reflecting social changes and capturing issues of wide public concern; it must be complex enough for a format that mandates unexpected twists and turns and in-depth investigation over a period of time; and it must be exclusive to CCTV and sustain a forty-five-minute broadcast. The show's narrative strategy emulates popular American investigative television programs, following the story as it happens and investigating what lies behind the surface news. As Zhang put it, this approach allows the event to take its course and encourages viewers to develop their own understanding of China's problems, fostering a new generation of Chinese who can think for themselves and become familiar with the diverse problems and dilemmas facing China and the world. According to Zhang, *News Probe* ultimately aims to encourage grassroots reform efforts that will bring modernization to every corner of the society. This is the essence of "enlightenment" in Zhang's conception. He takes seriously media's responsibility to become an independent "fourth power"[12] to guide society and to promote democracy and prosperity.

The year 2003, the second year of the Hu Jintao / Wen Jiabao administration, was climactic for *News Probe*. Zhang took over the program and initiated a number of directives. As Zhang put it, "We sharpened our goal in heavyweight investigative reporting, avoiding soft-edged stories. I encouraged my team to not be afraid of offending the powerful, though this was easier said than done, as there were constant threats from mobs and corrupt state organizations and law enforcement agencies." Besides the potential political consequences of ideologically sensitive reporting, Chinese journalists are also vulnerable to libel suits. The facts of a libel case in China do not always determine the court's decision, adding another measure of caution to journalists' self-censorship impulse. To protect itself against libel suits, *News Probe* keeps tapes of all footage for six months.

More than libel concerns, though, state censorship continued to limit the commercial and professional ambitions of Zhang's team. In 2003, when the SARS story broke, *News Probe* broadcast the first images of SARS patients from inside Beijing hospitals. A team of journalists using a concealed camera filmed the scenes. After the report was aired, Propaganda Department officials told Zhang Jie that one such report was enough. Many edgy stories were thus canceled before they went on air.

In spite of pressure like this, *News Probe* reestablished its reputation with a series of provocative stories in 2003 and 2004. "I realized by 2004 that our program would be more appropriately compared to *Frontline* on PBS than to *60 Minutes* on CBS," Zhang said. "In the next few years, though, the intensity of our investigations fluctuated as the political environment tightened or loosened. Our goal of performing a watchdog function remained until 2006, the year we started to inject 'enlightenment' into our surveillance function."

Questioned about the declining number of hard-edged stories in recent years, Zhang Jie suggested that there has been a deliberate turn to cultural and social "enlightenment." Zhang sees enlightenment as a balancing act between increasing pressure from the state to conform and pressure from viewers to do more hard news. After all, the traditional intellectual impulse to "guide society" has wide appeal among TV professionals. As Zhang told me, " 'enlightenment' in our usage is about teaching the Chinese about citizenry as we enter a modern civil society."

I asked, "So is the program going back to talking down to the public?"

"No," Zhang said. "The goal is for the media to enlighten the public as we explore a set of issues pertaining to how to become responsible citizens. We're inviting the public to come and discover who the quality citizens are and what constitutes responsible citizenship. We feature model citizens along the way and amplify the traits that make them superb citizens. For instance, Zhang Yimou made *The Story of Qiuju*, featuring someone who fights for her rights, so we'd be doing the public a good service trying to locate people like Qiuju. So our program aimed to encourage elements conducive to the building of a society that abides by law and is governed by moral principles." *Qiuju* the film is actually a portrait of futility, irony, and fickle fate as much as of the positive effects of fighting for one's rights, but Zhang Jie's point about offering useful explorations of the notion of citizenship in stories on *News Probe* makes sense. At the same time, though, didactic portrayals of "model citizens" in literature, theater, and film are notorious artifacts of the prereform revolutionary era, so anything smacking of model characters in the media runs the risk of receiving a cynical response from viewers. The Qiuju in Zhang Yimou's

1992 film is carefully constructed as an antimodel, a fully complex person whose noteworthy characteristics cut both ways.

Zhang Jie mentioned that in 2006, when one of their stories didn't get the censor's approval, they replaced it with a story that featured three community organizers who reflected on the challenges they faced when they ran for the local Condo Association's board (China has held direct elections for certain village-level offices since the early 1980s).

"What struck me the most was their adage that democracy starts from the neighborhood. The smallest units of community organization in China's urban center are boards of property owners in apartment complexes. The elected boards must confront builders and developers and the management of the apartment complexes. So the three people featured in the story all advocated that democracy in China must start with individual property rights. In order to protect your private property, you must form a union and take part in policy deliberation and implementation.

"The concept did not immediately kick in, as many of the condo owners in the city did not see the need to have an active voice in home owners' associations. They did not think it mattered and did not want to spend time and energy to have a stake in the association. If they do not bother to vote on matters concerning their own property, how do we expect them to vote for something less relevant to their immediate needs? This exposed our lack of understanding of the concept of citizenship and democracy. We wait for things to happen instead of making it happen. We wait passively for a savior to come and rescue us. We do not have the concept of standing up and fighting for your own rights. This is the Chinese tradition, waiting for a benevolent ruler to come and protect us. So the story featuring the discussion of citizen participation among three directors of home owners' associations speaks volumes about the lack of education about citizenship and community activism. I was one of the passive home owners they lamented. I did not want to donate my time and energy to fighting for our common benefits, but I wouldn't mind reaping the benefits if we scored in our fight against the builders and management companies who want to raise fees and reduce green space. Promoting the idea of individual rights and community activism and supporting the growth of nongovernmental organizations would go a long way toward fostering the idea of democracy and citizenship in China. So we try to promote rights awareness and the right to fight for and protect one's own rights. In the process, you need to learn the art of negotiation and compromise. Democracy is a balance between protecting one's own rights and observing the benefits of the majority. So our program started to do rights stories."

But almost as important to Zhang was his wariness in contributing to a "mean-world syndrome," what some call the excessive negative reporting on China's problems, and a desire to balance harder-hitting programs with those that captured the progress that China had made in recent years. Zhang told me a short anecdote.

"We did two stories right before the party's last annual congress meeting in 2009, one of which was about how a village in Chongqing experimented with democratic elections. Prior to that, the conventional wisdom was that rural Chinese were too ignorant to participate in any democratic process. The story featured two young local officials who tried to change the hostile attitude the local farmers had toward local government. Back in 1998, the lack of transparency in local government budgeting and high taxes caused a public revolt. Villagers smashed a signboard on the local government building. The party secretary-general and the mayor, both young men who took the offices trying to make a difference, were quite upset by the incident.

"Determined to change the dynamic, they decided to build a much-needed bridge that would connect the villagers with a local school separated by two rivers. Every year, during the rainy season, flooding from the river would claim the lives of a few local kids. The idea of building a bridge by collecting donations from the local people had been on the table for seven or eight years, but the villagers were too poor to come up with the CN¥60 per family needed to get the job done.

"The two local officials came to a compromise with the villagers, agreeing to find a less costly construction company that would drive down the cost by half so each family needed only to come up with CN¥30. The party secretary-general promised the villagers that all the unused money would be returned once the construction was done. One treasurer was elected from each of the four villages to keep the expenses in check. All four treasurers had to sign checks before they could be issued. The efforts paid off and there was a balance of over CN¥30,000 left after the bridge was built. Members of the local government were tempted to keep the money for other public projects or to make up for the back taxes some of the villages had yet to pay. But the party secretary-general insisted on returning the money to the villagers as promised. He convinced his cabinet members that regaining the trust of the people should be the most urgent thing to do. So they gave the money back to the villagers, CN¥9 per family. The CN¥9 brought smiles back to the villagers' faces and melted the ice between the government and the public. Most important of all, it reestablished their faith in local government.

"Soon neighboring villages began to follow suit, collecting money for

building bridges and other public facilities such as roads and electric gen-
erators. The Chongqing municipality praised the efforts of the villages. It
was a lesson in civil participation, democracy at its most fundamental level.
The villagers learned the benefits of public participation for the good of the
community. They also learned lessons about casting votes and respecting the
results of the voting. The officials learned the benefits of conducting local
business in a transparent and fair manner. They learned to trust the public's
ability in coming to a consensus.

"Eight years had passed when we showed up to do a story about the villages
in 2007. The places were still poor, but the investment in public projects had
reached more than CN¥30 million, of which the state funding was less than
CN¥5 million. Most of the collected funds came from money sent back by
migrant workers. It showed their love for their hometown. It was incredible."

Zhang turned sentimental, clearly moved by his own discovery of the
power of people who are in charge of their own destiny. I started to understand what he meant by enlightenment as a joint journey between his program
and his viewers. The message Zhang drove home was that the Chinese people
could be entrusted with self-governance, which is to say that the foundation
for democracy could be developed in China.

Zhang's enthusiasm for the messy process of democracy practiced by Chinese villagers was not a feint to cover for *News Probe*'s faltering edginess—he
seemed genuinely convinced that he and the show were on to something with
the new enlightenment project. "There were moments when the villagers had
to come to a consensus about the route while building a road. Issues arose
as to which houses the route should pass by. The villagers argued and even
got into fistfights. So the project halted for months, which frustrated local
officials, who threatened to call it quits. One official cursed the few villagers
for their selfish behavior and resigned. A new committee for overseeing the
project was elected as the villagers witnessed the completion of roads built by
other villages. It took this particular village three years to build a local road,
and the ordeal taught the local people about the messiness of the process of
democracy and the importance of compromise.

"It's too bad that while the critics endorsed our new approach, the ratings have not picked up, as stories of an enlightenment nature are not as
sensational as the muckraking, hard-edged, anticorruption ones. They don't
have blood or gore." Zhang's griping about the show's ratings revealed the
limits to his abstract enthusiasm for enlightenment television devoted to
civic-mindedness. "People with sound judgment would surely appreciate our
program, realizing the social significance of our program. Only uneducated

people would consider our stories meaningless. It is true that people watch TV for entertainment, but our program should not cater to the lowest common denominator."

The ratings slide was pronounced in 2005 when *News Probe* ran on CCTV-1, the most competitive channel on CCTV. That was also the year when a new policy directive forbade "cross-regional reporting," in which journalists from one geographical jurisdiction report on the goings-on in another region. News media regularly employed this jurisdictional trick to pursue hard-hitting stories (and higher ratings) without upsetting party officials in their own region—the ones they had to answer to directly. This had become an essential tool for professional journalists in China, facilitating reporting on many major stories, including mining disasters, illegal land-use cases, and even China's rural AIDS epidemic—but it had also drawn fierce opposition from local party leaders, who feared its consequences. City and provincial leaders pressured top propaganda officials to curb the practice, and in 2005, Beijing issued its directive, undermining watchdog journalism and granting local officials near impunity from press scrutiny.

At the same time that these rules constricting the news media's ability to engage in critical journalism were enacted, there was also continued commercial and official pressure to keep ratings up. Zhang suggested that resorting to salacious stories is always an option, that the directive against cross-regional reporting and the show's rejiggered enlightenment ethic don't prevent *News Probe* from crossing over to the dark side anytime it needs a little ratings boost. Zhang described the struggle at *News Probe*: "While the network is under pressure to conform to market logic, which measures programs with nothing but ratings, it is the responsibility of individual producers to balance out the popular with the public. So I set up a goal to not chase ratings so long as I am beyond the threshold set by CCTV. We were issued ratings warnings at the first and last season of 2008. The rule is that if a program is issued two consecutive warnings, then either the producer must be fired or the program must be canceled. So after we received a warning in the first season last year, we did several murder and corruption stories, which instantly brought up the ratings.

"While the watchdog function exposes the wrongdoings of others, enlightenment spotlights our own problems, revealing our own learning curve. So it turns audiences into participants. The exposé stories have not helped in curbing corruption. Neither has the execution of convicted high-level officials. While our political system might be responsible for the problem, our culture too is a contributing factor. Traditional Chinese society worships people with connections who can get things done, which breeds corruption and condones the violation of laws and regulations. So the key is to examine our culture, which continues to value networking and connections over rules and regulations."

"You mentioned the political system. Any signs of political reform?" I pressed on.

Obviously, neither *News Probe* nor any other significant media platform can say flatly that China needs comprehensive political reform *now*. One-on-one, however, some of the people I spoke to at CCTV, including Zhang, were surprisingly frank about supporting political reform, even in formal interviews. Still, in response to this direct question about political reform here and now, Zhang's response seemed to be a reflex of self-censorship. "Economic reform in the past seven or eight years has brought positive changes to China, but lagging political reform has complicated things. A seven-episode series we made last year, *Broken Ice*, traced major events and personalities in politics, economics, and culture over the past three decades. The first episode discussed events that contributed to the party's decision to 'open up.' In May 1978, the CCP dispatched high-level observation teams to the West to see how the system in the West functioned. Deng Xiaoping himself toured Japan and Singapore in December 1978. The experience cast a new light on their understanding of capitalism and socialism. The hard-line general Wang Zhen, for instance, saw with surprise that a laid-off factory worker could still afford to live in a two-story house. He marveled at the welfare system the British government provided to its citizens. He remarked that a combination of the UK's economic system with the CCP's political system would make a perfect communism. We included his quote in our program."

If Zhang's first impulse was to self-censor on the subject of political reform, his extended remarks were more daring and ended on a winking declaration. "There are several major areas one must pay attention to in order to understand China. One is the income gap between rural people and urban residents. Chengdu started to address this issue five or six years ago and has since brought down the income gap. The second area concerns the shape and speed of the democratic process. This has been on the agenda of party think tanks for a while. When I visited the Party School[13] a couple of years ago, I saw books and documents about the collapse of various foreign regimes in history. So the top leaders are thinking hard about this. A county in Cheduo held a mock election of the party secretary-general, the most crucial position in the county. We caught footage of the election, but our program was censored, as the election of a party leader is too sensitive a topic for TV. The point I am making is that democracy *will* be initiated from the top level in the future. I remember Premier Wen Jiabao said something to the effect that he believed that if elected officials could properly take charge of the village, then they could manage a county, even a province. Though I'm not sure if he included 'nation.' " Zhang chuckled. "Anyhow, the party has its plan, I believe. I must point out that democracy is not the end itself but a means to the end of a more fair and prosperous society."

"Or a 'harmonious society,' " I interjected.

"Tell you what; I had this idea of 'harmonious society' in 1994 at a conference in Taiwan. I defined the goal of media as helping to build harmony in society. Media freedom and democracy are means to achieve this goal. From this perspective, the problem with our watchdog type of programs in China is the tendency to simplify a complex issue and to demoralize the powerful and the rich and at the same time blow out of proportion the virtues of the underclass. For instance, we did a story about skyrocketing medical bills, which resonated among the public. The story became a media event, helping to push for medical reform. Later on, a friend of mine in the medical profession complained to me about the wholesale slandering of doctors and other hospital personnel. The majority of our doctors and nurses are hardworking and law-abiding professionals, my friend told me. I feel ashamed that we twisted facts in our zealousness to attack the medical establishment, partly for the purpose of ratings. So later I mandated that we treat fairly all parties involved in a story. Also, I stipulated that reporting of a few bad seeds should not be at the expense of the overall reputation of the institution. In short, the exaggerated bifurcation of the good and evil does little to build social harmony. The lack of professional standards in media reporting makes the situation worse. So I now frequently give lectures about 'news justice,' which I think is as important as judicial justice. So *News Probe* has a reputation for being fair, though our influence is not as wide reaching as *Focus*. As a result, people are more receptive to our queries for investigation and interviews. Our effort in the past thirteen years in this regard has paid off."

Returning to the issue of the media's surveillance role, Zhang said that whatever they do has to be in line with what the party likes to see, which is "scientific" and constructive surveillance that helps to improve the situation. "Also, media surveillance has to operate within what's permissible. There have been debates within CCP think tanks about whether media control should be loosened or tightened. Some think that transparency is better, but others are concerned about worsening social stability. The reality in China is that there are thousands of incidents of mass unrest every year, over ninety thousand in 2007, and almost one hundred thousand in 2008. You do the math and see how many revolts per day. No doubt that the central government is concerned. More media exposure would inevitably intensify the tension. As the public lost faith in local government and as their awareness of their rights increased, the clashes would continue to rise. What should the media do under these circumstances? It's a complex issue." Zhang was pensive. He had no answer to his own question.

"Looking back," Zhang said, "a significant change in Chinese media was the emergence of the media's watchdog function. *Horizon*, particularly one of its segments, 'Focus Time,' led the charge in exercising the media's watchdog function. 'Focus Time' also experimented with reporting major and breaking news, including the reporting of major disasters previously censored—what we call 'hot spots' or 'hard spots.' The public paid attention, and so did the policy makers. It was a training period for watchdog journalism and for CCTV. A year later, CCTV expanded 'Focus Time' into a ten-minute evening program. A year later it became *Focus*, and local stations all over China cloned the program. It dramatically changed the power dynamic between media and the state, as the latter now needed the former for information. Media was no longer merely the party's propaganda instrument."

The information that the party needs from the media in this reformulation of party and media relations is twofold. First, the state desires direct, original reporting of local conditions (corrupt officials, damaging environmental practices, workforce exploitation and abuse, ethnic tensions, etc.) in order to assist with administration. Because of the sheer size of the country and its population, and because of the nature and speed of its development, the party, even with its extensive networks, is simply unable to keep adequate tabs on everything. One is tempted to think of China as a control state par excellence, but in fact, says David Lampton, "China is under institutionalized: it does not have fully appropriate institutional capacity to justly manage an increasingly marketized, urbanized, and globalized system." [14]

The other kind of information that the state needs from the media is intelligence about public opinion and concerns. This can be more usefully read from the media (now including the Internet and social media) than from anywhere else, and as much from audience preferences for different media and media content, including the narrative content of popular soap operas, for instance, as from news reports and editorial choices.

News Probe became very popular in the late 1990s and early 2000s, a time when the public was slowly growing self-confident in developing its own opinion yet still trusted CCTV. "What we did was essentially leading and shaping public opinion," Zhang said. But the public, acting now as consumers of commercial media, soon began to influence media more than the other way around, driving media content via program ratings. "To me," Zhang said, "mainstream media are the media that deliver information demanded by the public. So starting from 2001, our program began to search for topics and styles of delivery that appeal to audiences. We did suspenseful stories, stories with hidden facts, and stories that captured certain trends and patterns in society, all the while keeping to stories of a personal nature. We did several major stories that exposed the corruption in mining accidents, medical malpractice, and mistreatment by law enforcement in 2001. So 2001 was the year of problem reporting. We also did follow-up stories to the major problems we tackled, providing updates on the issues. Our watchdog function was not as influential in affecting policy changes as that of *Focus* because policy makers paid more attention to *Focus*. We often joked that, though claiming to do media surveillance, *Focus* in effect was the extension of state surveillance, as it has become a channel through which the state is able to check the pulse of the public."

The official lines for the core values of CCTV news programs have been authority, truthfulness, richness, and liveliness. Investigative journalism is one of the few types of news programs that have actually adhered to these values. China's brand of cautiously tolerated watchdog journalism—encompassed by the phrase *yulun jiandu*, or "supervision by public opinion"—was given tacit official support in the 1990s. Yet China suffered a succession of crises in the late 2000s partially as a result of official corruption and negligence, which led to curbs on hard news, and on investigative reporting in particular, effectively neutralizing a vital form of power monitoring in China that has proven both effective and credible. *News Probe*'s "problem reporting" days largely came to an end in 2006, when it put away the watchdog and turned its investigative nose toward the scent of enlightenment. As Jingrong Tong and Colin Sparks summarize, "The situation of investigative journalism in China is precarious. There are serious pressures from both the party-state and advertisers that have reduced the opportunities for this kind of journalism." [15]

Zhang Jie didn't seem daunted, just overworked. Staying within the bounds of a regularly "tightened or loosened" political environment is an inescapable part of the professional regimen, and where the boundaries fall at any moment is less important than the way that Chinese journalists and media workers have come to imagine themselves as professionals, and the collective arc of their professional aspirations to be one thing and not another. Zhang Jie and all the other newspeople that I met at CCTV shared a determination not to be "mouthpieces." They pledged themselves, like Western journalists, to dig up the "truth," especially about injustice and abuses of power. They also sought to influence government and guide public opinion, imagining themselves in the traditional role of the Chinese intellectual: much-needed mediators between state and society.

4

DELIVERING THE NEWS:
PROFILES OF THREE NEWS ANCHORS

CCTV's forays into entertainment and lifestyle programming ended upon arrival of its new president Jiao Li, whose motto "Anchoring CCTV with News" returned the network to its core mission as journalists and opinion shapers. The newly consolidated News Center, which brought together five previously separate news divisions within CCTV, would be headed by Sun Yusheng, the former head of the News Division who was sidelined to the CCTV web division during Zhao Huayong's reign.

There was a genuine euphoria among seasoned newspeople at CCTV about the return of Sun, a veteran newsman who played an important role in launching newsmagazine programs during Yang Weiguang's era. I soon gathered, by talking to various people, that in this new round of restructuring, CCTV-1 would beef up its news programs, making it a predominantly news channel, with more and more frequent news programming. The proportion of watchdog-style news programs as well as international news coverage would be increased. To enhance CCTV's authority in news coverage, more timely and comprehensive coverage would be pursued. In practice, two twenty- to thirty-minute news segments would be added to CCTV-1's current programming schedule, one in the morning and one in the afternoon.

Efforts were also launched to make news programs on specialty channels CCTV-4 and CCTV-9 more targeted, intimate, attractive, and persuasive. The international-focused CCTV-4, aimed at overseas Chinese, would add European news and American news to the existing *Asia Today*; programs targeting Taiwan would be given emphasis on CCTV's website. Co-productions with Taiwan would be encouraged. The new round of restructuring essentially revived the propaganda function of the news, which was now cleverly cloaked in the ideologically neutral lexicon of agenda setting and opinion leading. By acknowledging the news function as a core mission at CCTV, the reforms took the pressure of ratings out of the news programming, in a sense, bucking two decades of movement toward commercialization.[1]

To maintain its dominance as the only national network with access to the most up-to-date party information, CCTV strengthened its lead in news programming by adding more news commentary programs and live broadcasts and by modernizing the stiff and outdated *National News Bulletin*. Two significant events occurred in 2009 that triggered debates on the efficiency and effectiveness of CCTV news programming. The fire at CCTV's new headquarters in February led to the appointment of Jiao Li as the network's new president in June. The same month Jiao took office, Luo Jing, the chief newsreader on *National News Bulletin* for the past two decades, passed away, prompting a belated call to revamp the evening news program, which had been in steady decline for the previous two decades. The nightly news broadcast that claimed a 40 percent market share in 1998 was attracting only 10 percent of viewers by 2009. A radical revamp seemed imperative.

The formulaic half-hour 7 P.M. program with stolid reports of leaders' activities followed by clips of the positive events in the nation was to undergo radical retooling. Starting on June 20, 2009, the prime-time nightly news would include fewer official announcements, more human-interest stories and critical reporting, and a more relaxed reporting style by its anchorpersons.[2] The *News Bulletin*'s compulsive vacuity had long been intensely ridiculed by critics and public alike. The standard joke about the state meetings and posturing statesmen reported on the *News Bulletin* goes like this: "There's no meeting that's not solemn, no closing ceremony that's not a success, no speech that's not important, no applause that's not enthusiastic, no leaders that aren't attentive, no visit that's not genial." Another joke satirizes the "three segments" on the network news: "The first ten minutes talk about how busy the leaders are, the middle ten about how happy people are across the country, and the final ten about how chaotic other places in the world are." As observed by a *Wall Street Journal* piece, for decades the nightly news broadcast has followed a strict protocol: a flowery anthem is played, then came the anchors with flat, emotionless voices reporting top leaders' activities of the day, followed by other government news.[3]

The *National News Bulletin* is the only regular CCTV program that has enjoyed "must carry" status—meaning all the country's broadcasters are required to carry the program every evening during its 7:00 time slot—since the early 1980s. Beginning with the broadcast of the Twelfth National Party Congress in 1982, the *News Bulletin* has also had the exclusive right to air major news items one day ahead of other media. The authoritative, rigid image of the *News Bulletin* was intentional and worked well enough for the party during the early years of Chinese television. As the reform era advanced and as the government's attitude toward the news media in general evolved away from "media control" toward "media management" and "media cooperation," the flagship *News Bulletin* lagged behind. Even Yang's pioneering decision in 1986 to lead with the breaking news of the *Challenger* explosion instead of the normal ranked rundown of the central leadership's activities did not fundamentally alter the *News Bulletin*'s structure; a little more than a decade later, the 9/11 attack was not broadcast as a major story on the *News Bulletin*. Instead, while other domestic networks such as Phoenix TV, Hunan Satellite Television (HSTV), and Chongqing TV broke in with breaking news coverage, CCTV ran only a brief report on the late-night news, three hours after the attacks.

As China's reform and opening have progressed, the *News Bulletin*'s authority has ebbed away. Especially with the flourishing of the Internet, the news market has been subdivided and channels of information have multiplied. Even as the *News Bulletin*'s news presentation became obsolete, CCTV still shied away from making major changes. The public outcry against the dull *News Bulletin* format finally drew the attention of the party's Central Committee in 2003, which led to a series of adjustments a few years later.

In 2006, the network tested out two new anchors but took them off the next day following complaints that they lacked the gravity of the older anchors, despite an online poll showing a 68 percent approval rating. In 2007, the program tried again and introduced another new presenter, the more relaxed Hai Xia. In the days that followed, three other new anchors went through tryouts. This time the changes were made more systematically. To ease the transition, each new presenter was paired with a veteran newsreader rather than holding down an entire program on his or her own. To prove that they intended to make the changes permanent, CCTV came up with a catchy four-part slogan: "Adding, not subtracting; training new people; veterans lead new arrivals; old and new advance together." Positive comments poured in. According to an online poll sponsored by CCTV-International, *People's Daily Online*, and Sina (a major Chinese website), the new presenters were deemed satisfactory by more than 85 percent of four hundred thousand respondents.

The power of the news anchor has long been recognized by those inside and outside of CCTV. Anchors with personal charisma build their celebrity status while helping audiences form connections with the program and network.[4] While the unique presentation styles of individual anchors attract audiences, CCTV news anchorpersons must pass the political test of the party. Entrusted with imparting the party ideology, they are larger-than-life personalities who carry the voice of the party-state.

Under Yang's leadership, news anchorpersons became popular icons. Yang explained to me that he has long thought that newsreaders for the evening news were too formal, failing to connect with audiences at a personal level. Aside from serious political news, he believed, news should be delivered in a more relaxed manner. He didn't think highly of the traditional anchor training that emphasized proper pronunciation and diction above all else and pointed out that several successful anchors and hosts at CCTV never underwent formal anchor schooling, sparing them the stylistic formality and impersonal rigidity that typifies trained news readers. Under Yang's direction, CCTV started to groom anchors with more individual appeal, a practice that brought quite a few individuals to stardom.

Bai Yansong

Bai Yansong is regarded as the most influential news anchor in China today. Born in Inner Mongolia in 1968, Bai's "intellectual" family (his parents were history professors) was repudiated during the Mao era. His Mongolian father, who died the same year Mao did, in 1976, was labeled an "antirevolutionary," and the young Bai himself is said to have spent time with his father in jail. Inner Mongolia was seen as a refuge for exiles at the time, and Bai grew up on a university campus where he developed a studious attitude and a strong Chinese intellectual's sense of "historic duty."

After graduating from the Beijing Broadcasting Institute (now the Communication University of China), Bai worked for several years as an editor and journalist on the *Chinese Broadcast Newspaper*. He never imagined himself on television, thinking he was not photogenic enough. And in fact he's probably right; his on-air look is a somber, almost frowning one—similar to that of Peter Jennings—that seems at first glance to give off all the wrong intentions for someone who is the lead carrier of the party's cheerful message.

Bai became known to the public when *Oriental Horizon* started to use regular hosts in January 1996, rotating him and three other anchorpersons, Shui Junyi, Jing Yidan, and Fang Hongjin. Bai and his co-anchors became the first generation of professional news hosts who functioned more than just as newsreaders. Now a senior journalist at CCTV, Bai has hosted almost all the live TV broadcasts of key events over the past fifteen years in China, including the Hong Kong handover in 1997, the completion of the Three Gorges Dam in 1998, and the Sichuan earthquake and the Beijing Olympic

Games in 2008. In 2008, he participated in the Olympic torch relay, handing off the torch to basketball superstar Yao Ming on Tiananmen Square. A political wonk with a touch of vanity, he reminded me that he also hosted CCTV's live broadcast of Bill Clinton's speech at Beijing University in 1998. Recently he established and began anchoring *News 1+1*, airing daily at 10 P.M., which quickly became China's most influential news commentary program. The *1+1* in the program's title refers to the show's dialogue format of one host plus one news commentator. As the flagship live news commentary program, *News 1+1* provides daily takes on the most current and critical topics in state policy and public affairs, as well as major breaking news. In this new program, Bai radiates authority and erudition as he cites the wider implications of each report and makes comparisons with similar events in history.

Bai is not only an incredibly sharp anchor, linking disparate events daily in his reports, but also a master debater. He spoke openly with me about how progress in news reform depended on similar progress toward political reform: "The new round of news reform is only a surface issue, contingent upon the path and pace of democracy and China's overall political reform. News reform will inevitably hit a glass ceiling without progress toward democracy and political reform. The bottom line is that news reform is part of the overall progress toward democracy and political reform. If you look back to Hu Jintao's Work Report at the Seventeenth National Congress of the CCP in 2007, you will find that the term 'democracy' was openly endorsed. The CCP leadership discussed the issue a lot more poignantly and in greater depth than many of us have so far discussed. Democracy and political reform have been part of the official CCP lexicon in the past couple of years. News reform must be and will become part of the political reform."

Bai declared that as for the journalist's responsibility, journalists needed to follow *guilu*, or a professional code of conduct.

"As I often remind people, there is no need to reinvent the wheel. My counterparts abroad have been perfecting the news profession for years. There are professional conventions to follow, no matter what your cultural origin is. News in China would have to follow the same professional conduct, becoming more independent and ensuring the watchdog function. News professionals ought to function within the confines of law while at the same time seeking the protection of law."

About CCTV's dual commission to serve the state and turn a profit, he emphasized that the market mechanism has been a positive counterforce to state control. Commercialization, as he sees it, is a liberating force for Chinese media. "It is better than responding to political pressure alone. The injection

of market forces should be viewed as progress. The market forces us to respond to the needs of the public. When the media rely more on advertising
and other forms of commercial income instead of government funding, they
respond more to audiences and thus the public." Bai's declaration puts him
squarely in the pro-market liberal camp as opposed to the antimarket New
Left camp of the Chinese intellectual factions.

And speaking of market, "What about CCTV's monopolistic position in
China?"

"As for monopoly, each country has its own way of doing things, not that
I consider CCTV's monopoly justified. I had commented on the pitfalls of
lack of competition before the new round of reform started. I don't consider
it a good thing that we only have one broadcaster. Things will change, either
via market force or via administrative force. It is possible that competition
might sprout from within CCTV and that CCTV might be separated into two
competing forces."

Bai cautioned me, though, that "the separation of public TV from commercial TV is to assume that there is a healthy commercial sector there to
begin with. One speaks of NHK in relation to Fuji TV and the *Asahi Shimbun*
or U.S. PBS in relation to U.S. commercial broadcasters. But there is not a
healthy and functional independent commercial news broadcaster in China,
though the sector is growing. All broadcasters in China including Hunan TV,
Shanghai Media Group, and the Hong Kong–headquartered Phoenix are hybrid entities responsive to both political and market pressure."

There seemed to be three perspectives on the issue of CCTV's monopoly.
One was a flat denial that a monopoly existed, an opinion espoused by Ren
Xuean, a producer at CCTV's Finance Channel, who insisted that since CCTV
occupied only a third of the China market, it didn't constitute a monopoly.
A second set endorses CCTV's monopolistic control. CCTV host Li Yong, for
one (whom I later interviewed; see chapter 6), was proud that CCTV had
no viable opponents. The third condemns CCTV's monopoly and argues for
opening up the market for fair play. Documentarian Xia Jun even goes so far
as to argue that CCTV is an illegal enterprise. As he put it, "It is not legally
registered as a commercial enterprise with the right to run commercials. It is
considered a not-for-profit public institution. In China, a commercial entity
without proper registration is not allowed to operate. CCTV has to confront
its status sooner or later—is it a public station or a commercial station? It is
a crossover between state and commercial. It is a commercial station taking
advantage of state monopoly, or a state-run TV station exploiting financial
operation."

And yet, even with its singular position, Xia and some others argue that CCTV doesn't receive sufficient resources for a state-affiliated network and echoes Bai's prediction of a breakup of CCTV into a commercial half that could compete without tying its hands behind its back and a separate, non-profit one that would serve as the state-directed outlet.

I suppose the network's current blend of state-commerce alliance is the consequence of the ad hoc reform initiatives of the early 1990s, when "growing out of a planned economy" took hold as the main agenda of economic reform. Such an alliance is the pattern in the Chinese film industry as well, as the state-run commercial enterprise China Film Group has emerged to be the biggest player in the Chinese film industry. The only difference is that private film firms such as Huayi Brothers have grown at the same pace and can now compete squarely with the China Film Group. But a powerful competitor for CCTV within the TV industry has yet to be allowed to emerge.

In fairness, CCTV's odd status is not odd at all in China, as state-run commercial enterprise is the new norm in China. As a state-run enterprise, CCTV is a microcosm of China as state capitalism. When the interests of the state and commerce are taken care of, what's left is the interest of the public.

Does Bai see the conflict between monopoly and public interest?

"The injection of a market mechanism to CCTV is a good thing, as it balances out the pressure from the state and allows us to respond to the needs of the audience. CCTV began to respect the audience's desire for programs of popular appeal only after we introduced commercials."

Bai is clearheaded about the key difference between public television in China and public television in the West, as he knows far too well that public TV in China would mean a TV broadcaster that caters to the imperatives of the government, not the public. "It would be disastrous if CCTV were to become a public television station when there is no single viable commercial broadcaster in existence in China."

I urged Bai to elaborate on anchoring CCTV with news, and he was forthcoming.

"Anchoring the network with news," Bai related, "is nothing new, as it was put forth when Yang Weiguang was our president. Nobody would dare to deny that news has been the foundation of CCTV as a default. The issue is the degree to which the leadership at CCTV carries out policies that seriously push for the foregrounding of news programming. So the devil is in the details. Also, I think there is a subtext here—or I wish that there would be a subtext—that would exempt news programming from the pressures of rating and marketization. I can't imagine outsourcing news production."

Here Bai discussed the issue of separation of production and distribution/broadcasting in Chinese TV, which has been a hotly contested topic in China's media industry. "CCTV has started purchasing and broadcasting entertainment, sports, and economic and financial programs from other production companies instead of broadcasting only in-house productions. TV drama has been the forerunner in this regard. Previously, CCTV screened only the in-house productions. The quality of its drama programming improved significantly once it started to purchase drama serials from elsewhere. Instead of making its own programs, CCTV has moved toward selling time slots for standard programs produced elsewhere. Anchoring CCTV with news would mean that everything else except news would be outsourced, following the market principle."

"The former head of the Propaganda Ministry Li Changchun actively pushed for the 'going out' policy for CCTV. How realistic is it for CCTV to reach out by anchoring itself solely on news when the network has yet to establish itself as an authoritative voice to the world in news programming?" I asked.

Bai gave a focused and succinct answer that suggested that CCTV could achieve real leverage in the world of media only when China as a nation achieved similar power in the realm of politics. "No doubt that CCTV's global influence is contingent upon China's global influence. 'Going out' depends on what you have to offer to the world. Initially we exported human capital and industrial products. Cultural and media products would inevitably follow as the overall influence of China continues to rise. The last export we can offer would be our value system. Twenty years ago nobody cared for our culture or media. A street product might get picked up by a big supermarket if it demonstrated its profit value. If its value continues to go up, then it might show up as a brand name in luxury stores. The point is that the world would have to listen to China's perspective on domestic and global events when China is too powerful to ignore. The world would need to listen to China's position on any particular political, military, and economic issue. Only then would the world pay attention to Chinese media."

"At present, then, won't programs about culture be more effective than news programs in 'going out,' given that the CCTV news has yet to find receptive overseas audiences?"

"Culture is not an independent entity. American culture is embedded in its soft drinks, cars, pop culture, fast food, et cetera. The same applies to Chinese culture. Building Confucius Institutes [institutes partnered with universities to promote the teaching of Mandarin] around the globe does not result in the exportation of Chinese culture. Obviously Chinese culture should be the foundation upon which an effective Chinese news program can be built. I particularly dislike the idea of wholesale adoption of foreign program formats. After many years of cloning others' programs, it is time for us to create our own. My current program has moved beyond mere imitation of news programs in the West. I spent all of 2001 emulating Ted Koppel's *Nightline*, but I have now moved beyond that. Although emulation is a necessary step, CCTV programming must be rooted in China's own cultural soil."

Some suggested that language might be an issue in China's "going out" effort. What is his take on this?

"Influence and what language one speaks have no direct correlation. I'll give you an example. I did the live report during Clinton's speech at Beijing University in 1998. I criticized sharply the poor quality of the simultaneous Chinese translation of the speech done by an American translator. My criticism in Chinese was widely translated into English in major news outlets around the world. No matter what language you use, if whatever you say is valuable, then other people will listen. The Chinese language will never outshine English to be the number one commonly used language in the world. Chinese is a difficult language to master."

Bai commented further that "there is a difference between having the venue for 'going out' and the ability to produce programming that would 'go out.' Instead of forcing your view on others, you have to learn to carry on a dialogue and locate a mutual ground for conducting a dialogue. For instance, during the Tibet riot on March 14, 2008, our official reporting found few receptive audiences overseas. So we failed to 'go out' on such a crucial event. But we 'went out' unexpectedly during the transparent and open reporting of the Wenchuan earthquake. There was no restriction and censorship during the earthquake reporting, and foreign reporters were free to come. You can 'go out' when you don't stop others from coming in. The Beijing Olympics 'went out' because it brought people in. Yes, there would be biased reporting, but this would eventually be counterbalanced by other positive and objective reports. So not to worry."

I asked Bai if the Chinese media policy makers are as sensible and confident as he is.

"Well," Bai said, "I am allowed to practice in China, am I not? My influence and authority are peerless in Chinese media, and I can say whatever I want to say without being censored. Don't forget that someone else above me makes the decision to let me have the platform to say what I consider sensible and wise. My position is not granted solely by the audiences."

"You mean there is a tacit consent from the policy makers."

"Yes," Bai responded. "In China many things don't go by a set theory or overt declaration."

"Is CCTV an ideal platform for you? What would be an ideal platform if not?"

"I have been courted by other broadcasters with more money, including overseas broadcasters. None, however, can match the CCTV platform in its broad reach and influence. I do not rule out the possibility of leaving if there is a place with even wider reach and influence. Money is secondary to my desire to be heard by more people. During the live coverage of the 2003 Iraq War, only the CCTV report reached every corner in China, not Phoenix, nor any other media firm that might have paid me a lot more than CCTV. That said, my colleagues and I could surely use a more open and transparent platform, a platform with more freedom. My current program provides better leverage in story content than any other programs at CCTV partly because I've proven myself to be reliable and harbor no ill intentions. I would continue to agitate for more independent journalism and hope that one day I could represent my own views on air, not just the views of CCTV or the party-state. The day will come, sooner or later."

There was a moment of silence as I pondered the scenario of CCTV turning directly into MSNBC, or Fox, bypassing the "neutral" stage of CNN.

For the time being, Bai is focusing on making his program *News 1+1* a quality news commentary program. "The program started at the end of March 2008. It is China's first live TV commentary program. During the preparation period, I told my team that the program would do two things: capture the ongoing change in Chinese society and push for democratic progress in China. Otherwise the program would be pointless. The first mission is public, but the second we keep close to our chests. We can certainly discuss the aspect of democracy here as an academic topic. Frankly speaking, pushing for democracy is far more important than simply documenting the change in China, and I don't shy away from any story that pertains to democracy. For instance, we commented on both the Wen'an and Shishou incidents.[5] I do not underestimate the value of our reporting on these stories. We are contributing to the progress of China's democracy."

Bai is proud of what his new program has accomplished. "At least in Asia, our program is peerless in providing incisive comments and perspectives on major news events. I looked, and not many programs in the U.S. do this either. My program alone is not enough to make a real difference, I must emphasize, which points to the pitfall of isolated instead of systematic reform. I called it showcase reform. But at least it's happening. Last year we had between 2 billion and 3 billion hits on our program website, by far the most on CCTV. So that is the impact of our program."

Bai suggested that the success of his program resulted in the addition of news commentary being one of the most prominent news reform agendas in the new round of reform carried out by the then-new CCTV president. "My program has built a good foundation for news commentary programs to develop and expand, which is to say that we have tested the water for the others and it proves to be safe. So now the policy makers and indeed everybody can proceed with confidence—that is the value of my program."

Given his stature at CCTV, I asked Bai whether he would like to assume a leadership position at the network.

Bai rules out the possibility of climbing the corporate ladder as he enjoys being an independent thinker. "I abandoned the route to politics a long time ago. I don't anticipate major changes in China during my lifetime to alter my personal trajectory. I was the only one at CCTV who walked away from three offers of a producer's position six years ago, two daily news programs and one weekly program, all influential and wielding tremendous power. Administrative positions would inevitably conflict with the position of a professional journalist, and being a newsperson is where my heart and talent lie."

I wondered what kept him going, now that he had achieved the level of influence that he wanted.

"Not money, and not fame, but a fulfilling life," he replied. "Also curiosity. Curiosity, for instance, about how far China can go. I would have never imagined sitting where I am now twenty years ago. All I wanted was a color TV twenty years ago. China evolves so rapidly that it is futile to have a five-year plan. A hometown or a birthplace can disappear within one generation. If you are not careful, you can easily lose your soul in this rapid change." Here Bai lamented the loss of a moral compass and humanity in China: "The Chinese are falling faster than the Americans in this regard."

I followed up by commenting on how disturbed I felt with the naked money-worshipping mentality prevailing in China. "Well," Bai retorted, "this is a stage one must go through." He cited a famous phrase that discusses three stages of changing priorities in life: "In the first stage, the priority is your relationship with material needs; in the second stage, it's your relationship with others; and in the last stage, it's your relationship with yourself. I discovered that the trajectory of China's reform is similar to the three steps of personal growth. The first two decades of reform addressed people's relationships with material needs, and the goal was to put sufficient bread and butter on the table and a roof over your head. The next step is to solve the relationships between people, and the goal here is to build a harmonious society. The last step is to address one's need to be in touch with oneself, and that is the toughest stage. What is China's core value and belief? What is our soul? This is the last stage we'll inevitably confront. I often remind my fellow travelers to slow down. Why? Because you have left your soul behind. The accelerating speed China is traveling at is scary. But it is also exciting. And that is why I won't want to trade my place. I might want to move to Europe to enjoy peace and tranquillity during my twilight years, but my formidable years must be spent here, at the forefront of change in China."

Bai has created some enemies along the way to megastar status. While in the United States to film a travel program, Bai gave a speech at Yale University, "My Story and the Chinese Dream Behind It," in which he narrated the evolution of his own life against four decades of Sino-U.S. relations. But Bai's "Chinese dream" was apparently not shared by his detractors, who thought the speech pompous and self-absorbed. To the New Left, Bai is the epitome of insufferable "liberal media" elitism. His public opposition to boycotting the French supermarket chain Carrefour after pro-Tibet demonstrators in France interfered with the Olympic torch relay did not endear him to Chinese nationalists either, particularly the online variety. Bai is passionate about issues such as social injustice and government and corporate corruption. His "uprightness and resoluteness" no doubt make him an eminently suitable anchor for *Horizon* and *Focus*, but his self-righteous combative tone does turn off some viewers, who call him a pretentious bully.

Asked about the perception of those who regard him as arrogant, Bai emphasized that he is of Mongolian, not Han, origin, and so does not have to adhere to Confucian modesty. "Being a Mongolian, I speak my mind," Bai said. And although this habit of candid speech has courted controversy, it has also won the trust of his superiors at CCTV, enough to earn him his supremely influential and wide-reaching program, unmatched for sheer popular exposure.

Yet in December 2009 *News 1+1* did run into troubles with the censors. A story by Bai's alternate host, Dong Qian, put a spotlight on a much-publicized anticorruption campaign in Chongqing, endorsed by the then-secretary of Chongqing's Communist Party, Bo Xilai. The story raised deep concerns about the campaign's brutality and questioned its legality. Bo called CCTV's president, Jiao Li, who was a friend and colleague from Bo's time as a governor of Liaoning Province. The producer of *News 1+1* was swiftly transferred to another program, and Dong Qian was briefly banned from the airwaves. Even

Bai Yansong had to learn to be constantly vigilant about what was permissible on his own program. *News 1+1* would eventually be vindicated in March 2012, when Bo Xilai was taken down as part of the party's political shakeout.

Jing Yidan

Jing Yidan, a longtime leading anchorwoman at *Focus*, comes from Heilongjiang in the far northeast of China. Born in the late 1950s, Jing experienced the same hardship endured by many during the Cultural Revolution. She took her first media job as a newsreader at her provincial radio station, where she stayed for five years before entering the Beijing Broadcasting Institute as its first female master's student. Prior to moving to CCTV-1 and the News Channel, where she now resides, Jing worked at the Economics Channel, where she anchored the first CCTV show ever to be named after a host, *Yidan Topic*. There, Jing established her reputation as a coolheaded, calmly composed, yet compassionate "big sister" figure with wide audience appeal.[6] Commentators have noted her use of the inclusive pronouns "we," "us," and "our," causing one academic observer to label her habit as part of the "politics of compassion."[7] Politics or not, Jing speaks eloquently and passionately both in formal studio settings and in live, unscripted broadcasts.

Now in her fifties, Jing retains her physical appeal, beautiful in a nonthreatening way. On the day we sat down for a chat, she came late but apologized right away, explaining, "There was a last-minute special taping." The previous week, on July 5, 2009, a major riot had unexpectedly broken out in Xinjiang and Jing was engulfed with responsibilities: "We have dispatched several reporters to Ürümqi, including Zhang Quanling, whose live report on location during the Sichuan earthquake was widely praised. I'm in charge of the reporting here from CCTV's headquarters."

"For *Focus*?" I asked. She nodded. We then started to talk about *Focus*. Jing reflected, "*Focus* had its golden period in the late 1990s, under Yang Weiguang's leadership. We have lost our edge and sharpness over the past several years. I have been thinking about this. Does it mean that whatever motivated us to do the program, which was the watchdog function of the program, no longer holds its appeal for us? The motivation or passion is still there, but it has receded. Many factors have contributed to the retreat. The shifting media environment limits the power and influence of the media's watchdog function. Obviously policy makers' attitude toward the media's watchdog function and the frequency with which our immediate boss utilizes our program to this end are all factors that have contributed to *Focus*'s weakened influence.

Another factor has to do with the arrival of similar programs that clone the *Focus* format, which naturally reduce *Focus*'s uniqueness. *Focus* captured wide attention because it was the only watchdog program in China at the time. Watchdog programs proliferated, so *Focus* is no longer the only one to watch. This is like Shenzhen[8] in its initial development, which captured wide attention. Shenzhen's appeal diminished when other cities started to enjoy the same Special Economic Zone status. So *Focus*'s appeal dwindled as more programs like it diverted audiences. And then there is the challenge from the new media. The power of traditional media has been overshadowed by the instant accessibility of the new media. All of these have overwhelmed *Focus*."

Jing was focused and methodical throughout our conversation, and as she continued, she contemplated the evolution of the concept of watchdog journalism in China: "The concept of 'watchdog' was a relatively new term to the Chinese public when it was introduced to and popularized in China by *Focus*. As the term has become a fixture in the popular vocabulary and psyche, the expectations of the public have changed. They demand more and are in turn disappointed as *Focus* has stayed the same, which accounts for the feeling of program stagnation. During the first few years, the stories that appeared on *Focus* shocked people, as nobody had ever seen a news exposé before, let alone a story that took a shot at the state agencies. That initial shock is now replaced by high and at times unrealistic expectations, which make it harder for us to keep up, even though we have expanded our coverage both in depth and in scope. *Focus* is no longer refreshing. So people's expectations, the proliferation of similar programs, and the tightening public opinion environment together have contributed to *Focus*'s diminishing popularity. But I believe that 'watchdog' has become part of the public lexicon and is here to stay. It might ebb, but it will not be erased entirely. I believe especially that public monitoring of political events and social justice has now become part of the Chinese consciousness as China continues its march toward modernization. The scale of implementation might vary among different programs, but the basic tenet of media's watchdog function will not change."

Jing has been an ardent advocate for children of migrant workers, now commonly referred to as "children left behind and in waiting." Her repeated calls for the central government to address the issue led to a poignant story by *News Probe* that spotlighted how these children often had to stay behind in rural areas—usually with grandparents—when their parents moved to urban centers for jobs with better pay.

Jing told me that she became aware of the issue while working for the Economic Channel's *Economic Half Hour* in the early 1990s. "I started out by doing stories about migration. As an urban resident, I began to see an influx of migrant workers in Beijing and did stories about them out of my professional curiosity. I wanted to know who these hurried travelers with few belongings I ran into on the subway were. This was in the early 1990s. The stories I did caught the attention of a migration and population expert. He contacted me, praising my efforts but pointing out that my stories lacked depth and that serious discussions concerning social ramifications of a massive floating population were needed. We invited him over to discuss how to pursue the story further. He unpacked a set of complex factors that have contributed to this phenomenon. It made me realize that migration is a pattern in development and must be addressed at the policy level. I have since raised the issue many times in the Consultative Conference." Jing is a representative in the National People's Congress and a former member of the National Committee of the Chinese People's Political Consultative Conference, a government advisory body. So I asked, how much influence does a member of the People's Congress have over policy matters?

"I have one vote," she said wryly.

She grew increasingly concerned with the destabilizing social impact of this mass migration. "Now the children of these travelers have followed in their parents' footsteps and become second-generation migrant workers. The older generation might have returned home as they grew old and frail. I have kept an eye on the migrant population over the years. When they were building the Xidan Bookstore in Beijing, every time I passed by it I would observe the migrant construction workers toiling away. It dawned on me that these people were here to enrich our cultural life by building this gigantic bookstore. But what did the city offer them in return? What opportunities do we have for them to enjoy culture and civilization? There was a movie house nearby, so I asked them if they ever went to the movies. Too expensive, they said. How about TV? No TV in their dorm. They are the floating population, uprooted from their native soil but not absorbed into the mainstream urban culture. The chances for them to ever walk into the very bookstore they built would be zero to none. The realization brought profound sadness to me. As time passed, I noticed the addition of the second generation. I watched little kids hanging around as their parents labored to earn a living. Then the little kids grew into school-age children. They no longer hang around, but stayed home—they have nowhere to go. The urban school districts would not take them, as they do not have Beijing resident permits, which are required for entering local schools. They grew up illiterate—ignored, looked down upon, or humiliated by the local kids. How could we turn a blind eye to these children and allow resentment and hatred to grow and erode these young minds? We have an obligation to not only shelter them but also educate them. We must nurture their souls. Illegal schools have been built for the migrant children, but they could be demolished at any time. This is a failure at both the policy and societal levels. So I started to shift my attention to the second generation of migrant workers, preparing to do a long story for *News Probe*. The state did respond by urging schools to accept these migrant children. But simply enacting a new policy does not solve the problem of societal bias and cultural discrimination. During one of my interviews, I asked a girl who had been ordered to attend one of these urban schools whether she would be happy to go there. The kid stared at our camera and said that she would not want to go to the city school, as kids there would bully her. My mind raced. Growing up in such a hostile environment, would she harbor resentment, indifference, or kindness toward the society? Would she grow up to have a sound mind and body? Would she be a productive and functional adult? Are we as a society accumulating wealth at the expense of these children? Some say that this is the price we must pay for urbanization and modernization. But it is not fair to apply terms such as 'price' and 'sacrifice' to kids. It does not have to be this way. The issue can be addressed, and should be addressed immediately! I am worried and anxious—we have no time to waste." Jing's eyes glistened as she momentarily lost her coolness. We averted our eyes. She quickly gathered herself.

"Leaving home to earn a better wage has become the norm. If you walk into a village now, chances are you will not run into many male adults. There is a phrase that describes this dire situation. People associate the elderly with the number 99, as September 9 is the folk festival for honoring the elderly; women, with 38 for International Women's Day on March 8; and children, with 61 for Children's Day on June 1. So people now call the rural population left behind 'Army 993861.' It drains the vitality of the entire village. A young nanny from Sichuan Province we once hired told us that she could not bear returning to her hometown. She could not find someone to talk to, as people of her age had all left. This is the reality of China's villages today."

It was clearly a topic dear to Jing's heart. "We have over 200 million migrants, and this is one of the major issues in China. If you choose to ignore it, you won't ever really understand the Chinese situation. Aside from the story I did for *News Probe*, I also produced a special program, *Voices*, that provided a platform for people to discuss these issues. The segment with the girl not wanting to be sent to a public school is from this program. Endorsed by the People's Congress, *Voices* allows for multiple perspectives to be heard. We have raised the awareness of both the public and the policy makers about the severity of this issue. The government has started to pay attention. They now make a point of visiting migrant children's schools over the Children's Day holiday. These kids are less marginalized now. Media have played a significant role in raising these issues."

Jing said that the media have played a positive role in raising another major issue: poverty. Jing used to bring her daughter along to various interviews. Her initial goal was to spend more time with her daughter. She discovered with delight that the places they went exposed her daughter to people from different walks of life. The experience helped her develop empathy, and now her daughter actively participates in various charitable works. "My daughter's growth makes me see how impressionable kids are and what we can do to influence their minds."

I asked if being a mother makes her more attuned to women and children's issues, particularly women and children in poverty. "Sure," she said. "My attention has shifted from the migrant population in general to issues concerning women and children in particular. Does being a woman bring a different perspective to male-dominated programs such as *Horizon* and *Focus*? For a long time, I was the only woman at *Horizon*. Initially I was not aware of the gender issue. I paid lip service to mothers on Mother's Day. I would comment on issues concerning mothers, especially mothers from disadvantaged families. Naturally, I talked about the issues of senior citizens on Senior's Day and children's issues on Children's Day. After a while, my colleagues joked that I was now in charge of all programs that have to do with mothers, the elderly, and kids. Then, little by little I started to consciously promote women's topics in our program. It works well with my own strength, as I am not suitable for discussing topics with a sharp edge or major current events—these should be reserved for Bai Yansong. Cui Yongyuan is good at topics with wisdom and humor. So my niche is to project a female perspective and spotlight women's issues. My topics are soft edged. No less significant, though. They come from my heart and at the same time are desired by the program. So a good match. Bai, Cui, and I have over the years developed our own styles and cultivated our own topics.

"Now I have more and more female colleagues joining the team—a good thing. Their reporting brings in subtleness and a soft touch that only women can provide. For instance, during the earthquake reportage, a colleague of mine, Li Xiaomeng, did a story that touched many hearts. She ran into a villager on her way out of the disaster zone. They struck up a conversation. She asked, 'Where are you going?' He answered, 'Back to my old house.' 'Why?' 'To see if there is anything left.' She told him not to return, as it was still danger-ous. 'It's my home,' he said. 'How do you get food now?' she asked, changing the topic. He showed her the special coupon issued by the government for food aid. As they continued to chat about unstable life during the recovery, she urged him repeatedly not to take the risk of going back to his old house. He was undaunted. They finally parted ways. She told him to please be careful back there. 'Sure.' He walked away, then turned back, giving her a quick wave. 'Miss, thank you for being so kind!' Tears instantly welled up in Li's eyes as she watched his lone figure down the shabby road. Trying to maintain her composure, Li turned her back toward the camera. The camera captured her shaking body as she sobbed. The raw emotion conveyed by a young female reporter captivated millions, and the segment of the program became an instant icon in the media and among the public. So the power of the media doesn't only come from fists and loud slogans. It can also come from soft and small moments."

Given that Jing was one of the few females I spoke to at CCTV, I could not help bringing up the issue of gender. "What is the main challenge you face as a woman working in the Chinese TV industry?"

Jing was very candid, but her answer de-emphasized her gender and fo-cused more on her personal disposition. "A personal challenge to me is that I am not particularly sharp, yet *Focus* needs sharp and aggressive reporting to maintain its edge. My temperament is relatively calm, so the question is how to adapt my relatively balanced approach to the needs of the program for a more provocative edge. To this day, in comparison to my more *Focus*-like col-leagues, I continue to be less adept at the sort of in-your-face, hand-to-hand combat style. I am less capable of handling live reports of extremely complex cases. So over time, a consensus has emerged that I am more suitable for dis-tance reporting and providing in-studio summaries and commentaries."

Does that mean that programs such as *Focus* and *Horizon* are not good fits for her?

"No. Both programs do stories that touch people's nerves. They elicit pain. The pain can be sharp or dull. I am more suitable for doing stories that elicit dull pain. Those pains are caused by long-term and accumulative problems and require thoughtful reflection and historical perspectives—that I can do. So I bring to the programs depth and weight, which complement the pro-grams' more immediate and short-term shock."

"So it's about balance? And you complete the equation?"

"No, I disagree with your characterization. I must correct you. The pro-gram depends on everyone, so we complete each other."

With characteristic modesty, she was "correcting" what she thought was my suggestion that her contribution was more important than others'.

Jing mentioned a couple of other young colleagues she admired, including Cai Jing, who is about twenty years younger than Jing, and best known for her empathetic reporting during the SARS episode. Our conversation flowed from gender issues to generational gaps. Jing said that hers is the oldest generation at CCTV now. I asked if the new generation is different from her generation. "There are differences," Jing said. "For instance, Cai is a lot more rational and analytical than I am. She has broader knowledge and a wider perspective. Her stories bring in a more international perspective, which I don't have. My generation is not as attuned to global affairs as her generation." There is a rarefied honesty and unpretentiousness in Jing's assessment of herself, qualities rarely seen among the celebrity media people I encountered in China or elsewhere.

"I have always been very self-critical. To put it nicely, my image has always been traditional and restrained. To put it in a less flattering way, I'm old-fashioned. The younger generation is more modern and cosmopolitan. They can go right to systemic problems and add a global perspective. Also, they are brave enough to tackle some of the psychologically twisted stories and apply an analytical framework from the most up-to-date social and psychological theories. For instance, Cai is particularly attuned to stories on the Internet. She did a story about how someone filmed herself killing a cat and posted the footage online. I would have found the story too disturbing. I can only approach topics of common concern such as migrant workers and their children. The gap has to do with both their contemporary knowledge and broader perspective. I ultimately see my duty as a media professional is to help people connect with each other, and building bridges for various parts of the society to communicate with each other. So we are professional bridge builders."

Cui Yongyuan

Another CCTV show that was considered a breakthrough was *Tell It Like It Is*, a panel-format talk show that encourages "straight talk" from the host and active participation from the audiences. The show was the outcome of a party-directed effort for CCTV to add programs about real people with real popular appeal. *Tell* avoided current affairs topics, focusing instead on the everyday lives and concerns of ordinary people, from moral dilemmas to interpersonal relationships and environmental change. Launched in 1996, the show "quickly found an enthusiastic audience for whom host Cui Yongyuan's quirky personality was as interesting as the topics under discussion."[9] Known for a natural and relaxed style, Cui differentiated himself from his more serious-minded CCTV colleagues.

Growing up in Tianjin as the son of army officers, Cui belonged to a privileged social group that was shielded from the worst of the Cultural Revolution. Their People's Liberation Army credentials afforded them freedoms that others were denied, and Cui's verbal skills and personality developed with few restrictions. Cui attended the Beijing Broadcasting Institute, and upon graduating he worked at China National Radio in Beijing. He came to CCTV around the same time that Bai Yansong was recruited. Cui first joined *Focus*, where he demonstrated exceptional oratory skills blending humor with serious social commentaries. This led to a new job hosting *Tell It Like It Is*, which was designed to suit his particular talents. In addition to his verbal skills, his natural confidence attracted a large number of followers. Viewers respected him for his willingness to listen, his ability to empathize, and his capacity to harness difficult and emotional moments on the show, so much so that Cui was featured twice on CCTV's popular Chinese New Year's Gala, playing the straight-talk man in comic skits performed with Zhao Benshan and Song Dandan, two of China's most popular comedians.

The initial success of *Tell It Like It Is* relied heavily on Cui's approachable and humorous demeanor. Yet behind the surface cheeriness, Cui was serious-minded and cared about building a quality program that would both enlighten and entertain. This impulse ran up against ratings pressure and censors' scissors to an extent that it took a toll on Cui in 2002, right at the apparent peak of his career. He withdrew from *Tell* and disappeared from television altogether, at least for a while. While announcing his intention to leave, Cui revealed that he had been battling insomnia and depression. He also cited anxiety over the negative impact of low-quality entertainment programs as a contributing factor to his depression. As discussed by Yu Shi,[10] Cui asserted that many of the talk shows planted respondents in their live audiences to ensure that emotions could be stirred up as needed. Cui despised such tactics and considered the practice a breach of professional ethics. At an interview given on China Radio International in 2007, Cui said that he was mentally tormented by what he saw as the corrupt practices of many CCTV programs in their naked pursuit of market share. "I thought I could change things. I fell into a depression when I realized that nothing would ever change. After seeking medical treatment, I am now coming to terms with my own anguish. I am not able to change the society, but society can't change me either. So we cancel each other out." In the same interview, and on a more positive note, he seemed to put his faith going forward in the ideal of professionalism: "I am a media professional. If I can get people who watch my program to develop an interest in history and independent thinking, then the achievement will be invaluable."[11] Cui was not the only media professional who felt this way—many others joined in his chorus against programs that promote a blind, materialist culture, numbing viewers' social nerves and diverting their attention from serious issues.

During my interview with Cui, I asked him about the significance of *Tell*. Cui replied, "The breakthrough at *Tell* was the exception CCTV made to allow *Tell* to go on air without a preapproved script, which defied CCTV's standard practice of preapproval. A predrafted script would not fit the talk-show format, so CCTV conceded and ushered in the method of post-screening—do it first and delete the problematic parts afterward. Though *Tell* was never a live show, it was allowed to tape before approval was granted." Cui told me that genuinely live shows with studio audiences didn't start on CCTV until the Beijing Olympics.

Cui went through years of clinical depression but returned to host a new forty-five-minute show named after him for the News Channel, *Xiao Cui Talks*, in 2003. *Xiao Cui* carries forward the legacy of *Tell*, which is to provide a forum for public discussion of social issues, but *Xiao Cui* does not mean too much to Cui at this point in his life, certainly not the way that his work on shows such as *Horizon*, *Focus*, and *Tell* once drove him. He keeps doing it because he needs the CCTV platform to stay in the game. "I really don't think *Xiao Cui* has much of an impact. It pales in comparison with the more edgy print media and the new media. We are way behind in our ability to engage in sharp topics and ignite passionate debate about sensitive issues. Often after we finish recording, we go home and read similar stories in the more daring *Southern Weekend* [a notoriously hard-hitting weekly newspaper in Guangzhou] and feel embarrassed by how bland and lukewarm ours are. When we go online to search for similar stories or topics, we are reminded of our own backwardness. This is why CCTV is having a new round of reform to revitalize the old network. The new round of reforms might not deliver a renewed network, but the fact that we're doing it is encouraging. It means that the people in charge realize that we are falling behind and need to catch up. Television was a glorious medium when I started out in the 1990s, an envious profession that everyone wanted to be part of, and a respectable one too. The golden era is long gone, and now we are the butt of jokes. The Internet loves to make fun of CCTV." He's right—CCTV is often called "Hee-Hee-TV" by Internet users, so much so that during Google's China standoff in

April 2010, the popular Chinese blogger Han Han commented, with his trademark sarcasm, that Google's lofty ideals of "freedom of information" failed to resonate with the average Chinese and that Google would have connected with the Chinese public better if it had picked a fight with the unpopular China Central Television instead.[12] Back in 2009, Cui pointed out, "Cell phones, too, often spread messages ridiculing CCTV. It's a sad situation since people like me have worked so hard to build this network up." *Xiao Cui* was upgraded from the News Channel to CCTV-1's 10:30 P.M. slot.

"I am anxious about China's rise," Cui continued. "For instance, numerous Internet incidents remind me of an era plagued by political movements that produced mass destruction. It is scary to envision another mass mobilization that would create another chaos. Understanding history would help people avoid falling victim to the attention-grabbing events and speeches prevalent on the Internet." Cui's fear of the Internet-induced chaos is shared by many of his countrymen. He mentioned the so-called human-flesh search engines, crowd-sourced detective work that aims to hunt down and punish perceived wrongdoers by getting them "fired from their jobs, shamed in front of their neighbors, and run out of town," reported the *New York Times*.[13] Though the Chinese human-flesh search engine is widely endorsed for bringing down corrupt government officials, *Invisible Killer*, a Chinese film made in 2009, offered a cautionary tale of the engine's potential for misuse. The movie tells the story of two people having an affair who are hunted down by disapproving netizens for their infidelity. The film's producer called for laws to control cyber harassment and misinformation. Cui lamented the questionable quality of this supercharged online activism for its vulnerability to manipulation and deceit. Quite a few people I spoke to at CCTV offered cautionary tales about Internet-induced mass uprisings and the need for information regulation. Given that national security and harmony continue to trump all other concerns in China, I wonder what Cui and his compatriots at CCTV might think of the Chinese state's recent crackdown on China's ultra-leftist websites, which came to the defense of the sacked populist political figure Bo Xilai.

Despite his concern for chaos, Cui considers the Internet an overall positive force in Chinese society. As he puts it, "It allows multiple voices and grassroots voices to be heard. So we can hear opposite opinions previously not allowed."

However, it seems that, unlike his colleague Bai Yansong, Cui has lost his zest for television. Though disappointed in what he sees happening at CCTV, Cui is remarkably attached to the network. It hurts him to see its reputation tarnished over the last few years as, in his view, commercialization has eroded programs of social responsibility. The new round of reform gives him some hope: "It is very simple, much like a track and field race. [110 meter hurdler] Liu Xiang was able to break a world record because of the people around him. With *Southern Weekend* to our left, [Hong Kong–based TV network] Phoenix to our right, and CNN in front, we are in good company and will have to run hard and fast to stay in the race."

Speaking further about his hopes for the new round of reform at CCTV, Cui added, "It is harder than building a brand-new station from the ground up. But you must confront the problems. As we speak, CCTV is conducting internal auditions for deputy division director positions, which is a pleasant surprise. In the past such positions were assigned, not selected based on merit. I withdrew from the competition because I think it is essential to let the younger generation have the opportunity to step up and shake things up. The CCTV population is aging and we need fresh blood. Many of my contemporaries, such as Shui Junyi, have stepped aside to make way for the young people."

"Is the job hard for you still, after all these years?"

"Yes, it's exhausting. Very exhausting. I grew up being taught to take my responsibilities seriously. It is ingrained in the consciousness of my generation, the generation growing up in the sixties. It grew more imperative since I became a media professional. I started out doing radio in 1985 after getting out of college. It was the heyday of radio. I entered TV in the 1990s, when TV became all the rage. There was no Internet back then, so TV was the most influential medium in China. TV is in the public domain so should be protected and utilized properly for the benefit of the public. But what I've seen defied my expectations. I still cannot accept the reality of public TV that doesn't benefit the public."

Would it be possible to split CCTV into a commercial network and a public network?

"Not likely in the short run," Cui said. "CCTV will only change when the overall direction of China changes. It bothers me that we can't have real public TV in China. Even a tiny country like Romania has three public stations. Many of our practitioners do not even understand what public TV is."

I thought about Bai Yansong's point about public TV being premature in China, given the Chinese state's strong ideological grip. "Knowing that change is beyond your capability, why aren't you settling?"

"I continue to insist on my belief and to seek pleasure in my persistence and resistance. China today paradoxically offers many options, and you can choose to do what you think is right and where you want to be to realize your vision. I choose to stay put here at CCTV because there has to be someone who does not give up. We have done many productive things over the years. For instance, I have a platform for multiple voices to be heard. I have also experimented with new program concepts and formats. For instance, I applied the reality show formula to a main-melody* program, *My Long March*."

He told me that in 2006, he suspended *Xiao Cui* to prepare for making *My Long March*, a reenactment of the Red Army's epic journey of escape from besieging Kuomintang forces beginning in 1934 and ending in 1936. To commemorate the seventieth anniversary of the Long March, a team led by Cui retraced the Red Army's path in a televised fund-raising event for rural development. In an interview with China Radio International, when asked about why he created the program, Cui was recorded as saying that "there should be someone who keeps talking about history and takes it seriously, the media, for example. This is the responsibility of a public TV station. My personal belief is to influence anyone who is under the influence, and of course, the more, the better. If you can enlighten people, then the job is worthwhile.[14]

"Though I'm still technically working for CCTV, I have moved out of CCTV proper now and have rented my own production facility here, footing my own bill and paying my own staff of over fifty people. I am the only one among my team here who receives a base salary from CCTV, as I am still counted as a CCTV employee. Actually I prefer not receiving salary from CCTV at all. I wanted a complete break, but CCTV would not relent because it meant that I'd have the freedom to engage in commercial activities, which are banned for CCTV employees. Many people have left CCTV over the past few years for commercial opportunities. To me, the platform provided by CCTV still means something."

I had heard complaints from Cui's colleagues about how he could get away with whatever he wanted to do. "At times I wonder if CCTV is Cui's private shop," one person commented sarcastically, noting that Cui was able to launch any program he fancied. Given his talent and the power he commands at CCTV, I asked Cui whether perhaps he would consider doing an evening talk show that tackles issues of popular concern, be they social, cultural, or political.

"We'd have to wait and see. The last thing I want to do is to have a show that falls behind the print and new media in terms of sharpness and contemporariness. Then the pain and the frustration would start all over again. I don't wish to continue living like that. But if there is a real platform for me to

---

* "Main melody" is a term describing shows promoting the party ideology.

do real in-depth programs, then I am all in. I interviewed three ambassadors the day before yesterday. They requested a summary of questions beforehand and wanted to arrange for preinterview meetings. I said no, as I wanted to meet them when I saw them at the interview. This is my way, and I want to have control over how I do things."

Retaining Integrity: Battling Censorship and Self-Censorship

As Cui and the others mentioned, controlling the message is key both to the journalist and to the entity that he or she is directly accountable to: the Communist Party. It is a constant battle, and despite institutional conversion and ownership deregulation, the party-state still filters media content by censorship. Compulsory censorship has been imposed so that all programs must be censored before and after broadcasting. The party has tightened its control over news materials in spite of the relaxation of operations. Immediately after the affirmation of a cultural industry approach, the Seventeenth Party Congress report in October 2007 emphasized that the core value of socialism must be internalized into the Chinese psyche. Obviously CCTV and especially its news programs must shoulder the responsibility of solidifying the socialist ideals. If the programs produced deviate from the socialist core, the producer, without any doubt, would be fired and the official in charge of censoring the program would also be fired. The system thus encourages self-censorship, and program producers are even more cautious and strict than the state regulators.

In practice, the party-state continues to control its major "mouthpieces" and politically sensitive content while allowing "limited pluralism" in nonpolitical areas. Under an authoritarian political regime, businesspeople avert political risk so as to preserve economic profits, and news journalists are no different, opting to work within the system once they realize that there is no alternative.

Cai Jing, the young reporter Jing Yidan so admired, told me that "instead of complaining, one should focus on working within the constraints and creating more space by pushing the envelope." She emphasized that it is important not to lose faith in justice and truth, and not to be corrupted by cynicism.

But it can be hard not to be infected by the weariness that documentary filmmaker and CCTV producer Chen Xiaoqing exhibited when I spoke with him. "I live a simple life these days, doing the best I can to perform my job duty," he said, "even though I no longer take to heart the program I am in charge of." He has had way too many run-ins with the censors to fight for the integrity of his program. "The more heart you put into it, the more you will get hurt. You absolutely cannot reason with the censors. They simply tell you that you're not allowed to say this and that you must say that. You have no choice but to follow their orders; doesn't matter that the facts point to a different conclusion. It hurts that you cannot say what you want to say. I know better now how to gauge the censor's limits. Shi Jian [a veteran news producer at CCTV] said something that was excellent. He said not to say things that are untruthful, keep silent if you have to lie, and don't be proud if you lie under force."

But this is not to say that CCTV is incapable of good journalism. In fact, CCTV earned plaudits for its serious coverage of the Iraq War, matching or even exceeding the major Western news services at providing multivoiced objective coverage.[15] Watching this happen, journalists and observers could speak optimistically about maturing broadcast capabilities and catering to the public's "right to know." The quality Iraq coverage, though, benefited from the state's ideological disinterest in the war. The free hand lent to the media on Iraq was immediately withdrawn and replaced by heavy-handed state management of the SARS story, making it clear that "right to know" journalism could be pursued only to the extent that it served the government's interests. At best, the contrasting cases spoke to the media's developing flexibility and readiness to play different roles under different rules, an increasingly skilled schizophrenia. As Zhang Xiaoling puts it succinctly, "Caught between stern decrees and restrictions on the one hand, and swimming in a 'sea of commercialization' on the other, few Chinese journalists have much energy left for democratic ferment, and few are inclined to risk their jobs to challenge the status quo. They adapt to current 'Chinese characteristics,' striving to maintain a 'complete understanding of the policies for reports,' and taking care 'not to be too conservative on the one hand, nor to bring any negative influence on the other in the coverage of any breaking news.'"[16]

"I might not know what to do without restrictions," Cui Yongyuan told me semi-seriously. "I'm not sure if I'm up to par with the global standards on such an issue, as I am trained to do things in a certain way." He admitted, "It would be difficult for me to break out of the old mode." His remarks are self-deprecating, but underlying it is a hard truth: self-censorship has become so ingrained in his professional code that Cui noted, "I am so used to stopping when I still have more to say. Hard to teach an old dog new tricks. Furthermore, how much independent thinking ability do I still have left in me, after so many years of succumbing to the will of the party? Am I well informed enough to carry a show that requires independent thinking?" Cui seemed to be oscillating between self-doubt and elevated self-assurance, all the while maintaining a pensive distance between his vision of professional duties and ethics and the vision imposed upon him by his employer.

Though news practitioners like Cui and Chen might feel frustrated by the restrictions that CCTV's role as mouthpiece puts on them, without exception the newspeople I talked to all displayed a deep devotion to professionalism, thinking of their work as a specialized skill with a unique set of "methods and ethics" intrinsic to what they believe is a critical role for the news media in China—methods and ethics, moreover, that should be independent of the state's oversight and often end up creating tension with their party mouthpiece role. Similar to their Western counterparts, Chinese journalists balance ratings-driven demands for news as entertainment against their professional ideal of journalism as an essential agent of the public interest. Unlike Western journalists, they must also balance professional aspirations against the old reality of their official commission as mouthpieces of the party. Self-censorship is second nature in this environment, but so is the determination among journalists to keep testing the limits of the censorship regime, and as the party-state struggles to accommodate the growing sophistication of the Chinese population, there is play in the system. The efforts on the part of journalists to advance their profession come up against a fear of retrenchment, but the constant push from journalists themselves and from the developing society is toward a less ideologically hamstrung media.

In addition to the general idea of a news media with a professional code independent of state directives, a host of subsidiary Western concepts including "muckraking," "watchdog journalism," and the news media as a "fourth power" or "fourth estate" have clearly taken hold in China. These terms were in common use at CCTV. And while no one openly espoused that cynical axiom about how to succeed in the news business—"if it bleeds it leads"—it's clear that everyone was confronting the reality. But as extensively as it borrows from the Western media canon, contemporary Chinese journalism is not Western journalism. A term that doesn't derive from the Western press but does tell a lot about Chinese journalism is the notion of "enlightenment journalism." This partly could be a face-saving term of art—a cover for Chinese journalists who know that at the end of the day they are still party propagandists, compromised by self-censorship even when the hand of the Propaganda Ministry is light—but it is also a genuine ideal to some extent. To what extent is difficult to pin down, except to say that it is consistent with the traditions of the Chinese intellectual, ideals that resonate with Chinese journalists.

Western journalists claim to do their work in the service of maintaining an informed public, bringing the public information that they need in order to make informed decisions in democratic societies. Media scholars have concluded that Western journalism is not quite so transparent. Decades of research suggest that at a minimum the news media are powerful "agenda setters," effectively telling people "what to think *about*," if not quite "what to think." Current scholarship disagrees about the extent to which Western news media do, in fact, also try to dictate what to think, especially in cases of large media conglomerates such as News Corporation. In theory, though, professional journalists in the West make a clear distinction between news content and editorial content.

The CCTV journalists that I talked to regard themselves as intellectuals, and in the tradition of the Chinese intellectual, their work is not just about *informing* the public; they also imagine themselves performing a vital service of *guiding* public opinion. This, of course, is more or less what the Propaganda Ministry, having advanced from outright thought control in the revolutionary era to a more subtle mechanism in the reform era, nowadays aims to achieve through China's news media. When asked how much control of her programs she had, Jing Yidan responded in a relatively unperturbed fashion, "It depends on the nature of the story. If it's something that threatens national safety and security, then we all need to observe rules and regulations set by those upstairs. For instance, the Xinjiang [riot] story must follow the tone and limits set by the state. Other than that, we have ample room for control and improvisation."

If the news media were suddenly released from their mouthpiece charge, they would certainly make some different choices about what to cover and how, but it is not clear that they would on the whole be any less inclined than the party leadership to shape the news in a radically different way than they do now.

Meanwhile, of course, as the crown jewel of China's contemporary news media, CCTV is highly prized by the party-state and closely associated with its central authority. The advantages and disadvantages of this position are plain. It has size, regulatory precedence, and enough resources to afford the highest production values and some of the best, most innovative talent available. At the same time, during extended media crackdowns, CCTV is under even closer scrutiny than distant, lesser competitors, and it is inescapably branded as the establishment spokes-network in the public eye. The restlessness of CCTV's news programming, with its constant revamping and restructuring, is indicative of the network's anxiety under pressure to deliver loyalty to the party-state, reliability to the market, and credibility to audiences. CCTV news, and perhaps Chinese journalism as a whole, seems to be in a state of "continuous revolution," reinventing the way that it does the news with each cycle of loosening and tightening under the censorship regime, all the while trying to secure small but permanent footholds toward a more independent professionalism.

5

RISE OF THE POWERFUL NATIONS
AND THE FINANCE AND ECONOMICS CHANNEL

In November 2006, a twelve-part, ten-hour-long documentary, *The Rise of the Powerful Nations* (*Power*), debuted to instant fame, matching the attention awarded *River Elegy* more than a decade earlier. Though the two share similar messages—China must learn and adapt or else stagnate and perish—*Power* does not comment directly on Chinese culture. Instead, it depicts the evolution of European statecraft from monarchy to democracy, examining the nation-building process and the territorial expansion of countries such as Portugal, Spain, the United Kingdom, Germany, Japan, and the United States. It covers major historical events including England's Magna Carta, Europe's great voyages of discovery during the colonization of the Americas, the industrial revolution, and the collapse of the Soviet Union. The narration bears an emphatic tone common to Chinese historical documentaries, and the soundtrack is equally imposing. The documentary cites attributes of the "powerful nations" that China might emulate: Spain had a risk-taking queen; Britain's nimble navy secured vital commodities overseas; the United States regulated markets and fought for national unity. The series highlights successes in statecraft such as core human values, constitutional government, education, and the blending of modernization with tradition. While covering a number of important social factors, the series shows how trust between the public and leadership was a key factor in the rise of the powerful nations. In addition, the series identifies a combination of political, economic, and cultural factors that contributed to these nations' eventual decline. Interviews with noted historians and academics such as Paul Kennedy, author of *The Rise and Fall of the Great Powers*, and Joseph E. Stiglitz, a Nobel laureate in economics, give the documentary added credibility.

The idea for producing *Power* was rumored to have been inspired by a Politburo study session in November 2003. Following Hu Jintao's call to consider world history when determining China's developmental path, the Politburo moved to commission an academic study of powerful nations, culminating in a book entitled *The Course of Development of Major Advanced Countries in the World since the Fifteenth Century*. The Politburo also invited two university-based historians to give tutorials on foreign history. They lectured on the histories of the major advanced countries, focusing on their ascendance to "world power" status in modern times. The news about the Politburo's world history sessions was aired on the radio as Ren Xuean, a producer at CCTV's Finance and Economics Channel, drove down Beijing Third Ring Road toward CCTV. The idea of making a popular documentary that would trace the rise and fall of powerful nation-states suddenly dawned on him.

Stimulated by the theme of "learning from the West," Ren consulted a team of Chinese historians specializing in European history who briefed the Politburo on the subject, including Qian Chengdan, a historian of modern English and European history at Nanjing University. "It is important for China to be able to draw lessons from the experiences of others," Qian encouraged Ren. Qian would later become the intellectual force behind the documentary. Qian and a team from Peking University's world history faculty participated in Ren's project, preparing the historical framework for the documentary. The final script was drafted by Ren and Chen Jin, a research fellow at the Central Bureau of Compilation and Translation. CCTV then sent out production teams to the featured countries to shoot footage and interview scholars and historians. Shooting took about eighteen months to complete. Editing took another year.

From the perspective of someone watching the program from one of the "powerful nations," the documentary might appear to be an example of China's new style of propaganda; that is, on the surface, China is more open to outside perspectives, but what is learned is ultimately selective. The documentary highlights only historical events that emphasize social stability, industrial investment, peaceful foreign relations, and national unity. These are presented as more vital than military strength, political liberalization, or the rule of law. In the ninety minutes devoted to examining the rise of the United States, for instance, Abraham Lincoln is accorded a prominent part for his efforts to "preserve national unity" during the Civil War, while Franklin D. Roosevelt wins praise for creating a bigger role for the government in managing the market economy, though Roosevelt's wartime leadership receives less attention.

Unsurprisingly, the views presented in the series coincide with policies promoted by the Chinese state: they also resonate with the outlook of the historians who worked on the series. Qian, who also appears in episode twelve, focuses part of his research on explaining why England became the first modern country. Qian's answer is that "the English were able to make constant adjustment to new social conditions in order to avoid violent, bloody revolutions."[1] Specifically, he points out that "since the 'Glorious Revolution' of 1688 the English have learned a valuable historical lesson from their tumultuous past that reform, instead of revolution, is a better solution to the demand for social change and progress."[2] As continental Europe was swept by revolutionary tides, England enjoyed more than a century of peaceful development. This emphasis on England's "peaceful rise" resonates with the image that the Chinese state attempts to project to the world while confirming Qian's "emphasis on piecemeal social reform and avoiding ferocious class struggle."[3]

Chinese historians began writing about the outside world beyond China's own sphere in the wake of the Opium War (1839–42) out of the strategic need to know more about its Western adversaries. After the shattering defeat by Japan in the Sino-Japanese War of 1894–95, interest in foreign history grew considerably; yet the motivation for Chinese historians to embark on the study remained essentially the same: to discover the secrets of success in the West (also Japan) and the causes of China's decline from its vaunted status as the "Middle Kingdom." For Liang Qichao, a history-minded reformer, a "historiographical revolution" was needed so that history writing could be rendered useful for constructing the new Chinese nation. The study of "world history," chiefly Western and Japanese history, became part of this endeavor. History was expected to offer useful tips about how to achieve the nationalist goal of reclaiming China's past glory.

The production of *Power* represents a fresh effort to rebuild China's glory tinted with a Eurocentric notion that equates modernization with Westernization. It is worth noting that the Chinese leadership of the 1990s, headed by Jiang Zemin, urged Chinese schools to educate students about China's modern history. As Edward Yang puts it, it was generally agreed that "Jiang gave the directive to make the 'Modern Chinese History' course mandatory on college campuses, hoping to inculcate students with the notion that '[a country's] backwardness will cause it to be bullied by others.'"[4] By emphasizing the need for modernization via the prism of Western nations, *Power* was an extension of this goal. However, instead of mining China's own history for lessons, *Power* examined the past glory of the Occidental others, analyzing "how some countries leaped ahead in gaining wealth and power and even became 'bullies' of others."[5] The message here is clear: China must move in the same direction lest it continue to be "bullied." In his preface to a book on the series, then CCTV president Zhao Huayong said that the documentary was an effort to search for distinctive features and the underlying principles of nation building among the featured superpowers.

The documentary debuted in November 2006 to enthusiastic audiences. The number of viewers for each episode averaged 4 million, according to Ren. The miniseries was aired three more times, which is unprecedented for a CCTV documentary. The success was a pleasant surprise to Ren, given the buffet of more conventionally entertaining programs available to Chinese viewers, and he was impressed that the audience embraced a history documentary with such an avowed pedagogical aim. The DVDs are so popular that bootleggers got into the action, defying the conventional wisdom that documentaries are tough sells in the DVD market. "In Taiwan, pirated copies of our documentary are still all the rage, *even now*," Ren emphasized during our interview in July 2009, three years after the show originally aired. "When the director of China International Television Corporation, the copyright holder of the program, browsed a high-end electronics market in Beijing the other day, he was stopped by a vendor who tried to sell him a pirated copy of *Power*. 'This one is harder to get than the porn movies,' the vendor whispered."

In online discussions, Chinese netizens mostly agreed that *Power* was an unprecedented event for Chinese television, though some pointed out that its endorsement of freedom and equality bears a resemblance to *River Elegy*.[6] One online posting proclaimed that *Power* had powerfully influenced the thinking of Chinese people, the same sort of reception *River* had received two decades before.[7] As is often the case, *Power*'s success caused many to try to read between the lines, with some suggesting that, like *River*, *Power* foreshadowed new political reform efforts and served as evidence of the Chinese leadership's desire to learn from Western society, including its political and legal systems. Most people agreed that the show is a good education for Chinese people, preparing them for China's ascension to world-power status. One blogger, Sun Bin, argued that *Power* ultimately suggested that U.S.- or UK-style democracy would be China's long-term goal—though China should be made into an open society before turning into a democracy—and that China would be ready to play by the rules of the modern world, compromising when needed.

On the patriotic Tianya Club Internet bulletin board, an article introducing *Power* attracted more than two hundred messages from netizens within three days, including some long, densely woven posts.[8] In their passionate endorsement of the show, netizens teased out several themes they see as the show's principles to becoming a "great nation": innovation is essential; aggression through force is to be avoided at all costs; rule of law must be enforced; the country must develop economically in a sustainable manner; and government must play a primary role in nation building.

Along with the widespread praise, criticism also emerged. Some charged that the show only touched upon the issue of economics and avoided real analysis of politics. Some took issue with *Power*'s omission of the repression by Stalin in the late 1930s.[9] Some pointed out that the episode on the United States mentioned only freedom from want promoted by President Roosevelt, omitting the three other basic freedoms on Roosevelt's list: freedom of speech and expression, freedom of religious worship, and freedom from fear.

Ren anticipated that there would be reactions to the program, but not this explosive and long lasting. "The overwhelming reaction attests to the hunger we have in learning about what other people have done to reach the point where they are now. The program is our reflection and position on the trajectory that others have taken so far," Ren said.

The documentary was influential beyond China. The former prime minister of Singapore Lee Kuan Yew was quoted as saying that he liked it so much that he asked Singapore TV to dub it in English and broadcast it, praising its nonideological stance.[10] The documentary has since been dubbed in English and shown on the History Channel in the United States. News coverage and analysis appeared in the *New York Times*, on the BBC, and in other major media organs around the world. Some see it as an attempt by the Chinese state to assure the world that China's emergence is a peaceful one. Others see it as a sign that China is increasingly open to discussing its growing international power and influence. As Joseph Kahn writes, "Until recently China's rising power remained a delicate topic, and largely unspoken, inside China."[11]

Commenting on the recognition overseas, Ren said, "In hindsight, the program not only benefited the Chinese but also global audiences, as it provides a window for the world to take note of China's perspective on the world." Ren gave me an English version of the program with subtitles done in Singapore. "It took them less than two months to do the subtitling. Our program came out on November 13, 2006, and they added English subtitles by January the next year." Ren lamented that there are not many CCTV programs that have English subtitles and that this reflects the Chinese media industry's insular and inward-looking attitude.

It is interesting, though, that Chinese officials minimized the importance of the series, defusing the wide speculation about what possible political changes the documentary signals. He Yafei, an assistant foreign minister, said in an interview that the documentary does not represent a change in China's thinking about projecting power.

Regardless, the show captivated both my daughter and me. To my daughter, it was an early education in world history that she had yet to be exposed to at her school in the United States. To me, the documentary is a far cry from the stereotypical rhetoric circulated at middle school and college during my school years in China. The world history textbooks from my era denounced the nations featured in the documentary as "colonialists," "imperialists" who brought to the world injustice, violence, and exploitation. It was quite surprising to see a CCTV documentary discussing the rise and fall of nations previously deemed oppressors from an institutional and technical perspective in a rational tone. The eschewing of the victim's view toward the countries that historically made China suffer is certainly refreshing. In fact, *Power* often overlooks the violence of Western colonialism and imperialism. This sort of revisionist historical view has now become mainstream in Chinese history, with few official conflicts over the proper ideological stance.

"Are you a history buff? Was it difficult to make the documentary?" I asked Ren as we settled down at the teahouse inside CCTV's media center.

"Not easy." Ren shook his head, admitting that he is no expert in world history and that limited historical knowledge meant a lot of catching up for him and his team. "We eventually became quasi-historians, after three years of hard work," Ren said.

"We made the documentary to help the Chinese public know more about the world. We want to help our audiences understand what it means to be a great power and how a nation becomes a great power. Frankly, making the documentary was my own journey of searching for answers to these critical questions. China has always been keen to learn from the achievements of others. As China opens up to the outside world, we need a more rational understanding of the world." By "rational," Ren meant to steer clear of the outdated official discourse that equates the West with the colonial and the imperial.

"In my opinion, the successful experiences of these countries have much in common," said Ren. "On the one hand, you have to respect tradition. On the other hand, you must have the courage to innovate. That's what I learned from studying these five hundred years of history."

Power was the product of CCTV-2, the Finance and Economics Channel, known within the network as the most innovative channel. It went on the air in May 1973, the same date when China began broadcasting in color. The channel has undergone several major overhauls since, and much like everything else at CCTV and in China in general, it has been under a permanent state of restructuring. In July 1996, still early in the era of media commercialization but almost two decades into the broader reform era, CCTV-2 was officially defined as a predominately economics channel. The channel's new definition seemed to have brought legitimacy to its relentless pursuit of profit in its early programming, which aggressively blurred the line between advertisements and regular programs, reflecting the pattern in the Chinese media industry in particular and in Chinese society in general. Commercialization was so all encompassing that a new joke has started to circulate that in China one would forsake sex for money.

By the late 1990s, in addition to the standard television commercials inserted within and between programs, CCTV-2 had three special programs that were more or less devoted to extended commercial promotions. They were *Gongqiu Rexian* (Market Place), *Shangwu Dianshi* (Business Television), and *Shang Qiao* (Business Bridge), lasting, respectively, half an hour, twenty minutes, and five minutes. The price for getting a commercial on any of these three programs was CN¥20,000 per sixty seconds in 1998. Apart from these programs of unabashed infomercial, many "noncommercial" programs carried concealed advertising as a result of deals struck behind closed doors between the producer and commercial sponsors. Together, the three long-form sales programs, along with *Dianshi Gouwu* (*TV Shopping*), a direct retail program launched in June 1998, took up about five hours of CCTV-2 programming per day. That is to say, commercial promotion accounted for 30 percent of the total airtime of the economics channel in the late 1990s, not taking into account standard commercials inserted between and within other programs.[12]

CCTV-2: The Finance and Economics Channel

Though CCTV-2 was redefined as an economics, life, and service channel in 2000 and officially became the Finance and Economics Channel in October 2003, the pressure of ratings forced the channel to venture into producing noneconomic-related entertainment programs as well, thus ushering in reality and competition programs like *Happy Dictionary* and *Lucky 52*, both cloned formulas imported from the United Kingdom and the United States. As the entertainment programs gained momentum, the channel launched *Win in China* in May 2006 by Wang Yifen, the former host of the channel's popular talk show *Dialogue*. Wang watched *The Apprentice* while in the United States and wanted to develop a similar show on CCTV-2. As Wang recounts, *The Apprentice* inspired his theme for *Win in China*, which was to promote the entrepreneurial spirit.[13]

In spring 2008, the station decided to retrench and trimmed its female-targeted programs. Cooking and household management shows were cut to make room for male-oriented, big-muscle financial programs. In September 2008, during the financial meltdown, the channel started a live program, *Target Wall Street*, inviting domestic and international experts to give in-depth analyses of the causes and ramifications of the financial crisis. The nightly program at 9 P.M. saw a 53 percent increase in its ratings from programs in the same time slot a year before. On October 27, 2008, a new economic commentary program, *Observation Today*, was launched, transforming the channel from providing news and information to offering discussions and commentaries on overall economic policies and directions. The fall 2008 reform not only helped with retaining loyal audiences but also brought in urban viewers with professional backgrounds.

By the late 2000s, there were five major areas in CCTV-2 programming: economic news and information programs such as *Global Information Billboard*; financial programs such as *China Financial News Report* and *Chinese Stock Market*; in-depth magazine-type programs that discuss economic events and personalities such as *Dialogue, Economy and Regulation*, and *Fortune Story*; consumer service programs such as *Life* and *At Your Services*; and finally entertainment programs such as game shows and quiz shows that help sustain the channel's overall ratings. Overall, 60 percent of the channel's programming was related to the economy, and 20 percent focused on the stock market and related financial news.

Then came another channel redefinition in September 2009, as the channel was yet again renamed to CCTV-Finance & Economy, focusing exclusively on broadcasting financial and economic programs. To prepare for the launch of the new name, three lucrative entertainment programs, *Special 6+1*, *Yong's Happy Club*, and *Quiz Show*, were relocated to CCTV-3, the Comprehensive Arts Channel, on July 27, 2009. With audiences being predominately consumers of domestic interest, CCTV-2 was unfavorably compared to CNBC, whose target audience is professional investors and the business community. "Would CCTV-2 become CNBC, then?" I asked the baby-faced assistant general director of CCTV-2, Xu Wenguang, who is the brainpower behind several heavyweight finance shows such as *Target Wall Street*. Xu said that pushing for further channel specialization was the impetus behind the renaming, but by no means was CCTV-2 the equivalent of CNBC yet. "There is no comparison between CNBC and CCTV-2," Xu said. "CNBC is a service channel for the business community. CCTV-2 is a hybrid product of China's unique situation. China's stock market has yet to grow and become the major focus of

CCTV-2." CNBC focuses exclusively on live programs for investors and business interests during the weekdays, yet CCTV-2 cast a much wider net, trying to lure both investors and ordinary consumers. Xu said that "with programs of noneconomic and financial nature flooding the pipeline, CCTV-2 had been falling short of being the specialty channel it set out to be. It is futile to compare programs in this fashion."

Though Xu was at the forefront of innovative economic programming, including overseeing two of the most influential financial programs, *Economic Half Hour* and *Economic News*, he expressed his reservations at what he saw as the pitfalls of never-ending programming overhauls at CCTV. Xu said that during the first stage of the push for a programming overhaul, CCTV basically emulated Western program models: "*Horizon* and *Tell It Like It Is* deftly lifted successful formulas from American television. As Chinese television continued to copy others' successful formulas, problems arose, as making newer and more novel programs became the goal itself, resulting in the constant negation of existing programs and never-ending shift of schedules. Sometimes we risk losing track of when our own program is on."

Xu emphasized that frequent program reshuffling had resulted in shorter program cycles that prevented quality programs from maturing into their own niche and establishing their brand. Xu lamented that CCTV had yet to allow a program to go through its natural cycle of birth, growth, and aging. He marveled at the longevity of U.S. programs such as *60 Minutes*. The impatience and shortsightedness very much reflected the general mind-set in China's ongoing transformation, resulting in many prematurely ended programs. He told me that he had urged his colleagues to have long-term strategies in program planning, and to this end, creating a brand name is a viable way to ensure the longevity of any particular program.

Although economic and financial programs under the helm of Xu Wenguang predominate CCTV-2 programming, a robust area of growth for the channel actually resides in the less high-minded consumer guide and lifestyle programs that promote a consumption-based lifestyle that conforms to the Western notion of modernity.[14] These programs speak to the aspirations of the newly emerging Chinese upper-middle class as they acquire their identity as an affluent class through personal consumption. Not surprisingly, these lifestyle programs are the most lucrative in attracting advertisers and thus help the channel maintain its good ratings.

Aside from regularly scheduled programs, CCTV-2 also produces special-topics programs related to China's overall developmental policy. Ren Xuean, the director of special programs who brought to life *The Rise of the Powerful*

Nations, is the man most associated with these programs. Like most of his colleagues at CCTV, Ren majored in TV news at the Beijing Broadcasting Institute, now the Communication University of China. After graduation, he had a brief stint teaching at BBI. He joined CCTV-2 in 1993 as a beneficiary of CCTV's contractual labor system under Yang Weiguang's reign. Ren stayed at CCTV-2 all these years, producing special economic programs on reform and development. He says that the programs he produced over the years prepared him for the production of *Power*.

As he recounted, a twenty-episode special-topics program he produced in 1995, *Harvest: Stories of Moderate Prosperity in Chinese Villages*, was the first television program documenting the achievement of village reform in China. His production team selected fifteen villages to examine the impact of reform on villagers' daily lives. The documentary highlighted how the concept of a market economy gradually developed and took effect and how economic reform brought about changes in interpersonal relationships within communities. The success of the program led to another special-topics program on urban enterprise reform, the sixteen-episode *Experimental On-Location Target Report* in 1996. Another one, in 1997, the twelve-episode *Market Economy and Professional Ethics*, sought to refute charges of negative impacts of market reform by illustrating positive regulatory changes and the establishment of the rule of law brought about by the market economy. These programs functioned to champion further economic reform, which puts Ren and his colleagues in the liberal camp of the Chinese ideological spectrum.

After the successful execution of three major topics programs, Ren was promoted to the position of producer in 1997. By this time, pollution had reached alarming levels in China. Ren was compelled to produce another special-topics program, *Generations of Natural Resources*, the first TV documentary that provides a systematic assessment of China's environmental issues. It advocated environmental protection and questioned the commonly perceived wisdom that natural resource–rich China was immune to environmental degradation.

Ren took over *Economic Half Hour* in 1998. The same year he produced another special-topics program commemorating the twentieth anniversary of the implementation of economic reform. The special program featured twenty individuals whose lives had been positively affected by opening up and reform. The individuals featured ranged from seasoned politicians and businessmen to migrant workers and farmers. In 1999, Ren produced the six-episode series *Talking About Farmers' Burden*, which broached the topic of heavy taxation on Chinese farmers. Ren left *Economic Half Hour* in 2000 to produce a new program, *Security and Stock Market*, and was soon promoted to deputy director of CCTV's Economic Division.

Based on the theme of the programs under his reign, Ren and his team belong to the liberal wing of the Chinese intellectual and media camp, which champions further marketization. Or maybe he is merely carrying on the tasks assigned by the more liberal-minded top brass. "Were these assigned programs by CCTV?" I asked.

"All were self-selected programs by our production teams," Ren said, "not programs by order from the party. Our programs all deal with what we see as issues of urgent public concern."

The end of 2003 brought Ren the welcome opportunity to produce *Power*. The actual production of *Power* started in 2004 and carried on until the second half of 2006. Ren said that *Power* is not a historical documentary but a special-topics program, what he associates with news programs, as it is highly relevant to the contemporary situation. Ren said that the production of this program made him see more clearly the process of globalization, the price of modernization on a global scale, and the limited choice China has in its march toward modernization. "You'd be abandoned if you do not participate," Ren said.

When asked about the fear and suspicion the West has about China's rise, Ren said that, first of all, it is not in the Chinese blood to expand beyond its borders; second, mistrust breeds disaster. "You want to be trusted, but you distrust others," Ren said, pointing out Western hypocrisy.

Ren discussed how the lack of mutual trust and respect had led to misrepresentation. Ren said that one of the things he would like to achieve via his documentary was to make people in the featured nations see that the Chinese are curious about their history and wish to learn from the paths that others have taken. In return, perhaps they would want to study the five thousand years of Chinese history and come to a more objective conclusion about China. I reminded him that the West has paid intense attention to China and that there is a whole field devoted to the study of China in the United States, the United Kingdom, and some other European countries. I explained that the Western visions of China were shaped by a set of deeply rooted and preconceived notions about China, which led to conflicting views about China that swing between positive and negative extremes. The mistrust goes both ways, I said, mentioning my reluctance to do a book on CCTV, knowing that people at CCTV would not feel comfortable talking to a U.S. scholar. "Would CCTV open its door to me? Not likely. The lack of access to information in China is the root of many of the misconceptions about China," I told him.

"Would one of the major networks in the U.S. or UK do a prime-time program about Chinese history at the same scale of what we did for the history of the major powers in the West?" Ren asked, more as a statement than a question.

"I am afraid not, at least not on the commercial networks in the U.S., because the audience demand is simply not there. Ordinary Americans are not interested in learning about Chinese history, or their own history, for that matter," I said.

"Well," Ren said, "*Power* corrected Chinese people's misconception of the U.S. as being a place with no culture and history. Take this as our contribution to the American people.

"This leads me to conclude that when China has opened up, the developed countries around the world are shutting down, closing their minds," Ren said further.

I felt compelled to clarify. "Commercial networks are driven by economic not cultural logic. But U.S. public TV has done quite a few documentaries on China." I talked about the documentary done by the Canadian Broadcasting Corporation and the Discovery Channel, *China Rises*, for which my college was entrusted with putting together a website about China studies for the *New York Times*' educational website.

Ren concurred but said that the lack of interest in understanding China among ordinary Americans suggested the deep-rooted imperialistic mentality that treats others as nonentities. Given that Chinese people from all walks of life are so motivated to learn and absorb knowledge about the world outside, "I come to the conclusion, based on our eagerness to learn, that China will become a major power," Ren said.

"China is already a major power," I said. And I could not agree more with him about the insularity of the American public when it comes to knowing the world beyond the United States. I reminded Ren too that the resentment toward China's rising power among the average American has much to do with the dismal economic reality, as cheap imports from China have taken away jobs in the United States. Then there is the same nostalgia that permeates every culture—the West also wishes to hold on to its old glory.

By the way, I asked him, how did he select which old glories to be included in the documentary?

"The criterion for inclusion of nations in the documentary has to do with historical dominance and influence." To Ren, capitalism or socialism itself tells us nothing. What matters are lessons that can be valuable to China's future development. Ren was fatigued with the old thinking that divides the world into capitalism and socialism. "Never mind which camp. Whatever works," he said. "There are variations within the socialist camp after all. Ours is different from Cuba and North Korea and different from the former Soviet Union; it's even different from our own previous path under the same socialism label. To me, the current Chinese-style socialism is about building an affluent and harmonious society together."

I asked about the human price of the economic restructuring. Ren answered, "Well, economic reform is in effect the redistribution of wealth and benefits. We are used to it now. It hurts to see my uncle, a formerly revered factory worker, now occupying the lowest rank of the society after the reform. He eventually adapted and took up driving. He understands that reform is good for China and his personal loss is justified by the progress China has made in the past decades." Here again, collective pride trumps that of the individual.

Our conversation shifted to CCTV's function. When asked about CCTV's dual function of serving the party-state and serving the Chinese people, Ren found the dichotomy dubious, as he maintained that the people and state are not necessarily at odds with each other. Indeed, in his reasoning, the Chinese state is the same as the Chinese people, and he noted, "CCTV is funded by the state, so we are obligated to carry out the state's mandate in serving the people." Ren argued that media professionals around the world should be in awe of Chinese media workers' extraordinary ability to carve out a space in addressing issues of public concern while fulfilling their obligation to the party-state. Thus, Ren implicitly acknowledged the rift between the state and the public. But he insisted that CCTV is a public TV network and therefore serves the public.

There seemed to be a common confusion or willful neglect by Chinese media professionals in their understanding of what public television is. In the United States, the United Kingdom, and Europe, public TV is funded in part or whole by the state, but it maintains independent control over programming and personnel. There is of course no such thing as government state TV in the United States and the United Kingdom, except for the Voice of America, the international radio station under the control of the U.S. Information Agency, which has no presence in the United States itself. In China, there is no such thing as public TV. I was often met with blank stares in China when I tried to clarify the conceptual differences.

The only person who spoke clearly and eloquently about the curious blurring of state-public service in Chinese television was Xia Jun, the once iconoclastic director of the controversial documentary *River Elegy*. In his book published in 2006, *Chinese Television at a Crossroad*, Xia devoted a whole chapter to dissecting the curious status of CCTV. Titled "The Paradox of CCTV," the chapter raises the questions of whether CCTV is a monopolistic operation, whether it is a state-run or a commercial enterprise, and whether it is a public or commercial station. Xia's conclusion is that CCTV has no clear functional distinction and thus transgresses and violates the rules of the game through its sheer power as China's only state-backed and commercially operated national network. Xia and I had lengthy discussions about CCTV's curious status during our interview. As Xia made clear, CCTV does not operate in a monopolistic manner in its market practices, yet it unintentionally ends up monopolizing resources and much of the market anyway, as it has the public airwaves in their entirety at its disposal.

Not that Ren does not see the gap between the needs of the party-state and those of the public; he proudly claimed that CCTV "is at the government's service yet at the same time satisfies the public's needs, their demand for information and knowledge." In Ren's elaboration, at times the Chinese public is not seen as the client of CCTV and his programs are considered to be doing a favor to the public while carrying out their duty to the state.

Our conversation shifted to the pronounced technological sloppiness of some of the programs on CCTV, which has further tarnished CCTV's reputation. "Does the issue have to do with what people commonly perceive as the inertia of a state-run enterprise?" I asked. Ren maintained that the problems are twofold: on the one hand, there is the culture of a particular institution; on the other hand, there is the qualification of a particular individual. "The problem has nothing to do with whether a station is a state or private enterprise. It has to do with a station's corporate culture and an individual's professional training and commitment. We're lagging behind major Western firms in realizing the importance of fostering a conducive corporate culture." Ren said that Chinese media as a whole have yet to realize the importance of cultivating a positive corporate identity.

"Perhaps competition is also a crucial factor in motivating a firm to perform better?" I suggested, alluding to the charge of a CCTV monopoly.

"This is a typical Western framework," Ren said, again punching back. "I don't deny that competition is good. But CCTV does not have monopolistic presence in China. In fact, the state has more restrictions on CCTV than on local stations. Certain things are allowed elsewhere but not on CCTV." Here Ren turns to CCTV's sliding market share as proof of CCTV's nonmonopolistic status. "CCTV only occupies 38 percent of the Chinese TV market, which means two-thirds of the population watches other programs." Ren's remarks point to the fierce competition within the Chinese media market, where CCTV's ratings have been eroded by formative domestic challengers such as Hunan TV and Phoenix TV.

Getting back to the issue of how to help CCTV improve its quality, I brought up the disenchantment and complaints I had heard from CCTV employees. Chen Xiaoqing, one of CCTV's heavyweight documentary producers, had related to me his sense of alienation, and Xia Jun had lamented that the room for flexing one's critical and professional muscle is so limited at CCTV that many people's talents were wasted. Ren replied, "Again, CCTV has yet to learn to cultivate and nurture its talents. Obsolete training methods, departmental infighting, and recruitment not tied to market principles have hampered our ability to achieve optimum potential. The gap remains huge between us and the world-class media firms in terms of organizational structure, professional quality of our employees, management skill, and a healthy corporate culture. But the problem does not inherently belong to state-run enterprises."

The point Ren drove home is that a state-run network *can* be made into a world-class firm: "As we talked about earlier regarding capitalism versus socialism, the system itself is not necessarily the root cause. Other more mundane factors do have an impact on a firm's performance." To make his point, Ren mentioned that there are many state-run enterprises in China that are highly efficient and profitable. "For instance, China National Offshore Oil Corporation, a state-run company, is doing very well as a result of quality management and a healthy corporate culture. China National Petrol Corporation, another state-run enterprise, is not doing so well. The problem is not with ownership but with management, and perhaps the ability of a given CEO. I am not defending state-run enterprise, as I am all for further economic reform. The point is that we must examine the overall operation of a particular organization, including talent recruitment, market research, and the quality performance of individual employees." I finally realized that his concerns and outlook were more about economics than politics, which made sense. In case I had forgotten, I was reminded that Ren works for CCTV-2, the Finance and Economics Channel. And I had the distinct impression that Ren, unlike some of the other CCTV producers and managers I'd interviewed, would have fit right in, in front of the camera, as much as he did behind it.

Before we parted ways, Ren made a point to remind me: "Everything is in flux in China today, and the term 'developing country' captures well the vibrant change occurring in China and elsewhere. At the same time, the 'developed' nations have stopped moving and stand on the sideline, passing out judgment." He went on to say that the rule of law has progressed steadily in China over the past decade and that their program *Economy and Law* is all about solving disputes via proper legal channels, not top-down coercion. "So this is progress. China has changed, and we need to acknowledge that. The U.S. does not have the patent on democracy. Other cultures also can have their homegrown governance based on democratic ideas."

Though Ren downplayed the benefits of references and making connections, it is hard not to compare the developmental path of China and its Western counterparts, as *Power* does bring up various dynasties in China while covering milestone developments elsewhere. The comparative framework has been in place in many other CCTV documentaries of a similar nature, including *River Elegy*, to which *Power* is frequently compared. What does the trajectory of CCTV from *River* to *Power* tell us about the network and China? Indeed, whatever happened to the man who helmed the controversial *River* two decades ago? What has he done since *River* was banned during the aftermath of the 1989 student movement? To better understand CCTV's transformation, I tracked down Xia Jun, the veteran CCTV producer who directed *River*.

6

XIA JUN AND CHEN XIAOQING:
DOCUMENTARIANS AND CRITICS ALIKE

In 1988, a six-part documentary series, *River Elegy* (also translated as *The River Dies Young*), aired on CCTV, delivered a poignant and pointed message about how agricultural-based and inward-looking China came to be defeated by maritime and ocean-based civilizations. *River* denounced traditional Chinese civilization and claimed that the revival of China could be achieved only through modernization and Westernization. In the documentary, China's Yellow River was seen as a symbol for a country that was once at the forefront of civilization but had dried up in modern times as a result of isolation and conservatism. The Yellow River's age-old silt and sediment are equated with the dead weight of Confucian traditions and the consequent Chinese cultural stagnation. For China to succeed, the documentary elaborates, it had to replace its regressive civilization with a more open and adventurous ocean culture like that found in the West. The film laments the ban on maritime activities during the Ming dynasty, which prolonged China's land-based civilization and led to its decline. The documentary captured the imagination of TV viewers, sparking debate about China's future and past. Deemed as having fanned the democracy fever among young people and therefore fomenting the 1989 student movement, the documentary echoed the reform agenda of the then premier, Zhao Ziyang, who was promptly ousted as the party voted to use force to evacuate Tiananmen Square.

With the return of hard-line conservatives to power, the director Xia Jun was forced into an involuntary career hiatus. But after more than half a decade wandering China's nether regions, he was eventually rehabilitated and returned to CCTV under the stewardship of Yang Weiguang in 1996 as a producer at *News Probe*, where he worked for four years before moving on to take over Beijing TV's entertainment channel.

Now integrated back into the Chinese media world, Xia is fully aware of the effect *River Elegy* had twenty years ago. "No single program today can replicate the impact *River* had."

Interested in gauging Xia's reaction, I asked him directly: "What about *The Rise of the Powerful Nations*—same impact?"

"*Power*'s influence is nowhere near that of *River*," Xia said. "Times are different now that we have multiple channels with competing programs. No single program can replicate the same exclusive success *River* had twenty years ago. Nowadays, audiences are more sophisticated culturally and are less enthusiastic politically. Most importantly, *Power* did not question and criticize China, which makes it less controversial. The program avoided talking about politics and focused on economic issues such as free trade and markets. It does not provide a complete picture. The logic of the West explored in the program is not complete without discussion of its democratic system. It's wrongheaded."

Xia's sharp tone perhaps suggests a tinge of professional resentment, but his assessment of the differences between *River* and *Power*, differences not just of content but also (and more critically) of historical and social context and reception, seems fair. *Power* and *River* depict the two sides of the same coin, both printed on a core of nationalism. While *River* evoked pessimism and anxiety in its urge to revive China by doing away with Chinese tradition, *Power* exuded confidence and optimism in its embrace of others' achievements as a way to welcome a revived China. While the optimistic turn suggests the progress of CCTV and China in general, the superiority-inferiority complex that characterizes the May Fourth generation's reflection of China's past rings true in both documentaries. This curious interplay of positive and negative feeling about China's future is described by William Callahan as China's "pessoptimism."[1] Both documentaries equate wealth and power with modernization, an interpretive scheme that privileges wealth over poverty, dominator over dominated, and inventor over emulator. The dynamic relations between Chinese culture and its Western counterpart are pared down to a comparison of their relative power, defined mostly in terms of competitiveness. A cultural utilitarianism operating in both documentaries examines the past for the purpose of serving the present, which, as Jing Wang puts it, "reduces the pluralistic manifestation of Western civilization to a monistic totality."[2]

I sat down with Xia in the conference room of his company, Chinese Culture Group, which takes up a section of the fifteenth floor of the Jinyu Plaza Office Building in Beijing's Haidian District. Xia looks a little pale, with a soft and slightly round physique, like many desk-bound affluent Chinese men I met whose daily routine involves more banqueting than exercising. I was rather curious about his experiences after the screening of *River* and throughout his "second incarnation" at CCTV and beyond.

Like many others, Xia graduated from the Beijing Broadcasting Institute, majoring in TV news. A humanities scholar in his heart, he stayed on to enter BBI's first graduate class, majoring in the history of modern Chinese literature. He joined CCTV in 1986, becoming the network's first employee with a graduate degree.

Upon arrival at CCTV, he participated in making *Great Yellow River*, a thirty-episode *National Geographic*–style documentary jointly produced by CCTV and NHK (the Japanese TV network) that celebrated the Yellow River as the origin of Chinese civilization. During the course of making the documentary, Xia was jolted by the naked poverty surrounding the crisis-ridden Yellow River. Xia grew frustrated with what he saw as the series' unmitigated celebration of the magnificence of the Yellow River as the cradle of Chinese civilization. Inspired by pioneering films such as Chen Kaige's *Yellow Earth* and cultural modernization movements, Xia gathered a group of like-minded young intellectuals from China's literary circle with the hopes of injecting serious cultural musing into CCTV programming. The result was the ground-shaking *River Elegy*, directed by Xia himself, the first widely viewed Chinese documentary with hostile attitudes toward traditional Chinese culture and the legacy of the CCP. *River Elegy* became an overnight sensation, stirring heated debate among Chinese intellectuals, the party leadership, and the overseas Chinese community. Soon after CCTV started airing the documentary series on June 11, 1988, the *People's Daily* published the film's script. Viewers and readers hand-copied and circulated the script among themselves. Seminars and symposiums were organized by various newspapers and journals and at university and high school campuses to discuss the series. *River* was credited with ushering in a new type of quality Chinese TV that integrates artistic expression with cultural and intellectual analysis and with introducing scholarly discussion about the impact of Chinese traditional culture to the public. Indeed, *River* made scholarly debates in a number of disciplines accessible to the general public.

River was a product of the uneasy mood of the late 1980s, an anxious time when political factions within the CCP contended for the direction of China's reforms. From the early to mid-1980s, the liberal-minded Hu Yaobang, then party secretary-general, advocated for open cultural and political policies, which helped to nurture a relaxed intellectual atmosphere. The years 1985–88 were a period of unprecedented intellectual and cultural diversity. Yet missteps in economic reform had brought economic instability and inflation, amplifying official corruption and nepotism. Opportunities for upward mobility were seemingly confined to a privileged minority. The Chinese public was growing increasingly restive as economic and political reforms appeared to stall, while reformers and conservatives at the top level quarreled over China's direction. There was a sense of a nation at a crossroads: one direction led to further marketization; the other suggested a return to Maoist socialism. The upheavals of the period would be repeated two decades later, in the spring of 2012, with the seismic political scandal involving Bo Xilai, which blew open a fractious Chinese leadership. The outcome of the battle remains to be seen, but it is symptomatic of the range of uncertainties China faces today—from the once-a-decade leadership transition to an economic slowdown some interpret as the result of an entrenched crony state-capitalism that has hobbled market forces and private entrepreneurship. In the 1980s, the jitters led to the student demonstration in Beijing in late 1986, which resulted in the ouster of the liberal-minded Hu and the subsequent launching of a campaign against "bourgeois liberalism" the following year. Tensions ran high in the top leadership, with the Zhao Ziyang–led reform camp continuing to argue for liberalizing reforms. In the midst of this economic debate, censorship of public expression remained relaxed, which allowed *River* to capture the crisis on Chinese television.

The ensuing debates on the documentary attracted attention from the pro-reform party leader Hu Qili, then a member of the Standing Committee of the Politburo and the Central Secretariat. Warned that the series might stir up student unrest, Hu asked MRFT to reevaluate it. Meanwhile, Zhao Ziyang and a few other Politburo members privately screened the documentary. While Zhao endorsed the series, a few members of the Politburo took offense at the documentary's harsh criticism of Chinese traditions and what they saw as an attack on orthodox party ideologies. Meanwhile audience enthusiasm for *River* was high and CCTV was under pressure to rebroadcast the series. Wary of the tension among the top party leaders, the MRFT ordered CCTV to revise the series before rebroadcast. The revision removed politically sensitive content and toned down the harsh repudiation of traditional Chinese culture. Gone were the sympathetic attitudes toward the 1986 student demonstrations and the call for the party to establish a regular dialogue with the public to address concerns about corruption, inflation, and government mismanagement. The sanitized *River* was aired in August 1988, triggering even more criticism from party hard-liners. At the Third Plenum of the Thirteenth Central Committee, Wang Zhen, the then vice president, accused *River* of being "counterrevolutionary," decrying its "ocean civilization" as promoting "bandit civilization and bandit logic." Zhao Ziyang and his liberal allies argued that artwork should be immune from political accusations. Zhao later issued two principles for dealing with the *River* controversy: the party should allow public debates without taking an official stand on the documentary, and any party leaders' personal opinions should not be taken as the viewpoint of the party as a whole.

Zhao's protection did not last long. The *River* fever came to an abrupt halt as the 1989 student uprising implicated the reform-minded Zhao Ziyang, dragging down the entire reform camp. *River* was accused of instigating the student movement, and an intense media campaign was launched to discredit the series. CCTV broadcast a self-criticism meeting on the evening news, denouncing *River* as bourgeois propaganda.

With the documentary repudiated, its creators, many of them having openly endorsed the democratic movement, were purged, detained, or forced into exile. Xia was promptly stripped of major responsibilities at CCTV. Instead of leaving China like many of his collaborators, he underwent a self-imposed exile, spending the next five years roaming around China's poverty-ridden rural areas.

An Independent Producer

Xia returned to CCTV in 1995, answering Yang Weiguang's call to help initiate the fledgling *News Probe*. "Many things had changed during my five years in exile. I returned to a different CCTV, now housing celebrated shows such as *Oriental Horizon* and *Focus*. Reform and opening up had brought changes to CCTV. And I was a changed person as well. When I made *River* at twenty-six, I knew little about the real world. I did not have a real in-depth understanding of the many issues facing China. My years wandering around China's countryside transformed me. I experienced the real China and realized that there was a gap between my abstract notion of Chinese tradition and how the tradition is lived through real Chinese people." He would work at CCTV for four years before leaving for Beijing TV.

Reflecting upon his unexpected early fame and career at CCTV, Xia said simply, "It is fate." He went on to elaborate: "I had my five minutes of fame because I was at the right place at the right time. The moment passed, and that's that. It was during the optimum period when the society was allowed to open up, and media, which was influenced by the cultural fever at the time, was receptive to this type of programming. The freedom was there for the program to appear on Chinese television. It all ended after June fourth."

Xia continued, with a mild smile on his face, "Obviously I was completely marginalized at CCTV after that, but luckily my skill and expertise were valued by other organizations so I became a floating independent producer. From 1990 to 1995, I spent five years wandering around China's rural areas, exploring topics of my own choice. I made a documentary about China's peasants in 1992 and then another six-part, two-hundred-minute one called *East*, which is an anatomy of ancient civilization in Asia. The documentary was never released," Xia stated flatly.

Like the May Fourth Chinese intellectuals who relentlessly scrutinized Chinese tradition, Xia described himself as a patriot. Though accused by the official discourse at the time of being unpatriotic and culturally nihilistic, *River* actually expressed a deep and profound nationalism in its mobilization of an ethnicity-based narrative. While it argued for a wholesale overthrow of the traditional agriculture-based Chinese civilization, contradiction exists between the intellectual and emotional content of such a rejection. As Jing Wang notes, though *River's* voice-over narration ridicules the delusions of patriotic dreamers in restoring a glorious Chinese empire, the sentimental emotions captured by the music and images betray a deep-seated nostalgia for China's old glory.[3] Even though the documentary preaches most eloquently the elimination of such nostalgia, its vision for the future is embedded in the same rhetoric of imperial nationalism. Xia never successfully severed his emotional ties to China's old glory. In both *River* and *East*, the reappraisal of tradition and quest for modernity are motivated by a contradictory compulsion to recover China's old glory while also pushing for Westernization.

"China is at a very awkward stage," said Xia. "I don't think intellectuals fully comprehend the level of China's dilemma. Urbanization and industrialization have unleashed a hard-to-tame desire for a more materialistically enriched life, resulting in vast disruption to life's natural balance and equilibrium."

Xia added that unlike others inside China and in more enlightened societies, he did not think democracy was the panacea for these issues. "Granted the right to vote, the villagers would very well vote to go for immediate gain at the expense of the environment. The villagers would veto birth control in favor of multiple births that do not end until a son is born. The villagers would vote to have the right to purchase a bride sold from a poor area elsewhere. Putting my feet in the shoes of the Chinese policy makers, the choice is a hard one. Democracy is a trend and an inevitable destination, yet the choice at the moment is not so obvious."

After some pause, Xia asserted that democracy in China might actually lead to disastrous outcomes. "Democracy does not provide the immediate remedy for the issues plaguing Chinese society," Xia said. He mentioned the case of Deng Yujiao, which had caught wide public attention in 2009. Deng, a leisure center waitress, killed a government official on May 10, 2009, after he sexually assaulted her. Police had originally wanted to charge Deng with murder but backed down amid the public outrage. The court found that Deng had acted in self-defense but had used excessive force and therefore was guilty of intent to harm. But the court did not sentence her to prison, citing a psychological evaluation that found her mentally unbalanced and thus having "diminished responsibility" for the crime. By finding Deng guilty but not punishing her, the judiciary managed to satisfy both the public and the law enforcement authorities. Deng was set free after a short trial, one month after the homicide. Xia questioned whether the law was properly followed and whether the outcome of the case created a good precedent. "The handling of the case was heavily influenced by political but not legal concerns. Law caved in to public sentiment. Is this what we want in arguing for democracy?" Xia seemed to be equating democracy with simple majority rule.

It is interesting to see how Xia has moved from the position of a radical Occidentalist to someone with a self-professed understanding of the logic of China's agrarian-based civilization. It's also worth nothing that he has not harbored anger and hatred toward the Chinese party-state for being penalized but has instead come to empathize, albeit in a reined-in fashion, with the party-state for the conundrum China faces. The mixture of pessimism and optimism Xia exuded and his fatalistic tone reminded me of a passage from Mencius's writing, which had perhaps shaped the thinking of Xia's compatriots: "When Heaven is about to confer a great destiny on any man, it first disciplines his mind with suffering, and his bones and sinews with toil. It exposes him to want and subjects him to extreme poverty. It confounds his undertakings. By all these methods it stimulates his mind, hardens him, and supplies his competencies."[4] My recollection of this famous quote in association with Xia was quite ironic, for it was Mencius, the itinerant Chinese philosopher born in the Warring States Period (roughly fourth century B.C.E.), a little less than two hundred years after Confucius, who was one of the principal interpreters of Confucianism, which was a philosophy that Xia himself had sought to eradicate two decades ago. Like Confucius, he traveled around China for forty years, attempting to impart wisdom to rulers, but was time and again rebuffed. Disillusioned by his failure to effect changes, Mencius retired from public life altogether.

"Perhaps there will be nothing [waiting for me] in the end," Xia said with a tinge of sentimentality. "There might never be an opportunity for me." Xia left CCTV in 2000 to experiment with running a lifestyle channel leased from Beijing TV as a private contractor, an opportunity that gave him the freedom to run his own media entity. He emphasized that his freedom was worth the price of losing CCTV as a major platform. He reminded me that his former CCTV colleagues have little moral or professional control working for CCTV.

Is he granted more freedom or space now that he is an outsider?

"The space outside is small as well," he said. "Media is a highly controlled area across the board in China. I left CCTV to take over Beijing TV's channel 7, the Life Channel on cable, as an independent contractor. I was getting really tired of politics so wanted to do something different." Xia's backer is a private firm, an unusual practice in Chinese media at the time, so his operation attracted much scrutiny, including state investigation. He paid a price for the bold move. "My original plan was to experiment with bringing private capital into media production. We started the operation in 2000 and continue to this day. We survived, but our scale is getting smaller and smaller. The revenue for the channel was over CN¥20 million when I took over. It reached CN¥500 million in 2008. Though operating privately, it is still a channel under Beijing TV, with the same censorship process as in CCTV. Yet economically, the channel triumphed, which suggests that the potential is there for Chinese media to make profits."

I asked Xia if it did not seem a bit contradictory for someone of his nature to be involved with a commercial operation. What were his motives?

"I am an intellectual in my heart, so not a merchant in the conventional sense. Chasing profit is not my ultimate goal. My goal is to maintain spiritual independence from the state, which can be achieved only via financial independence. I am not interested in wealth accumulation. Sure I want to provide for myself and my loved ones, but nothing more, nothing less." Xia said that he is not driven by commercial logic because it might lead him astray. "The lure of wealth has plagued Chinese society, and so many good people have caved in. This is why people felt that the society has lost its soul and moral compass. That said, I am interested in expanding Chinese TV as a commercial entity."

Chen Xiaoqing

Xia mentioned that leaving CCTV brought a renewed sense of freedom. When I relayed this to Chen Xiaoqing, CCTV's director of documentary programs, there was a touch of sarcasm in his response: "I hope so, though probably not. I feel that the old Xia's spirit has actually been straitjacketed today. His trademark sharpness and precision are all gone now. He caters more than he had to before. You have to cater [to sponsors] if you want to do projects. There is no way out. The difference is that instead of serving the party-state, you're now at the mercy of money. Perhaps we all need to find places that are right for us as individuals."

Perhaps this was an overly harsh assessment of Xia's recent career move, but like Xia, Chen is not someone who minces words. Chen Xiaoqing is a man in his mid-forties, a decade younger than most other middle managers at his level. A native of Anhui, Chen majored in cinematography at the Beijing Broadcasting Institute. He took an internship at CCTV's Military Program Division before graduating in 1986. A fifteen-minute documentary he made during the internship, *Soldiers Start Their First Steps Here*, was selected for broadcast on the CCTV program *The People's Soldiers*. Upon graduation, Chen entered the graduate school at BBI, again specializing in cinematography. While he was in graduate school, BBI held a conference and was fortunate to have the legendary documentarian Joris Ivens attend as a speaker. Chen's soldier documentary was screened as a sample student work. A scene that abruptly cut off a soldier's emotional moment caught Ivens's eye. He asked Chen, why not let the camera roll until the emotional moment came to a natural end? The idea was novel to Chen, who was taught to follow a strict shooting regimen: eight seconds for a long shot, six seconds of medium shot, and three to four seconds of close-up or extreme close-up. It had not occurred to him that documentary film was about capturing life as it happened and was not bound to follow any set structure.

Chen noted that Ivens, as well as the cinema verité tradition, became a strong influence on his documentary work. Ultimately, though, he regards Chinese culture and literature as his most important influences. "Filmmaking is more about your understanding of life than any style or method." He mentioned in particular the neorealist literary movement in China in the mid- to late 1980s as his primary source of inspiration—though this itself was an incarnation of Italian and French neorealist literary movements.

In 1989, after completing his master's degree, Chen joined CCTV's *Local 30 Minutes*, a curated program that showcased local documentary productions or productions about local events. Chen did not make another documentary of his own until 1991, when he was sent to report on flood-control efforts in southern China. There he shot *The Story of a Lonely Island* on location. The film became China's official documentary entry at that year's Cannes TV

Festival. Encouraged by the success, Chen started to toy with the idea of making an independent documentary about migrant workers from his hometown who worked as nannies in big cities. Anhui is known for its many girls and young women who leave home to eke out a living tending others' households. The idea of making a documentary about the Anhui nannies came to Chen when he was still at BBI. He frequently ran into these migrant workers during his long-distance commute between Anhui and Beijing. He found their habit of imitating well-to-do Beijingers fascinating and thought that their transformation reflected something about China's own changes in recent decades.

With support from Anhui TV, Chen made the film in 1993. *A Faraway Home in Beijing* became an instant classic, bringing both fame and financial backing for Chen's work. His next project, *The Dragon's Back*, about rural school dropouts, came out in 1995 to more critical acclaim. Chen suffered bouts of depression while he was making *Dragon*. He was clinically depressed for a year and half, losing his sense of purpose and questioning why he would want to continue working for CCTV. He seems to have come out the other side of depression with a firm grasp of the limitations and imperfections of contemporary Chinese media, and the implications of those conditions for his own life as a media professional. Resigned but not jaundiced, he is among the most thoughtful and clear-eyed people I talked to.

Though Chen hinted in our early correspondence that he'd rather not discuss his depression, by the time our appointment arrived, I could hardly fail to address the issue, since it had already become apparent from background research and in previous interviews that CCTV is full of serious-minded creators who regularly experience bouts of self-doubt, philosophical ambivalence, and in some cases, like Chen's and Cui Yongyuan's, clinical depression. Certain common themes, about ideals distorted or altogether thwarted by commercial and political pressure, were also emerging. I broached the subject with Chen with an open-ended question: "Are you happy where you are?"

"Doesn't matter. Work is work." He shrugged. "I'm the employee, so my loyalty lies with my employer." With a palpable disenchantment in his tone, he continued, "Prior to 1999, I thought I was part of the collective ownership of the network and worked hard to make the network better."

In 1999, Zhao Huayong took over as CCTV president, replacing Yang Weiguang. Yang had valued creative talent, Chen explained, so under his leadership, management put itself at the service of production talents. Yang's successor, Zhao, imposed a more formal operating style and put bureaucrats on a higher rung in the CCTV hierarchy. "The emphasis is now on management, not service." Chen felt slighted, and the sense of ownership gradually slipped away.

Chen reminisced that in the Yang era, someone like him could randomly walk into Yang's office to discuss a project. "Once President Zhao took the office, the first thing he did was to establish a system whereby proposals had to go through a regular command chain." The creative fire that he had felt under Yang was by now thoroughly doused. "I only have fifteen years left before retiring," he said.

Zhao's management style is one thing, but CCTV's accelerated commercialization troubled Chen even more. "National TV should represent the nation, not the moneyed interests. Now it all depends on who can sell more products and cater to more viewers. You're rewarded based on the amount you sell and bring."

Are there many others who share these feelings about the state of Chinese television?

"Certainly," Chen said. "Mine are hardly radical. Many have written articles and spoken to journalists about this. I don't usually do that."

When asked about whether he was optimistic about the future of CCTV under the then newly arrived president, Jiao Li, Chen was neutral.

"I don't know what will transpire after this new round of reform," he said. "It's an unknown territory." I joked that a new broom sweeps clean. "I don't know," Chen said again. "This is politics, which I do not need to know."

Perhaps the new president would protect quality programs from the ratings war.

"It all depends on whose criteria we are talking about, quality-wise," Chen said. "Quality according to the state machine, the general public, or the social ideals of intellectual circles?" he asked. "They are not equivalent."

He added that the program's midnight time slot, which on the surface seemed like a curse, was actually his good fortune, insulating the often niche programming from having to cater to more populist interests. Chen acknowledged, "Documentary programs are an endangered species," but because CCTV seeks to maintain a diverse mix of programming, they'll always find a place on the network. He wryly noted, "A better time slot would mean that I'd have to compromise by following the rules of the game. Then I'd violate my own principles."

Chen was right that the "lousy" time slot turned out to be a blessing. TV stations looking for content had driven a renaissance of documentary making in China in the early 1990s. Yet most of the documentaries failed to recoup their costs, let alone make a profit. Many TV stations suspended their documentary programming soon after trying it out. Regarding documentaries during the late 1990s, Chen had told a reporter at *China Daily*, "The development of Chinese documentaries was in decline. Many established directors did not have the opportunities to shoot documentaries for several years." With such turmoil, Chen was lucky to still have his own documentary slot.

When I asked Chen whom he hoped to reach with his programs, he responded, "Maybe people with a sense of social responsibility. Not necessarily intellectuals, as they would consider our program too shallow. And it's not that I am not able to make programs that appeal to wider audiences. I am pretty sure I can make more popular programs. At any rate, I value the current opportunity for us to make quality programs that might be valuable, from a historical perspective, to policy makers and audiences. That's all I need. But if one day CCTV has to choose between being an entertainment network or a propaganda network, then I'd choose to produce entertainment programs, as I need to bring food to the table for my family."

Chen regards documentaries as a kind of gateway toward high-culture television in China, the most nimble vehicle for ideas and information that would otherwise scrape against too many political and commercial barriers to make it to the air. In every other type of programming, he complained, the road is already laid out for you, especially the news. "No need for you to look for news, because news outside the boundaries does not exist. . . . You say whatever you are told to say."

And yet Chen reiterated that his program is not his but CCTV's. "Given that CCTV still wants the program around, I do the best I can to deliver quality stories with depth and substance. Occasionally we are asked to make a copy of a particular episode of our program for high-ranking party leaders at Zhongnanhai [the government compound in Beijing—sort of equivalent to Capitol Hill in the United States]. We are pleased that what we do might have some impact at the policy level. Historical documentaries are particularly valuable. Contemporary development has its historical precedents. History is full of lessons, which is why earlier historians tried to use history as a textbook for making policy suggestions. Our program approaches history as an investigation, piecing together and laying bare facts for audiences to come to their own conclusions. We do not seek to advance our own position."

Western media scholars and critics have lately subjected documentary filmmaking to withering scrutiny of its pretensions to superior objectivity compared to narrative film and television—so much so that raising the issue of how documentaries select and present information in a deliberate, meaning-making way has become a cliché. It simply doesn't need pointing out anymore. But Chen's insistence that his documentary practice aimed to separate facts from positions seemed to warrant a reintroduction of the old debate. It turned out that I was misunderstanding him. Chen quickly acknowledged that "your view on life is behind the inclusion and sequencing of facts." What he meant by "stating the facts but not preaching" is that his program does not force its views on viewers. Skillful manipulation of images and sound to communicate ideas is the stock-in-trade of the documentarian, but "not mouthing slogans." It dawned on me that he was not saying that his documentaries don't stake out a position. He was emphasizing that it is important to use the force of reason and legitimate techniques of audiovisual narration to get one's points across to a Chinese public that has long since learned to be very resistant to the overt forms of propaganda that prevailed during the Mao era and that persist today in much CCTV programming.

Chen was erudite and deeply vested in the theory and practice of documentary filmmaking. He told me that the style of his historical documentary films was heavily influenced by the Annales School, a group of twentieth-century French historians who understood history in terms of complex social development rather than easy political frames and formulas like Marxist analysis. The Annales School also famously rejected "great man" accounts of history that focused on kings, princes, emperors, generals, and other prominent leaders, instead studying the lives and habits of ordinary people among many other factors that contribute to the historical trajectory of particular societies. In something like that spirit, Chen's program turns its lens on ordinary Chinese, consciously recognizing them as part of the living history of China in this century.

Chen told me that his creative philosophy is further influenced by New Historicism, which pays attention to the "texts" and "discourses" of a historical moment, as well as Lucien Lévy-Brühl's work on primitive mentality, which suggests that people in "modern" societies think in a different manner from their predecessors, and other weighty Western historians and thinkers. "Their work has a profound impact on my entire production team."

I then asked if the actual program is in sync with his ideas about programming and life in general. Chen answered for his generation rather than himself. "I think that our generation was brought up to love what we do and that what we do becomes part of who we are." This appeared to be partly a dig at the latest generation of post-Tiananmen, post-socialist Chinese, who are less inclined to selfless service in the collective interest of the broader society. It may also have been partly an expression of generational regret and a rationalization of personal professional resignation. Certainly, Chen was not the only person at CCTV who downplayed his own foiled ambitions.

If Chen had his regrets, however, he had also cultivated a new professional

pursuit for himself beyond the confines of his CCTV position. His early, critically acclaimed documentaries about ordinary people led CCTV to invite him
to make a series of main-melody epics about legendary party figures. He made
documentaries about Zhu De, founder of the Red Army (forerunner of the
People's Liberation Army), and Liu Shaoqi, former chairman of the People's
Republic who was deposed by Mao and branded a "capitalist roader" during
the Cultural Revolution. Chen called the four or five years he spent churning
out these propaganda pieces "torture" and the finished products absurd. Still,
his skillful execution of the assigned tasks allowed Chen to advance his career
at CCTV, and along the way he also honed his skills as a historical researcher
and archivist, becoming a certified history buff.

As he was wrapping up the Liu Shaoqi documentary, Chen was approached by a group of young historians about making a documentary about
changes in China since the early twentieth century. Endorsed by CCTV, *A
Hundred Years of China* traced the country's evolution in the twentieth century by featuring the commonly acknowledged movers and shakers of the
time span. The fifty-two-episode series began airing on New Year's Day 2000
as a program commemorating the end of the millennium. With rare archival
footage, some never seen before, the documentary reached a wide audience.

I wondered how he had managed to put together this epic, complex history with such clarity and conviction. "History is not clear-cut and is open
to interpretation and factual manipulation, if not downright fabrication;
furthermore, history is usually written by and about the winners," I said.
Clearly this line of inquiry clicked for him, and our conversation gained a
new momentum and energy. As he nodded, Chen agreed that the official an-
nals record history as rulers would like us to see it. "On the other hand," he
said, "unofficial or folk history never ceased to exist in China, which attests to
the persistence of those outside the system. The gap has been shrinking with
the advent of film and photography and especially television. Some people
have documented leaders, and some have recorded average Joes. Different approaches yield different perspectives. Many interesting things can happen at
the same time but in different places, motivating our program, which seeks to
preserve history on television."

China has a long tradition of official historical writing. From the Han period (206 B.C.E.–220 C.E.) to the early twentieth century, more than two dozen
"standard histories" (*zhengshi*) were churned out by court historians, offering
the official and authoritative view. But Chen is right that outside this tradition,
there has also been a continued and energetic interest in private historical writing, motivated not only by the desire to complement and correct the official

history, but also by an interest in making history more accessible to the general public. The tradition flourished especially from the fourteenth century, giving rise to a different historical record. During the early twentieth century, when historical study in China entered a phase of professionalization, this alternative tradition maintained its attraction among historians, journalists, and other writers. The rise of the so-called reportage literature (*baogao wenxue*) from the 1930s on is a prime example. Reportage literature blended history and journalism, fact and fiction. The narratives are embellished with imagined dialogues among the protagonists and descriptions of their inner emotions, but the story line remains truthful to the unfolding of the real events portrayed.

Just as Chen was getting a handle on making archival documentaries at a leisurely pace, he was assigned to head up a new program on contemporary topics, to be called, simply, *Documentary*, in November 2001. The program aired at 1:20 A.M. daily on CCTV-1 and at 2 P.M. weekdays on CCTV-10. Chen served as senior editor and executive director, and initially he started out by making quality anthropological-style documentaries. A year into the project, as audience response failed to match the effort and budget devoted to the documentaries, Chen opted for a less elaborate product, shortening production time and trimming the budget. Previously, on average, it had taken six months to make one documentary. The long production cycle not only cost too much but also made it impossible for Chen to maintain a steady supply of finished documentaries for his program. He shortened the production cycle to fifteen days. He was coming to terms with the commercial imperatives at CCTV.

In the midst of dealing with the financial reality of maintaining the nascent program, in summer 2002 Chen was appointed general director of an ambitious project that would remake more than thirty documentaries originally produced in the 1980s and 1990s, many of which took the form of prescripted or illustrated lectures. Dubbed "special-topics films," the documentaries covered a range of subjects.

Already worn out from just keeping his regular documentary program *Documentary* going, Chen was not particularly excited about the new assignment. Regardless, he began carefully selecting thirty-five documentaries that he considered to be the cream of the era, all award-winning pieces. He contacted the directors of the works, promising them carte blanche on the reshoots.

Though Chen had to work with a tight budget of CN¥20,000 for every thirty minutes of film, all the directors responded with enthusiasm. The directors, most of whom were by then established producers at local TV stations, were excited by the prospect of revisiting the people whose stories they had recorded years before. Reshooting took a year to complete. The finished films captured changes over the past decade or so. Chen called the series the Weight of Time.

"Among all genres of arts and culture, the documentary is particularly adept at recording the reality and changes of human society. All the changes are caused by time. The phrase 'the weight of time' is perfect to describe our works," Chen said. The thirty-five documentaries were aired in May 2003. Other directors called to ask if they could join the project. So Chen commissioned more. The resulting documentaries eventually became the foundation for Chen's regular thirty-minute documentary slot, by then renamed from *Documentary* to *Witness*.

The name change reflected a shift in program emphasis from contemporary to historical subjects, and the revamped program reinvigorated Chen. Before the switch, the pressure of managing a program constantly under threat from low ratings had taken a toll on Chen's health. The struggle to adapt to a commercial practice against his creative instincts was no small feat. The focus on fleeting contemporary topics also did not sit well with his growing passion for historical subjects, and in 2003 he fell back into depression. CCTV took notice, agreeing to the changes and allowing him to spotlight historical subjects, a fair reward for Chen's accommodations in shortening and cheapening the production cycle.

Following the tradition of reportage literature, *Witness* sought to move beyond presenting an "official" view of history. "In the past, emperors could burn books and massacre dissenting scholars. Such is very difficult to accomplish nowadays," Chen said. "There will always be alternative voices that manage to be heard. We have grassroots audiovisual footage that provides alternative perspectives on the Cultural Revolution, for instance. What we are made aware of is often the end result of history, but my program reveals the process. Some commonly perceived sacred elements and moments can look absurd and ridiculous when cast in a new light, and things that were often considered trivial and laughable begin to gain new meaning and significance. We can tease out new elements that are touching. Actually, this is what *Witness* has been doing, reconstructing history within politically safe boundaries."

As his program strove to maintain a certain format in its style and approach, a formula inevitably set in, which played down directors' individual creative contributions. Chen was unapologetic about this, arguing that a consistent product is critical to retaining audiences. "Individuality is now the domain of the DV [digital video] generation. It represents a nonmainstream approach, unsuitable for national TV," Chen said.

Aside from managing *Witness*, Chen was now also in charge of several large-scale productions, including China's first commercial nature documentary series, *Forest China*, which hit China's TV screens in December 2007 to mixed reviews. A stunning production that brings China's natural habitat to the audience, the eleven-episode series took four years to finish. "The entire show was scripted, as we had developed a complete script and the production basically followed the script," Chen told me. The crew was sent to remote locales, exploring China's mountains, forests, and deserts. Before shooting began in 2004, the documentary directors were given a week of training by Michel Stedman and Peter Hyton, two veterans from the world's leading producer of factual television, Natural History New Zealand Ltd. They learned how to make their documentaries tell a story, emphasizing the idea of a narrative arc. On the advice of an animal expert, for instance, one episode in *Forest* tells the story of golden monkeys as they choose a new king.

Although the team was short on funding, having received only CN¥10 million from the State Forestry Administration and the Ministry of Finance, far short of what was ordinarily needed for an eleven-part series, Chen and his team pulled together. Chen was happy with the final product under the circumstances. "I would do it again if called upon to do another film on nature," Chen said. "Our choices and devotions have a lot to do with how we were brought up, in that we do not usually seek out things to do but wait for our turn. We give it a hundred percent when called upon."

Is Chen still interested in making his own documentaries? He told me that running *Witness* is a full-time job, leaving little time and energy for anything else, though he does perform several engagements on the side for extra money. Regarding his salary, Chen told me he made "CN¥10,000 a month, among the best paid at CCTV. I reached the top of my profession at thirty-five, so there is nothing more to look forward to." He gets additional income by giving talks at the rate of CN¥5,000 per lecture and writing food columns at CN¥1 per character, which amounts to another CN¥5,000 per month. "Being a food critic, I get to eat for free too," he gloated. So his total amounts to CN¥20,000 a month.

Shared Criticisms

Though Chen may not think much of Xia's current career moves and Xia might have issues with Chen's jaded pragmatism, the two are much more alike than they might imagine. As documentarians, they both shared an unsparing eye for observing flaws and a willingness to openly speak their minds—even if it is to criticize their colleagues.

Xia talks about his five years producing *News Probe* as "the program's most visible and bold period." He proudly said, "I was also at the forefront of making several major programs, including the one that commemorated the twenty-year anniversary of the reform and open-door policy, for which I was an executive director."

With the memory of my interview with *News Probe*'s current producer, Zhang Jie, fresh in my mind, I could not help asking Xia his take on Zhang's rationalization of the weakening impact of the program as the natural trans-formation of the function of *News Probe* from watchdog to enlightenment. Xia dismissed the enlightenment rationale, labeling it a lame excuse for not doing stories with a sharp edge and intellectual fire. "What is enlightenment? What does enlightenment mean to China? Are you going back to an old era that called for enlightenment via science and democracy? Or are you trying to teach the public about law and governance?" Xia considered the courage to confront China's reality the key to the program's success during his era. He mentioned an episode of *News Probe* he did in 1998 that had the nerve to declare that a Central Committee for Discipline Inspection under the CCP would not be able to perform the function of monitoring the party-state. The program called for an independent anticorruption agency. "*News Probe* has retreated from doing such daring programs. Audiences are abandoning the program because it no longer has the audacity to do hard, edgy stories. It is not sincere and has no noble pursuit. Enlightenment is a pretentious slogan, a clumsy attempt in covering up its own inadequacy while insulting people's intelligence. The depth and breadth of information people are able to obtain elsewhere, including from the Internet, are far more attractive."

Xia said that the intensity and sharpness of *News Probe* was greater ten years ago. "The power of expression, the sense of responsibility, and the enthusiasm have all diminished. I feel a profound sadness that we're going backward. A decade's struggle has brought us back to where we started fifteen years ago. Yang Weiguang created the splendid period of the 1990s. CCTV managed to return to a pre-Yang era. Isn't this a tragedy? The current CCTV is not capable of producing a real in-depth newsmagazine type of program—it doesn't matter what function it strives to serve. The overall quality of CCTV is not up to par. That is the key obstacle."

Xia noted that there are other problems plaguing Chinese television as well: "For one thing, most of the TV practitioners started out as technicians or as small-time reporters who learned the craft by practicing it without proper training and advanced schooling. Also, the TV industry has few highly quali-fied commentators or experts or intellectuals who can provide insights on contemporary issues. In China, TV practitioners are people who happen to work in the TV industry, where qualifications and knowledge are far from sophisticated or comprehensive."

Xia's observation about the lack of qualified commentators and experts is especially relevant today. As the routine of wholly scripted programs made way for more live broadcasting, anchors and producers tried to minimize the uncertainty any way they could. Spontaneous commentary during live broadcasts was new in Chinese television. News anchors tried to cope by deferring to the commentator to a greater degree than their Western counterparts and by adopting a less confrontational style. Producers reduced the uncertainty and the lack of official instruction partly by prescreening potential commentators. Experts known to be "dissenters" were avoided, as were scholars and others who only mimicked government lines. The best guest commentators would provide original insights without inviting official inquiries. Asked if she would be held responsible for the political blunders of guest commentators, *Focus* reporter Li Xiaoping said, no, but she had learned to be cautious in selecting guests nevertheless. Such a system required anchors and producers to have nimble judgment.

Li also noted that a certain amount of self-censorship is inevitable. Another measure to reduce uncertainty is to discuss the channel's editorial policy with the guest prior to a live event, in effect, coaching them—making remarks that "go off the track" less likely. Li recalled one expert interviewed during the Iraq War coverage saying that he understood not to address the "legitimacy" issue of the war.

As Limin Liang discusses in an article on the political dimensions of the Iraq War, reporters and commentators largely deferred to the government's line, but there were some opinions on the "periphery." On the military dimensions of the war, both U.S. and Iraqi media voices were featured.[5] Chinese analysts made their own interpretations of foreign media sources, not always representing them accurately, and often disagreeing among themselves. Jiang Heping, then the head of CCTV-International, referred to the channel's strategy as "detached and neutral" and said that he "wouldn't want to set a fire that would get CCTV-International into trouble."[6]

When I asked Xia about the increased reliance on expert commentators on CCTV, he replied, "Yes, this area is opening up. The trouble is that the experts can't always say what they want to say. The experts have become specialty decorators, serving as window dressing. No real power and influence. The bottom line is that CCTV has too many technicians but not enough thinkers, which obviously affects its program quality. CCTV in the past decade has been pretty much a bureaucracy. Everybody is a bureaucrat, functioning mainly as an administrator instead of a media professional. I left CCTV precisely because the organization has become a place for climbing up the bureaucratic ladder. This is not a professional arena but an administrative playground, which is a logical match for being a party organ. The ceiling is low at CCTV, and there is not much room for genuine discussion and reporting." He gestured with his hands. "An adult must stand no taller than a child, so the only option is to kneel down.

"And this makes it hard to find high-caliber people who are willing to come forward as commentators on CCTV because of the constraints CCTV imposes on them. They are worried about their professional reputation. It is hard for a true talent to dumb down. Mediocrity is the enemy of creativity. Whoever is in charge at CCTV should encourage innovation and creativity and carefully guide talented people through the censorship maze. Instead of stepping hard on someone who accidentally touched the ceiling at moments of excitement, might you remind him or her to be careful next time and to be creative within limits? There are certain lines that you cannot cross. For instance, you can't use scintillating language to report a mass demonstration because you might stir up more chaos and violence. Using a sensible and reasonable voice to direct public opinion fits the China situation. But there should not be a severe punishment when a commentator occasionally loses his balance. You have got to give people some freedom and leeway. This requires skill, courage, and an open mind on the part of the leadership." He told me he had no stomach for the way the system was set up as it was.

In the end, this political climate compelled him to leave CCTV. "I found the network suffocating. Given that I could not do and say what I really wanted, my talent was not fully utilized. I lost interest in doing the same programs. I left CCTV at a period of intense media attacks on the Falun Gong sect. My thinking was that, instead of attacking Falun Gong, we needed to use the opportunity to reflect and examine what has led to the rise of Falun Gong. To its followers, it was an oasis in a vast spiritual desert. Why repress it? The whole approach reminded me of the Cultural Revolution. I found the attack idiotic and could not stand it.

"It ought to be the mission and responsibility of CCTV to facilitate the process of China's contemporary transformation," Xia continued without further prompting. "To do that, you must face reality and open up to the world. You must provide a more fulfilling spiritual culture to battle what you think is a cult. You must represent the wisdom of our culture. Why prosecute Falun Gong when it is all that people have left? Falun Gong is not a religious sect to begin with. China is no doubt a difficult case, and whatever medicine you prescribe would come with side effects. But you have to gradually nurture a conducive spiritual environment." Xia said that the hard-line approach toward Falun Gong would only breed hatred. "You have to let people pursue something that they see as healthy, uplifting, creative, and forward looking. The pressure must be released and replaced with something positive. We understand that the government has a tight grip on the media because it wants social stability. But negation needs to be balanced out by encouragement of new ideas that would provide a positive spiritual guidance to people in despair."

As much as Xia is disappointed by the overall environment now within CCTV and specifically *News Probe*'s decline in watchdog journalism, Chen is just as dismissive of the *National News Bulletin*.

Chen's distaste for the program was brought up when I mentioned recently watching an interview with Yang Rui, a prominent CCTV-International anchor. Yang had just come away from hosting a live program about the recent rioting in Xinjiang, and a media scholar from the United States asked whether the program was initiated by Yang or ordered up by CCTV. "Both, as it is my responsibility to help maintain social order and harmony," Yang Rui replied impatiently. To me, the answer did not seem unexpected. Instead, it was rather predictable coming from someone who professes to be the voice of social responsibility. Chen had a different take: "Yang would have responded differently in private. But a question like this from a foreigner always gets on our nerves, so Yang was provoked." On the other hand, Chen suggested that CCTV has a credibility problem, with many Chinese skeptical about the news reported on *National News Bulletin*. "The world is complicated, so it's hard to say who and what to believe. But the presence of CCTV lets me know who not to believe." By which he meant, *not* CCTV.

"How about the BBC and PBS? Are they more believable?" I asked.

"Of course, at least on the surface. At least on the grounds that they allow for multiple perspectives and voices and they don't slap you with one definitive conclusion. Their ambiguity is in sync with the ambiguity of the society and people in general. We are different here. Here everything is thought about and plotted out beforehand. All is black-and-white."

Chen then went on to suggest that "people do not trust *News Bulletin* because the program has too often fabricated and distorted facts, so when it finally tells the truth, in the Xinjiang case, for instance, nobody believes it anymore." The crying-wolf analogy is quite bold here. "I see little gap between reality and what is reported on the BBC and PBS, but not with CCTV. CCTV does not look real."

CCTV may have gotten away with letting the emperor strut about with no clothes forever (to cite another folktale), if not for a little boy called the Internet. Xia noted the difficult position that CCTV is in, constantly forced to continue letting the emperor go out without clothes even after the populace has caught on to the fact that something is wrong. "As the Internet is making a bigger splash, CCTV is losing its dominance and authority. People can easily get news from print and the Internet. Why bother watching CCTV's nightly news? Yet the state continues to expect CCTV to guide public opinion. The Internet is the biggest challenge to the state's ability to control information," Xia said. "If one day you banned [the major Chinese website] Sina here in China, the company might move elsewhere, to Hong Kong or Singapore. It can continue its operation and the Chinese readers can continue accessing its site." Xia's prediction came true a year later—though he had the specific company wrong—when Google withdrew from China and set up its Chinese operation in exile in Hong Kong.

Indeed, the rise of the Internet has come at CCTV's expense: the sheer openness of information online (for those with the technical know-how to scale the Great Firewall) not only means fewer people bother to watch, but also means that instances when CCTV is forced to censor itself are even more apparent. With such a setup, it's no wonder that CCTV's news operations are the butt of jokes and its credibility diminished.

The Hu administration is carefully treading on dangerous territory. For more than two decades now, Deng Xiaoping's mantra of "stability above all else" has been the highest article of faith at all levels of government. Those who protest or petition to the authorities are accused of "breaching stability" and are subject to legal repercussions. At the scene of almost all conflicts, the police tend to be out in force as an instrument of the state rather than of social protection.

Xia said that this form of governance couldn't persist, as citizens now have more access to information. The total monopoly of information that was a bulwark of state power no longer holds. Furthermore, an environment where public anger and frustration have been bottled up for a long time can lead to an instant eruption of mass fury. Indeed, Weng'an, where a riot took place amid a swirl of allegations of official misconduct after a young girl died under mysterious circumstances, could be any county in China, and, according to Xia, CCTV is contributing to it by adding to the gap between perception and reality: "It's a pressure cooker. The harder you try to cover it up, the more dangerous once it blows up in your face. Without proper release, the mass discontent would inevitably lead to violent revolt."

Xia could not in good conscience continue to work for something he did not believe in. As he put it, he no longer wished to honor the authoritarian structure of a state-run network. "The space is not there for something really meaningful." He simply could not bear the stiffness of the system anymore. "This is like witnessing an incompetent person trying to accomplish a task. You very much want to give him a hand. In the end you did extend your help, but he gave you a kick in the gut. What's the point of being kicked around day in and day out? The help you extended is sincere, as you see clearly what the goal is, which is to maintain stability. You offer a better way to achieve that goal than repression and censorship."

Xia would eventually leave, having decided that CCTV's best days were in the past. Chen seemed to be nearing a similar point. Just as Xia spoke with reverence about CCTV and *News Probe*'s heyday, Chen would occasionally slip into a nostalgic mood. At one point, he recalled a time when he used to hang out with like-minded folks at CCTV, including the current deputy president, Gao Feng. "We had fun talking about programs and all that. Nobody would cater to his opinion simply because he was the most senior person in the group or ignore my ideas simply because I was the youngest. As time went by, the network changed and we spent most of the time complaining whenever we were together, which affected our mood. . . . Something must be wrong if everybody, from president to division chiefs and department directors to producers like me and ordinary technicians, all complain." He continued, "I have stopped socializing with people who work in the TV industry. With my new circle of friends, I was reluctant to reveal that I worked in the television industry, especially CCTV, for fear of being scolded and looked down upon. I would say that I'm a documentary filmmaker, which scores slightly better."

Chen lamented that the connection between people is more often than not reduced these days to one's title on a business card, which suggests a certain status. "A friend of mine said that without the title, a person would mean nothing, would be a nobody. A nobody who nobody would pay attention to. To gain respect and favor, people have resorted to name-dropping, suggesting connections with the powerful or famous. I'm in my mid-forties and would like to think that I am somebody even without my CCTV titles. Otherwise I'd feel hollow. For instance, I am currently writing a food column for four magazines, commenting on eating, something I enjoy. And this makes me fulfilled. . . . The point is that I have finally separated my job from my profession. I will have a profession that I identify with when this is all over."

7

THE CULTIVATED AND THE VULGAR: GAME SHOWS AND LECTURES

The third channel in the history of CCTV, CCTV-3 debuted on New Year's Day in 1986, initially reaching only Beijing and nearby provinces. A decade later, on January 1, 1996, CCTV-8, a Chinese opera and stage drama channel, debuted, also reaching only Beijing and nearby areas. In May 1999, CCTV-8 was designated as a TV drama channel, moving opera and folk music programs exclusively to CCTV-3. Thus, in August 1999, CCTV-3 officially became the Culture and Arts Channel. Amid the push for channel branding via specialization, the channel was renamed the Comprehensive Arts Channel on December 18, 2000, and began to beam its signal nationwide twenty-four hours a day. The Comprehensive Arts Channel broadcasts a variety of arts- and literary-related programs such as Chinese opera, singing and dancing variety shows, talk shows, and programs promoting music and literature. As a component of Chinese soft power, CCTV-3 later joined CCTV-4 (the Chinese-language International Channel) and CCTV-9 (the English-language Documentary Channel) to become the third CCTV channel to beam its programs overseas via satellite.

A mixed arts channel similar to France 4 or ARTV, the French-Canadian TV network, CCTV-3 has undergone countless programming reforms in the past decade amid ratings pressure, resulting in the cancellation or consolidation of many programs. Most shows on the channel today were introduced only recently. The channel now features a mixture of game shows, quiz shows, and other light entertainment. In China, any mention of such shows necessitates talking about Li Yong.

Li Yong, King of Entertainment

The flamboyantly unconventional Li Yong is China's leading variety show host. Li and his signature shows work at the limits of CCTV's accession to the world of "vulgar" commercial entertainment. Hugely popular, and jealous of any competition, Li aspires to be a loyal public servant, a marketable popular icon, and a rebel without a (political) cause—making him quite a good fit for the modern CCTV, a network he is proud to work for. In many ways, his attitude toward CCTV is the total opposite of Xia's and Chen's more jaded views. "I am nobody without CCTV," he told me.

The host of the game shows *Lucky 52* and *6+1*, the talent show *Dream China*, and the variety show *Yong's Happy Club*, Li is regarded as the king of pop TV. Known for his theatrical exuberance, his somewhat androgynous appearance and demeanor, and his outrageous outfits and unorthodox hairdo, Li is a cultural icon. He is so loved that a forty-nine-year-old chef from Hubei Province reportedly underwent three surgeries to look like Li Yong in the hope that he might one day perform onstage with Li. Li is widely recognized among the Chinese diaspora overseas. Televisions in Chinese grocery stores and restaurants in North America are routinely tuned in to Li's program. In fact, I became a minor celebrity at a local Chinese grocery store once my fellow shoppers realized that I had interviewed him. In 2006 Jim Yardley reported that in a study publicized by the state media, Li was called "the most valuable host in China, with a projected annual value of $50.8 million to CCTV."[1]

As we sat down for an interview on a Thursday afternoon in the summer of 2009, Li claimed that he never imagined himself becoming a television celebrity. Indeed, Li had little reason to expect stardom, given his origins. Born in May 1968 in Ürümqi, the capital of Xinjiang Province in far northwestern China, Li said that his childhood dream was to get away from his parents and family so that he could do whatever he pleased. Li's parents had moved to Xinjiang from Shandong Province, part of a migration encouraged by the party to develop China's frontier regions. Li's "going away" dream came within reach when he aced the National College Entrance Exam in 1987 and was accepted by both the Shanghai Theater Academy and the Beijing Broadcasting Institute. By then he apparently had some inkling about the career to come. His parents felt dubious about a future as a stage actor or *xizi* (opera singer), a disparaging term still associated with the underclass. So Li chose to enter the BBI, majoring in radio broadcasting. He graduated four years later, whereupon he was assigned a spot not at China Radio but at CCTV. Upon reporting to CCTV, he was sent to Tibet to help launch a co-anchored TV program on Tibetan TV. After six months at the co-anchor gig in Tibet, he was eager to return to Beijing to start a position as a news reporter and producer for CCTV-4, the Chinese-language International Channel. Soon, though, he moved over to CCTV-2, the Finance and Economics Channel, where he began hosting entertainment programs that became cash cows for the channel.

Li's spectacular run began in 1998 when he was assigned to host a game show at CCTV-2, *Lucky 52*. CCTV had bought a bingo-based game-show format in the summer of 1998 to compete with a hit game show launched by Hunan Satellite Television (HSTV) in 1997, *Citadel of Happiness*, which had inspired a wave of imitators on other provincial stations. HSTV has been a commercial juggernaut, taking advantage of its distance from Beijing to test the boundaries of what is permissible, and it often leads the way in developing the best in popular entertainment. CCTV responded with *Lucky 52*, based on the Philippines-originated *GoBingo* format but with a CCTV twist. The original show included an interactive element that allowed viewers to play (for a fee) and win money. As recounted by Li during our interview, the core attraction of *GoBingo*—winning money—did not sit well with CCTV's ideas about Chinese culture. In its Chinese variation, a host asks questions of four contestants who are randomly selected from the live audience. With a format settled upon, CCTV then set out to look for a host. The British consultant hired to help vetoed several candidates but eventually settled on Li Yong. Li's confident, relaxed style and ability to connect with audiences proved vital to the success of the show. In one incident, the shooting equipment broke down right before the taping. As the live audience grew impatient, Li was sent out to keep them entertained. His spontaneous chitchat was so captivating that the audience begged Li to continue telling jokes even when the equipment was fixed.

Li was unabashed about crediting individuality, his unique style, and personality for making his programs appealing. In both 2004 and 2005, Li led a list of China's ten most valuable TV hosts published by the World Economic Forum and the World Brand Lab. He topped the list for being "humorous and intelligent" and breaking with conventions. When I mentioned all the praise heaped on him, Li reacted modestly. "I would not have become a so-called celebrity without CCTV. I don't consider myself a celebrity. I am just a host, or a public figure. I don't feel like a famous person. I don't believe that my popularity will always be there. I know one day I'll 'fall off the stage.' Then I'll walk away myself. I won't have others push me away."

On-screen, Li is truly a larger-than-life persona. His easy smile on camera has won him millions of followers. Indeed he grinned throughout most of our conversation. He looked much shorter and skinnier in real life than he does on TV and was keenly aware of not possessing a classically muscular male physique. He was reluctant to stand up while posing for photos next to my sturdier-appearing fellow interviewer. Given his reputation for being fussy about outfits, I told him that it took me half an hour trying to figure out what to wear for the interview. I finally settled on a pair of jeans. He said, "I too am wearing jeans." But his were a lot more stylish than mine.

Confident as he appears, Li struck me as unusually thin-skinned to criticism. When I said that he seemed to be a natural-born entertainment host, he was taken aback, pointing out that he started out as a journalist and producer. Indeed reports about him often mention his initial resistance to becoming an entertainer as well as the great amount of practice and training he underwent to prepare for his role on CCTV-2.

Quick-witted but a bit too spontaneous at times, Li has been prone to on-camera gaffes. During an episode of *Lucky 52* themed to celebrate ethnic culture and diversity, for instance, Li commented during a question about Shaanxi Opera: "The old saying has it right, 'In the eight-hundred-mile Guanzhong Basin the dust flies, and 30 million lazy men sing Shaanxi Opera.'" Danwei, an English website devoted to Chinese media, reported afterward, "Viewers from Shaanxi were not amused. They filled online forums with passionate defenses of Shaanxi's climate and work ethic as well as calls for Li Yong's dismissal."[2] Li later apologized on his blog to the people of Shaanxi, though the tone was defensive, and he was still a bit defensive about the incident during our interview. One of Li's comments in an interview with Yardley speaks broadly to his foibles: "I don't distinguish the stage from life. My habits and flaws come right out on stage."[3] He also complained that he was unfairly targeted for his bloopers and that the mistakes of other hosts get less attention.

On a more serious disciplinary matter, in September 2006, Li appeared in pictures promoting Sunyard flooring products alongside eighteen gorgeous-looking models. Billboards bearing his image were posted in many cities and the pictures were also widely available on the Internet. Just a year before, SARFT had mandated that television anchors and hosts sign a self-discipline pact strictly forbidding them from taking part in commercial promotions. SARFT warned that anyone who violated the pact would be expelled from the industry, and in fact two program hosts were forced to leave CCTV for violations. In Li's case, his wife and publicist Ha Wen denied any rule violations, claiming that Li's appearance in the pictures was incidental rather than contracted. The incident prompted an investigation by CCTV's disciplinary inspection department, and the network editorial committee took Li off of the top ten host list for that year. In the end Li was too valuable to get a pink slip over the incident.

I told him how impressed some of my friends were that I was interviewing him. "You are huge in China," I said. His reply: "I merely follow Chairman Mao's teaching of 'serving the people.'" Li wasn't just being jocular: he genuinely seems to imagine himself, if not as an intellectual, then at least as a serious person and a responsible, positive influence, and he is averse to any suggestion of base motives.

Li also spoke about his "uniqueness" as a reason for his popularity. I asked him what exactly he means by his "uniqueness."

"Look at me," he said.

With a long, bony face, a wide mouth, and small eyes, Li is not classically handsome in Chinese terms, although in the right clothes he might cut a thin Marlboro-man figure in Hollywood. He may not be a Brad Pitt, but he certainly looks more camera ready than either Leno or Letterman. His long face is matched by long wavy hair, which is unorthodox at CCTV, where every other male anchor and host sports a standard formal hairdo. Essentially, he looks different and he acts different. He sometimes wades into his audience, talking to them as he walks around, tossing cue cards, feigning favoritism to female contenders, and mincing a few Latin dance steps. He continued, "The way I talk or walk is different from other people. It's uniquely mine. I don't follow rules and I am spontaneous."

Indeed, spontaneity is key. Li Yong is a highly visible personal embodiment of a classic struggle between native impulses—what feels right—and ingrained theory and thinking. In China, it is at least a three-way struggle now among the great social engineering project of the Mao era, the lesser reengineering project of the reform-era CCP, and the more spontaneous, bottom-up changes in the broader society as it adjusts to more choices, more complexity, and less certainty. It is also very significantly a struggle between generations, with the dividing point somewhere in the mid-1960s. Those born by the mid-1960s grew up mostly under the old regime, when collectivist values and purposes were dominant. However, those born later came of age after Tiananmen and have mostly known only of the "socialist market economy," with its overriding economic imperatives, its material attractions, its nationalist spirit, and its authoritarian party-state. Li Yong, born in 1968, has a foot in both eras, but if he still thinks of self-abnegating service to the collective, he thrives as an avatar of reform-era self-assertiveness. The apparent tension between an older political ideal and a newer lifestyle is reconciled in Li's public persona as a friendly, nonabrasive humorist wrapped in a colorful package.

In his autobiography, Li joked that by comparison to cool-mannered talk-show host Cui Yongyuan and icy-cold news anchor Bai Yansong, his own demeanor is like sunshine after a snowstorm. He considers his freewheeling style a breakthrough for CCTV. The national broadcaster has to maintain a certain core image, he says, but he is like the Tower of Pisa in Italy, notably slanted next to the upright structures all around him. His sweeping hairdo, frilly attire, and relaxed bearing are so unorthodox that Chinese media scholars organized a conference to consider whether Li Yong and Li Yong–style television should be encouraged or not. "It's risky to push the envelope when one's job is at stake," Li said. "A delicate dance for sure." Clearly, though, to his fans Li's easygoing flamboyance is a welcome refuge from the stiff recitation of scripted lines typical of CCTV hosts and anchors.

When asked what he was most proud of in his career, Li said, "Befriending audiences. The ability to connect with audiences is crucial in my line of work, and I stir up audiences to make the show more lively. The loud noises and atmosphere my in-studio audiences create in turn might bring in new viewers who happen to come across the show while channel surfing." He joked that if he can capture accidental viewers with loud noises for three minutes or more, they will register on the viewer meter, boosting the show's rating.

Li's popular appeal has earned him a highly prized place as one of four regular hosts for CCTV's annual Chinese New Year's Gala, a broadcast tradition since 1983. Aired on New Year's Eve, which depending on the lunar calendar usually falls in February, to Chinese audiences at home and around the world, the gala is essentially a variety show featuring China's biggest stars in live performances. No surprise, then, that it is the world's most watched program of its type, hence also an important propaganda platform. The gala regularly amplifies particular national events such as the Olympics or the Asian Games, but every gala promotes family reunion and harmony, themes appropriate to the New Year's / Spring Festival tradition of traveling home to be with family, but also resonant with the party-state's interest in fostering a comprehensive Chinese "family" unified behind its leadership. The "family" pointedly encompasses Taiwan, non-Han ethnic populations in restive regions like Tibet and Xinjiang, and overseas Chinese everywhere. Hence, supermodels and pop stars from Taiwan and ethnic performance troupes from around China are always among the invited performers, as well as the occasional Chinese pop star based overseas or even non-Chinese stars with large Chinese followings.

Everyone who watches the gala, of course, knows the propaganda subtext, and they take their medicine with a pinch or more of jaundiced bemusement, enjoying the stars, the skits, and the performances in spite of it. After nearly two decades, the gala broadcast rolls on with considerable inertia, but it is fraying at the edges. With growing competition and changing public tastes, it has been losing viewers in recent years. Li was signed up in 2002 and the show tweaked to include more pop singers in order to attract younger viewers. Li imagines himself as a kind of tailor for the show, stitching one performance to another and conveying the government's theme for the year.

Li's posting to the gala job, in spite of his unorthodox style, is a reflection of his enormous appeal and of the new reality at CCTV. Once unchallenged, the national network faces strong competition now from provincial, local, and Hong Kong–based channels, and Li Yong has become one of the network's best weapons in the ratings wars. Even so, with less oversight and more distance from the central censors, the competition frequently beats CCTV for sheer novelty, and sometimes the latest novelty becomes a major hit. In 2005 the competition hit particularly hard as CCTV failed to meet its ad revenue goals, and a new talent show from HSTV called *Super Girls* (similar to *American Idol*, but featuring only female contestants) became wildly popular. Li had his own talent show, *Dream China*, but *Super Girls*, which was much more about the competition and less about the host, left *Dream China* in the dust. Li tried to defuse any linkage with *Super Girls* during our interview. I pressed the point, telling him that I had just returned from HSTV, and asking him to comment on the fact that people frequently compare his shows with programs on HSTV. He tensed up immediately, saying, "First of all, there is no comparison between CCTV and Hunan TV, as CCTV, as the only national-level station, has its unique mandate and responsibility." He insisted that CCTV does not actively compete with local stations and that "the local stations are on the defense." When asked about the perceived threat from *Super Girls* in particular, Li simply shrugged it off, emphasizing instead that both 6+1 and *Dream China* preceded *Super Girls*.

Li is right that both his shows came before *Super Girls*, so if anything HSTV is guilty of imitating formats that Li pioneered in China, but which he in turn borrowed from the United Kingdom. In 2003 CCTV asked Li to come up with a new show for the 7:30–9 P.M. slot left vacant by another show that had been relocated to CCTV-3, the Comprehensive Arts Channel. After screening a number of British entertainment programs, Li and his team settled on the *Pop Idol* format for a show that would transform ordinary contestants into megastars. CCTV president Zhao Huayong green-lit the idea. Each week contestants rehearse for six days and perform live on Sunday evenings, lending the show its name, *6+1*. Li claims that seven is his lucky number: his college dorm room was in building seven, the end of the license number on his first car was seven, his house number has a seven in it, and he hosts a game show called *Lucky 52*.

Debuting on October 18, 2003, on CCTV-2, *6+1* was eighty minutes long, featuring three contenders whose lives would be transformed in front of millions of viewers. Similar shows featuring amateur singing stars had broken out across Chinese and Taiwanese television even earlier. CCTV was desperately trying to catch up with the trend. *6+1* was expanded to ninety minutes in April 2004, just before it ran up against the challenge from HSTV, which started to promote its *Super Girls* nationwide. Li's show is essentially a Chinese version of *American Idol* except that Li Yong hosts the show alone (no panel of judges), and the entire production relies less on the contestants and more on Li's personal style and star persona, a choice that proved fatal in the ratings war with HSTV's *Super Girls*.

Interestingly, in September 2004, during one of his visits to CCTV, Premier Wen Jiabao issued a directive to create more programs focusing on ordinary people. The foregrounding of ordinary people has been a consistent theme throughout the last decade. Serving the public indeed, Li and his producer wife debuted *Dream China*, a spin-off of *6+1*. Getting started, *Dream China* aired every day for one week straight during the October 2004 National Holiday week, promoting itself as an anniversary commemoration of *6+1*.

But by 2005, *Super Girls* was a popular phenomenon, sweeping China and crushing *Dream*. To differentiate itself from *Super Girls*, with its sixteen-and-above female contestants, and as a sign of CCTV's national reach, Li's *Dream* team solicited contenders without regard to geographical location, age, or gender. However, this approach only diluted the CCTV program's focus; trying to appeal to everyone, *Dream* failed to captivate anyone, while *Super Girls*'s targeted teen audience proved to be phenomenally active, not just voting (via text messages) for contestants, but also spontaneously organizing fan clubs and creating idols. Chinese teens, it turns out, are frequently in charge of the TV remote control at home. In addition, many *Super Girls* fans were the loyal followers of a popular HSTV serial drama, *Princess Pearl*, creating a kind of multiplier effect for the provincial broadcaster. By comparison to HSTV's integrated marketing approach, which aimed at creating an HSTV brand name for its sponsors and lucrative subsidiary markets, *Dream*'s focus on program alone was deficient and outmoded. *Dream* was also criticized for a traditional, monotonous, stale approach, evident particularly in its top-down awards ceremony, announcing the overall winner first rather than building suspense to the end. Finally, while *Super Girls* produced popular idols, *Dream* was never sure whether its focus was on creating new stars or cultivating the stardom of host Li Yong. A friend commented that "*Super Girls*'s grassroots and bottom-up approach delivered the Chinese dream to the contenders, whereas Li's approach kept the dream to himself."

Despite the support of SARFT, which clamped down on *Super Girls* and other rival programs, *Dream* was considered a failure and was folded back into *6+1* in 2007. Afterward, both Li and his wife Ha went on the defensive when asked about their take on *Super Girls*'s success at the expense of *Dream*. Li claimed that he had no interest in comparing his programs with similar programs elsewhere and that CCTV's dominance rendered such comparisons meaningless. His seeming nonchalance nonetheless betrayed his bitterness about *Super Girls*, which he wouldn't mention by name during our interview. Instead, he insisted that he had never watched "that" show. By Li's account, HSTV just doesn't rate against CCTV's vast resources, production quality, and national influence. In short, it makes no sense to compare the two, nor for CCTV to concern itself overmuch with HSTV or any other local station.

It was quite clear during our interview that Li did not wish to discuss HSTV. Any reference to the "competition" excited a defense of CCTV exceptionalism, and this was hardly an aberration. Virtually all CCTV people I interviewed officially denied any serious threat from the locals, implying or saying flat out that CCTV's unique status made it untouchable. Interestingly, people from the local stations more or less echoed this line, for their part denying any intentions to compete with CCTV. For now, it is a fiction that seems to work for everybody, though off the record many of the same people did acknowledge that the local stations are cutting into CCTV's market share.

Li continued on *6+1* after *Dream China* disappeared. Meanwhile, he started to toy with the idea of a celebrity talk/gossip show. The end result is a show that went on air in 2008, *Yong's Happy Club*. To make room for the show, Li had to nix *Lucky 52*. Li was the one who suggested canceling *52*, as the show's deliberate modesty gradually seemed more like naïveté amid rapid commercialization and audiences' shifting values. Li also seemed to have had enough of competing with *Super Girls* and the like and was looking to reinvent himself. Li himself said, "I had been hosting shows standing up for so long that I now want to host a show where I can sit down and relax." And in fact *Yong's Happy Club* does exude an ethic of easygoing enjoyment of nouveau middle-class urban existence.

In a brilliant move that sets it apart from genre-defining exemplars like *Oprah* and *Cristina*, Li and his Hong Kong and Taiwan producers decided to make China's essential pastime—eating—a central feature of *Happy Club*, with Li hosting a multicourse banquet as he chatted with guests. The talk is usually about the life experiences of the celebrity guests. Running Saturdays in prime time at 7:45 P.M., the show was hailed on its official website as ushering in a new program type on Chinese TV. Li says that his new program is about more than celebrity: "The celebrities on my show are not there to discuss their success stories but their views on life. The show aims to promote a positive outlook on life, as optimism brings success." The debut episode got the show off to a strong start by landing megastar Jackie Chan as the featured guest. The key to the show's success, though, is its unusually effective leveling of celebrity and audience. The fantastically tacky set with its mixture of frilly Georgian decor, modern condo appliances, and techno bits reflects Li's own style and the faux-haute ornamentation of China's new consumer class. Li himself, meanwhile, comes off as not all that flamboyant; instead he is comfortable, fun, and affable. Having guests sit down for a meal during part of their interview, though, is the show's particular genius, having the effect of putting aside celebrity to engage in the most Chinese of all pastimes.

Asked about American anchorpersons or hosts that he admires, Li mentioned Walter Cronkite, Tom Brokaw, and David Letterman. "But I can only admire them from afar instead of emulating them, due to the differences in cultural background and the contemporary environment." Here again, he seemed to want to associate himself with serious-minded work, and not with "trashy" entertainment. Taking the closest match from his list, I asked him about Letterman. Li acknowledged that he is no Letterman and that the best he can do is make fun of himself rather than politicians and celebrities. "Chinese are traditionally apprehensive of poking fun at the expense of others. Obviously political satire is out of the question, though my programs are not meant for political satire."

Indeed *Yong's Happy Club* is not much like *Late Show with David Letterman*. But while it might be true, as Li suggests, that Chinese are traditionally reluctant to publicly satirize their leaders, it is much more the immediate practical politics of his position at CCTV that keeps him from doing anything like a Letterman show. The nightly political satire would be career suicide for Li, given that the Chinese media are strictly forbidden to criticize top leaders. Still, within the confines of what is permissible on the entertainment side of state television, Li continues to think himself a bit of a rebel. Unable to say anything politically untoward, Li expresses his unconventionality through his appearance, mannerisms, and speech. In addition to his flowing hair and flashy attire, he uses a trademark punching gesture on one show while on another he has taken to flicking away question cards in Lettermanesque fashion. He also injects bits of slang into his speech even though censors forbid hosts from using the Hong Kong and Taiwanese phrases and accents that are popular with Chinese youth. In a 2006 interview in the *New York Times*, Li discussed the limits that he works within. He said that he had tried out a new gesture—blowing kisses—to add to his trademark punch. So far, though, it had always ended up on the editing-room floor.[4]

Finally, he was open, but positively crotchety, about the Internet—uncomfortable with the demands of adapting to a new technology and disdainful of the online public. Does he try to utilize the Internet to further connect with the audiences? No, he said, "I strongly dislike the Internet. I do what I do and don't give a damn about what other people think. The Internet is a digital hell now that I am forced by my employer to utilize it and to construct my own blog." So to the extent that Li thinks of himself as "serving the people," he seems to have an image of the traditional Chinese intellectual in mind, conceiving of a public in need of "guidance" from above.

The Lecture Room

This notion of guidance similarly drives Wan Wei and his cultural powerhouse of a show, *The Lecture Room*, which features, not surprisingly, lectures by Chinese scholars. It is the flagship program of CCTV-10, which was founded on June 9, 2001, and specializes in science and technology programs as well as educational, cultural, and social programs.

CCTV-10 began in 2006 to promote the slogan "two services and one effect" to emphasize the channel's duty of effectively serving society and the public. The "society" here meant the party-state, while the "public" meant ordinary viewers. "Effect" refers to whether the program appeals to the viewer and is therefore measured by ratings. Topics of current events were said to be more effective in attracting audiences. Traditionally, the channel had collaborated heavily with academic institutions to produce pedagogical programs, some of which were literally taped programs with professors or scholars delivering lectures. In 2007, as the central government started a new campaign for media professionals to produce content that would be closer to the realities of people's daily lives, the channel pushed forward a format reform that took into consideration TV as an audiovisual medium. Serialized storytelling with thematic consistency was identified as a good way to retain audiences. The push ultimately transformed many lofty yet dull educational programs into popular ones.

The Lecture Room had begun its life as an unpopular show broadcasting the latest scientific and research findings. It wasn't until it settled on a formula featuring literary scholars and historians who interpreted Chinese classical texts to an in-studio audience that it found success. Gone were the hard-to-popularize science topics and less dynamic scientists. The remaining literary scholars were instructed to talk about history in an accessible yet engaging manner, suitable for both refined and popular tastes. Scholars such as Yi Zhongtian, Liu Xinwu, Yan Chongnian, and Yu Dan appear regularly on the program and are now household names in China.

The program now ranks second among all CCTV-10 programs and has received wide recognition among netizens. Several scholars turned lecturers on the show have become celebrities with lucrative book contracts that brought them millions of Chinese yuan in profit. The books themselves frequently become bestsellers, and their releases have become public events, frequently drawing huge crowds. The show's most formidable producer, Wan Wei, was unabashed about the commercial success of *Lecture* in terms of both ratings and print. "We made three million in three years!" he exclaimed during our interview. Wan was the producer who resuscitated the program after its initial suspension and oversaw the revamping. According to Wan, the financial success of the show in its current format is a significant sign that there is room in Chinese television for quality programs that teach people about Chinese classics and traditional thought. "Audiences are capable of recognizing lively programs of cultural value," Wan emphasized. He, of course, was the one who transformed the stiff *Lecture* of its early days to the lively program of its current format. How did he manage to do that?

A cautious man with a slight build and an undistinguished look, Wan took over *Lecture* as the show's third producer in September 2004. The first thing he did was to identify the show's target audience as middlebrow with diverse interests. He then modified the program format to make it livelier by training its guest lecturers to shake off their rigid academic style and cultivate a relaxed approach. "Colloquial language became the key in retaining audiences," Wan said. Lecturers were asked to make history simple and personable, focusing on events with appealing anecdotes while avoiding overloading viewers with historical facts. Personalizing history and telling it as if history were a narrative story were considered keys to a successful lecture. The hosts essentially functioned as narrators of stories grounded in history and literature. "Three time-tested cards at the producer's disposal are suspense in terms of narrative strategy, name recognition in terms of star hosts, and the mainstream nature of the program. Mini-cliffhangers within each lecture and a big cliffhanger at the end of each lecture are routinely utilized to emulate the technique of dramatic programs, with ups and downs and occasional pauses for detailed description," Wan elaborated to me.

Criticism of kowtowing to the lowbrow at the expense of historical accuracy and academic rigidity, while difficult for the scholar-hosts to swallow, did not bother Wan a bit. As he put it, "Channel 10 is supposed to impart knowledge to the public in a popular format. Narrating history or interpreting classic texts in a dramatic way does not mean that we trivialize history or the Chinese classics."

Wan personally holds the conviction that history is open for interpretation. His belief may not be rooted in prevailing revisionist historiography, but the populist side of him believes that history is colorful and multifaceted and that different narrators bring to history different personalities and voices, which makes each of their interpretations unique, novel, and unconventional.

Wan was a computer teacher at a middle school upon graduating from the Beijing Normal University in the mid-1980s, a forward-looking and exotic position at the time since computers were still relatively new in China. A friend who was then the director of CCTV's Science and Technology Division encouraged him to come and work for him. Given the rigid employment policy at CCTV, it took Wan ten years to make his way into the network. Wan finally landed a spot at CCTV on August 1, 1994, with the help of an old drama-troupe buddy from Beijing Normal University who was then working for CCTV's program for senior citizens *Dusk Is Red*. Wan was entrusted with making documentary shorts that featured inspiring senior citizens. "I was finally able to align my profession with my passion," Wan said. His life up to that point had been buying time while chasing whatever fancy came along. Wan worked hard at *Dusk* and was rewarded with a promotion to be the head of the program in 2002. He was sent to *The Lecture Room* in September 2004 to help shape up the beleaguered program, which was just coming out of a period of suspension due to poor ratings.

Wan told me that the idea of producing *Lecture* was initiated by Gao Feng, the deputy president of CCTV and the head of China's Central Documentary Film Studio. Gao's intention was to provide eager learners who were otherwise shut out of the academic world with access to inspiring lectures by college professors, turning television into an educational tool. In its primitive stage, the program simply recorded and broadcast classroom lectures deemed educational and inspirational. While the newly enacted rating scale within CCTV was putting the dismally rated show on the spot, in May 2002 a colleague of Wan's from *Dusk*, Nie Chongchong, was brought in to revamp the show. Instead of randomly recording available lectures, Nie began to focus on scouting for lectures by the most renowned scholars. He also redefined *Lecture*'s audience as "middle school students," not in terms of their education level and age but in terms of their tentative knowledge of the topics explored by experts.

The turn to the popular was a decisive moment in the evolution of *Lecture*. Both the program format and content had to be adjusted to cater to middlebrow audiences. Lectures by lesser-known scholars were included, and nonspecialized topics were provided. An initial ratings breakthrough came when Yan Chongnian, the well-known historian of the Qing dynasty, gave a lecture that told the story of the great men of Qing, mixing anecdotes with historical facts. Wan and other colleagues suggested that Nie record more talks by Yan, thus introducing the idea of planning and producing talks by tested speakers and on topics *Lecture* deemed popular. Serial lectures were introduced to allow a maximum run for topics that proved popular. Serial lectures were carefully plotted out with Yan, a strategy that eventually led *Lecture*'s ratings to the top of CCTV-10.

Prior to Wan's arrival, there were no such things as preproduction and postproduction. It took Wan half a year to train his staff for production and programming standardization, during which time he scouted possible locations for a permanent studio for production and broadcasting. Wan's tale of what he had to do to professionalize his staff confirmed the frequent complaints I heard about the lack of professional training of many CCTV production staff members, a testament to the imperative of reform on hiring practices. As Wan waited for his staff to turn pro, he took the time to sift through one hundred or so taped lectures already on the shelf, plotting a viable content niche. He eventually decided that traditional Chinese culture would be *Lecture*'s emphasis.

Wan spoke about his own transformation from feeling aversion to traditional Chinese culture to becoming an advocate of it: "I knew little about Chinese culture growing up during Mao's era, when classical Chinese thought and literature were repudiated and smeared. As a concerned patriot, I wanted to find a way to renew our nation and saw traditional Chinese culture as an obstacle to China's modernization. Many of my contemporaries had gone overseas to study Western thought and technology. Interestingly, many of those who had left for the West returned to China around 2003 and 2004, not due to lack of opportunities for material gains overseas but due to their sense of cultural alienation living in their adoptive countries. The returned 'sea turtles' assured me that Chinese culture was a worthy topic."

"Sea turtles" (*haigui*) is a label for the Chinese returnees from overseas. The Chinese word captures the idea of growing up at sea (the West) followed by a return home to the shore. While influenced by sea turtles' remigration fever, Wan grasped the essence and value of Chinese culture and history by talking to Yan Chongnian and Liu Xinwu, two speakers whose lectures struck a chord with the audiences. Meanwhile, a wave of hit drama series about the Qing dynasty had aroused popular interest in Chinese history, which made it relatively safe for *Lecture* to focus on Chinese history and culture. Wan now had guidelines for topic selection on *Lecture* firmly in place: traditional Chinese culture, speakers with strong personalities and unique insights, and opinions that, so long as they do not oppose the party-state, do not need to adhere to orthodox scholarly positions. Wan believed that *Lecture* should reconstitute the speaking privilege of Chinese intellectuals, who had traditionally enjoyed more influence over culture and politics than their European counterparts. The key was to encourage Chinese intellectuals to be better public speakers—a leap of faith considering the decades of political turmoil that had muted Chinese scholars. Wan had to carefully cultivate his lecturers' oratory skills.

Coupled with trendy topics and unorthodox perspectives, the newly effective scholar-speakers delivered lectures that courted much critical and popular attention, even controversy, making *Lecture* the "talk of the nation." Among the early popular lecture serials, Liu Xinwu's nonconformist interpretation of the Chinese classic *Dream of the Red Chamber*, in particular, caused a stir. *Dream* is one of China's four most renowned literary classics.[5] It tells the story of the wealthy yet declining Jia family in the late Qing dynasty, featuring the young protagonist Jia Baoyu, heir to the Jia family's (mis)fortune. Baoyu's complicated courtship with his cousins Lin Daiyu and Xue Baochai is the main plotline of the epic novel. After a series of family tragedies, Baoyu renounces worldly possessions and becomes a monk. The novel had been so fervently studied that "Redology" emerged as a subfield of Chinese literary criticism. But as Liu saw it, Redology was too academic and highbrow for the general public. He was determined to approach *Dream* not as an academic exercise but as a devotee of the novel who would unearth the less noticed elements of the sprawling narrative.

A renowned fiction writer, Liu is known for the satirical tone in his short stories and essays that confront social problems and highlight hypocrisy in human relationships. Liu held editorial positions at a number of prominent government-sponsored publications throughout most of the 1980s but relinquished all his state affiliations after the 1989 student movement, which he had endorsed. Liu turned to study of *Dream* in 1993 and has since published essays and research monographs on the topic. An ardent promoter of Chinese classical literature, Liu considers *Dream* an equivalent of *Les Misérables* by Victor Hugo. Given that Hugo's literary environment was more nurturing than that of Cao Xueqin, the author of *Dream*, who lived in an era of harsh literary inquisition during the Qing dynasty, Liu considered *Dream* all the more eminent, a treasure of world literature that ought to be better cherished by his fellow Chinese. As Liu put it, it's a tragedy that Chinese people know more about Shakespeare than about Cao Xueqin. So his task was to publicize the novel by discovering fresh insights about its narrative and social critique.

Liu presented his alternative take on April 2, 2005, and instantly drew people's attention. In his lecture series, Liu postulated a new theory, one that is now known as "Qinology," which focuses on a less important character in the novel, Qin Keqing, the beautiful and flirtatious wife of Baoyu's nephew who has an affair with her father-in-law and dies mysteriously before the second half of the novel.[6] When taking a nap on her bed, Baoyu has his first dream about traveling to the Land of Illusion, where he has a sexual encounter with Two-in-One, who represents Xue Baochai and Lin Daiyu, his two competing love interests. Two-in-One's name is also Keqing, making Qin Keqing a significant character in Baoyu's sexual experience. One of Liu's theories is that Qin Keqing represents Qing dynasty emperor Kangxi's deposed son, which brings up a new line of political and sexual intrigue. Liu's alternative take on *Dream* outraged the establishment Redologists, who denounced Liu's theories, insisting that "*Red Chamber* is not *The Da Vinci Code!*" Liu was further accused of inventing theories that bore no scholarly grounds.

Clearly Wan's third criterion for his program, that opinions expressed do not need to adhere to orthodox scholarly positions, did not bode well for acceptance by the scholarly establishment. *Lecture Room* was charged with misleading and misinforming the public by providing Liu with a platform on CCTV that legitimized Liu's unfounded claims. But Redologists had little support from the general public, who rallied behind Liu and *Lecture*. In a poll conducted by Sina and *Beijing Star Daily*, 76 percent of the respondents thought that Liu expanded public awareness of the classic novel; 31 percent believed Liu's theory to be innovative. In response to the question "Who has the right to dissect and analyze the *Dream*," 73 percent chose "Anyone who loves the novel"; less than 1 percent said only Redologists. Liu maintained that "Redology is like an abundant gold mine, everyone has the right to dig."[7] Liu insisted that the novel is in the public domain and is open for multiple interpretations and hoped that his lecture motivated more people to read it.

As Wan put it, the *Dream* lecture turned *Lecture* into a cultural phenomenon. Debates raged that went beyond comments on individual lectures, focusing on the role of *Lecture* in creating the Chinese classic and history fever. The scholarly community expressed concerns that what was being preached on *Lecture* might not be all that conducive to the "proper" study of Chinese classics and traditional thought. In an article published in an English-language journal out of the United Kingdom, *Social Sciences in China*, Mei Xinlin and Ge Yonghai use the term "second-hand reading of the classics" to categorize the role of *Lecture* in creating what they see as cultural deficiencies.[8] As they summarize, "First, the audience, eager to become culturally enlightened, find themselves in the passive role of mere receivers of scholars' interpretations of the classics, lacking the role of autonomous readers. Second, the media, motivated by commercial aims, opt for an inappropriate cultural strategy and over-reach their proper role. Third, scholars, taking their orientation from the powerful mass media and following the commercial logic that the audience is king, settle for a misplaced role and degenerate from being 'guides to the best in culture' into merely catering to mass taste." The critics called for a concerted effort to switch from "second-hand reading" led by the media to self-initiated "autonomous reading" to rebuild a public intellectual sphere. The establishment community is clearly not comfortable with losing control of intellectual and scholarly discourses.

The charge of commercial incentive might have some merit, as Liu's controversial lecture did wonders for both *Lecture* and the novel's renewed popularity. Between January and August 2005, more than fifty *Dream*-related books were published, making 2005 the year of Redology. Amid the intense popular interest, the Oriental Press paid a handsome fee for the copyright to Liu's lecture transcripts, which they published in August 2005, under the title *Liu Xinwu Uncovers a Dream of Red Chamber*. The book topped the charts across the country. More than two hundred thousand copies were sold in just three months. The *Red* fever further spawned the production of a serial TV drama, *Dream*. Armed with the popular endorsement, which translated into solid ratings, Wan was unfazed by the resistance from the scholarly community. As he sees it, his is a bridge for the scholars inside the ivory tower to come out and speak to the public. "This was what Gao Feng had in mind when he initiated the idea of *Lecture*. Our public is hungry for knowledge and spiritual nourishment and our program helps them better understand Chinese classics and motivates them to seek out other Chinese classics," Wan said.

With a winning formula in hand, the remaining daunting task is to find dynamic speakers with inspiring personalities to match radical topics from the literary classics. The next ideal speaker Wan had in mind was Yi Zhong-tian, a professor of history at Xiamen University whom Wan's team spotted when he appeared on a Phoenix TV show. Wan invited Yi over to give a couple of talks on the legendary figures of the Han dynasty Liu Bang and Han Xin. The talk material came from Yi's published book of the same topic. Once the talk was over, Yi left to do a show for Sichuan TV. Wan and his team followed Yi to Sichuan, attempting to talk him into doing a serial lecture on *Romance of the Three Kingdoms*. Yi did not consider himself an expert on *Kingdoms* and instead wanted to talk about *Water Margins*, a more familiar topic to him. Wan reiterated to Yi that *Lecture* was not about experts reporting scholarly findings but about making Chinese classics accessible to laymen, a significant contribution to the preservation of Chinese culture.

"Surely you're knowledgeable enough to have your own take on the novel?" Wan recalled prodding Yi in Sichuan. Still, Yi was reluctant. Wan knew that Yi was concerned about his professional reputation amid the outcry over Liu Xinwu's lectures on *Dream*. "Why worry about this now that you're in your sixties? What do you have to lose?" Wan tried to make Yi see that being on *Lecture* to reach out to the wide public was worth the possible risk to scholarly reputation.

"To convince potential speakers to get onboard *Lecture*, many times I had to sit down with them and plot out their lives for the next several years. The issue of academic reputation always comes up first. Discussions on content and program format came later," Wan said. Yi finally relented but requested that he himself alone dictate what would be covered and how. "No problem," Wan promised. Yi signed up with Wan to focus exclusively on preparing the lectures.

"It really is a full-time job preparing for an engaging lecture," Wan attested. It was relatively easy when Yi lectured on the Han dynasty, since it was based on his published book. But the preparation for lectures on *Kingdoms* took Yi half a year. The effort paid off and Yi became an instant hit when it was broadcast in 2005. The slim Yi may appear frail, but he is robust on the rostrum. His lectures are humorous and accessible, breathing life into history. "Representing people through stories, history through people, culture through history, and human nature through culture" is how Yi summarized his approach in relaying history to the public.[9] Yi's unconventional reading of some of the historical figures drew large audiences and helped to build further momentum for *Lecture*. His lectures were so popular that CCTV-10 contracted him for additional lectures about *Kingdoms* that aired on Sunday

throughout the following year. The Sunday lecture series was a special program, separate from the regular *Lecture Room*.

As Yi continued his lectures on CCTV-10, Wan started to plan on ink-
ing a book deal for Yi. Under Wan, *Lecture* signed a two-year contract with a
speaker, during which the speaker was forbidden from giving the same lecture
elsewhere. In return, *Lecture* guaranteed a book contract based on the lecture
with a royalty of at least 8 percent. The pay of CN¥1,000 per lecture that
CCTV provided to its speakers is worth hardly anything compared to the
financial gain that comes from book and audiovisual publishing. The book
contracts aim to retain the loyalty of star speakers amid fierce competition
from local stations. Wan wanted exclusive rights to his star speakers, and a
good book contract was absolutely essential, so Wan worked hard to deliver it.

Given that CCTV is not allowed to be involved in direct commercial deals,
China International Television Corporation, a marketing branch of CCTV,
was put in charge of copyright issues related to audiovisual and print publications. While CCTV retained the rights to the DVD copy of the lectures,
the book rights were granted to authors alone. Yi's TV credentials attracted
multiple publishers, several of which were also Yi's previous publishers. Yi
did not want to hurt the feelings of his friends at various publishing houses
by choosing one over the others, so Wan made an arrangement for China
International Television Corp. to auction the publishing rights, a rare practice
in publishing in China. The auction took place in May 2006, attracting thirty-
five publishers. Shanghai Literature and Arts Publishing Group gained the
right to publish Yi's book by offering him an unprecedented 14 percent royalty on total sales volume. The initial print run of the book alone surpassed
550,000 copies. Within the first week, Shanghai Literature and Arts Publishing Group received orders for 650,000 copies from various book distributors
all over the country. As the book is priced at CN¥25, Yi was estimated to have
made CN¥2.27 million within a short time span.

The program has brought both fame and wealth to its speakers. Being
a speaker on *Lecture* now carries great prestige. Lesser-known speakers can
have instant recognition or at least attention when they announce their association with the show. The reputation of *Lecture* gradually spread to the
overseas Chinese community in the United States. For instance, in April 2010,
an announcement from the China Institute in New York about a visit from a
university president in China felt the need to highlight the visitor's status as a
Lecture speaker. Fame and wealth aside, Wan emphasized the other aspect of
the show's transformative power to many of its speakers. "It provided them

an opportunity to discover life beyond the narrow confines of academia. So *Lecture* is an inspiration for the speakers themselves as well for the audiences."

Predictably, while endorsed by many for his ability to offer history in a folksy fashion, which appealed to the grass roots, Yi was harshly denounced by the academic community for not sticking to historical facts and for misleading the audience to believe that his narratives were entirely factual. By then, Yi could not have cared less about the opinions of his own scholarly and critical community. Wan, on the other hand, welcomed the controversy because it helped to keep *Lecture* in the headline, which sustained the show's momentum. This momentum would reach its climax with the debut of Wan's next speaker, professor Yu Dan from Wan's alma mater, Beijing Normal University.

Yu Dan, *Lecture Room*'s Reluctant Beauty Scholar

Yu Dan is on the faculty of the TV and Film Department of the School of Media and Arts at BNU, known for her experience as a media strategist and consultant for several major media groups such as CCTV and News Corp. (China). Wan had always been captivated by Yu's colorful language and mesmerizing personality. Yu was Wan's old pal, dating back to his *Dusk* era, when Yu was a consultant for the show. Wan recalled how people avoided talking right after her during meetings, as she was a hard speaker to follow. "Ordinary Chinese language from her mouth became something explosive," Wan told me.

Yu was invited to the strategy sessions for *Lecture* after Wan took over the show. Wan thought that Yu would be a perfect speaker for his program, but her expertise on media seemed far removed from the classical Chinese culture that Wan had in mind for his program. A random chat at a conference both attended changed Wan's thinking. Yu asked Wan how *Lecture* was doing and what was next for the program. Wan said that they would continue covering traditional Chinese culture, maybe branching out into classic texts such as the *Analects*. "Oh," Yu said, "I know *Analects* inside out." It turned out that Yu had majored in classical Chinese literature in college.

Growing up with her grandmother in a courtyard in Beijing after her parents and grandfather, victims of political turmoil in the 1960s, were exiled to rural areas thousands of miles from Beijing, Yu began learning the Confucian classics at age four. Her grandma further taught her to sing Kunqu Opera (one of the older forms of Chinese opera) and to write Chinese calligraphy with a brush. Traditional Chinese culture thus took root in her from a young age. Yu later taught classical Chinese literature at Beijing Normal University.

She also taught courses on traditional Chinese philosophy. She stood out with her ability to explain in vernacular language the *Analects of Confucius*, the primary source of China's Confucian tradition. Wan soon learned that Yu's deft incorporation of news stories, folktales, anecdotes from daily life, quotes from the *Analects of Confucius*, and her personal insights about life and society had captivated many of her students. As her reputation grew, Yu was invited to give lectures to larger audiences at BNU, often to thunderous applause. These lectures would serve as rehearsals for her successful foray into televised lecture series.

Yu's knowledge of Chinese history and classical literature and her eloquence in articulating her thoughts in a simple and accessible manner made her a perfect candidate for the show. Wan was convinced that Yu would be the perfect speaker to branch out, leading *Lecture* out of history and literature and into Chinese philosophy and traditional thought. Wan had been scouting for a candidate to talk about traditional Chinese thought but had yet to find someone who could deliver what he wanted. When Wan heard that Yu was an expert on the *Analects*, he could barely contain his excitement. "I wanted her to be my next speaker! I knew she would be huge," Wan said to me as he reminisced about his role in the making of Yu Dan into a megastar.

As Wan recounted in a colorful manner, to achieve his goal he first invited Yu to be a regular consultant for the program. She agreed and asked what she could do to help. "The first thing is to find us a viable speaker for the *Analects*," Wan said to her. Yu brainstormed with Wan about the qualifications that would be crucial for the potential speaker. Knowing far too well that it would be impossible to find such a person, Wan kept on bugging Yu, calling her every so often to ask whether she had found the ideal speaker. After months of failed searching for that ideal candidate, Wan slyly invited Yu over for another strategy meeting, taking Yu out for dinner at an exclusive restaurant. The gourmet food, the boutique wine, and the pleasant surroundings put Yu in a good mood, so she started to talk about ways of relating the *Analects* to the public, as if she were the speaker. She would elicit from the classical text philosophical ideas about human existence that would apply to people's daily living. She would be attuned to audience responses, frequently revising lectures to be in sync with the needs of the audiences.

Wan seized the opportunity to press on: "Such a waste that you're only a media scholar with authority to comment only on media issues."

"Why is that a waste?" she shot back.

"What's the use talking about media in China?" Wan replied. "Is there any use for these media theories you preach, given that media's propaganda function is paramount in China? But if you were to talk about traditional Chinese culture, you would at least help to spread Chinese culture. How many people regularly attend your lessons at your college? It would be a different story altogether if you were to give a lecture at our program. There is no comparison in terms of audience outreach and influence. And you would be addressing the value and impact of Chinese classics on contemporary society instead of media theories with little direct relevance to ordinary folks."

Yu took the bait and soon launched a cultural sensation.

Lecture recorded seven *Analects* lectures and aired them during the National Holiday break in 2006. The lectures did not create an immediate reaction, but Wan started to discuss book publishing with Yu. When China Publishing House offered to print thirty thousand copies, Wan, sure of Yu's success, countered with 1 million copies. Though initially shocked by Wan's audacity, the publisher relented after Wan threatened to walk away from the deal, compromising at six hundred thousand copies. To coincide with the book's publication in November 2006, Wan aired a rerun of Yu's lectures at the same time. In conjunction, Wan held a book-signing event at the Zhong-guan Village bookstore at Beijing Book Building as well.

"Yu did not think many people would show up, so she invited many personal friends to come and be her cheerleaders," Wan told me.

One of her guests was the renowned CCTV host Jing Yidan. The first thing Jing commented on upon arrival was that Zhongguan Village was having a huge traffic jam, which was caused by none other than the thousands of people lining up to buy the book. Wan got what he'd aimed for—the crowds lining up for Yu's book made headline news on media around the country, calling attention to Yu's lecture on his show. At the time I interviewed Wan in July 2009, Yu's book had sold more than 4 million copies.

Not surprisingly, the book, which included both the content of the TV lectures and the original text from the *Analects of Confucius*, stirred up controversy within academia over what the classics scholars saw as trivialization and simplification of a classical text. As media analyst Joel Martinsen observed, Yu's "willingness to pick and choose what she likes from the *Analects*, and in some cases to misread what the text is actually saying, has drawn criticism from orthodox interpreters."[10] Critics, some of them Yu's colleagues at BNU, complained about the sloppy scholarship in Yu's approach. Elsewhere, nine graduate students from Peking University and Tsinghua University led the charge against Yu, demanding on the Internet that the media cease their adulation of Yu Dan, *Lecture Room* cease broadcasting Yu Dan's programs, and Yu Dan apologize to the entire nation. Writing in *Southern Metropolis Daily*,

Zhao Yong charged that Yu Dan's scholarship was calculated to uphold the mainstream government line and that her thinking and her lecture style resembled that of a scholar-official from feudal society.[11] *Lecture* itself was criticized for representing only one voice, one tone, and one format. Yu countered by calling her book "a collection of my personal readings of the ancient sage's thoughts which I have accumulated over decades." Yu was quoted in *China Daily* as saying that "I am not an expert in Confucian studies, but rather a media scholar. It is only that, as a great fan of Chinese classics such as the *Book of Songs*, the *Analects of Confucius*, and Chuang Tzu, I am willing to share with people my understanding of these centuries-old pearls of wisdom."[12]

"How has *Lecture* handled such criticism?" I asked Wan. Did he anticipate such strong reactions?

"We were prepared," Wan said. "There was a scholar in Shanghai who raised many issues concerning factual errors. For these types of errors we apologized and made public corrections. When it came to scholarly positions, we insisted on protecting our speakers' rights to their opinions so long as these opinions were presented in a civil manner. We chose to ignore harsh criticisms based on one individual's scholarly position."

Wan told me that Cui Yongyuan, the renowned CCTV host who was a crusader for high-quality programming, thought that the discussion on the *Analects* was one of the most valuable discourses in recent years. "Yu's lectures are about returning to one's own cultural roots," Wan said. "Hers was not meant to be scholarship in the first place. It was about bringing the *Analects* to the public and the reality of contemporary society so as to call attention to the relevance of our own cultural tradition."

As criticism from the learned society raged on, the public endorsed Yu's interpretations and her style of delivery. Netizens gave bountiful kudos to Yu's "enlightening lectures" in their blogs and online forums. They uploaded the video clips and quotes from her lectures, praising Yu for providing a remedy for the lost souls in a rapidly changing society. A twentysomething fan I encountered in Beijing in the summer of 2008 told me that Yu's lectures helped her to look at life from a new perspective. As cited in the *China Daily* article, one netizen posted on his blog that "Yu's reinterpretation of the more than 1,500-year-old classic drags me away from online magical-realism novels during the National Day holidays. Listening to her lectures was the happiest moment of each day. During the period of time after watching the TV lectures, I suddenly found that what Confucius said are simple truths that are not at all lofty but can be applied to my daily life."[13]

In an interview with me in January 2011, which was later included in a

TV documentary, *What Does China Think*, Yu attributed the popularity of her work to the stresses of modern life in the increasingly materialistic China. "People want spiritual guidance, so they are thrilled to discover the contemporary relevance of China's ancient wisdom." Yu's photogenic on-camera presence also helped. Smartly dressed, with precisely tousled short hair, Yu appeared professional and commanding. Yet she seemed extremely sensitive about her image as a serious scholar instead of a media star. At one point during our interview, she stopped and told our cameraperson to mount the camera on a tripod. "Mobile camera is for pop stars. I am a media scholar doing a serious interview here," she explained to me. So we adjusted our shooting style.

Back in 2009, a month before I arrived in Beijing in May, an English version of the book *Confucius from the Heart* was released in England by Macmillan to mixed reviews. It nonetheless brought Yu international fame.

Given the degree of fame and wealth *Lecture* had brought to its star speakers, the program must have become rich as well.

"No connection," Wan flatly denied. "Their personal profit had nothing to do with our program, as *Lecture* was not allowed to profit from our programs. And I told my team not to leer over the newly realized riches and fame of our guest speakers, as theirs is the result of their work and we're merely here to produce our program."

"Your team must at least feel a sense of achievement."

"Yes. We're happy to have done something valuable for society," Wan declared without hesitation. "It is not at all easy for media practitioners in China to realize one's own value and aspiration. We were able to do what we wanted to do professionally and our professional aspiration turned out to benefit the society as a whole, which certainly does not come every day in China. Frequently, programs of lofty ideas brought low ratings, which risked cancellation. Programs of high ratings are often at the expense of social responsibilities. We managed to strike a balance, and this brings us a sense of achievement."

Wan told me that the attention showered on *Lecture* in recent years brought it tighter scrutiny within CCTV, so efforts were made to tone down the programs' media exposure. The now relatively low-key approach was matched by the program's continued focus on spotlighting Chinese classics. Yu soldiered on to lecture on Zhuangzi, the ancient Chinese philosopher whose thinking had a profound impact on me and many of my peers during my younger years. Yi Zhongtian was called back to tell stories of major Chinese philosophers. New speakers were added to cover other historical figures, thinkers, and classical novels. Meanwhile, Wan was leaving the show. "My work is done," Wan said. "I left the program on May 8 of 2009. I was promoted to take the position of deputy director of the Education Division within CCTV. I will oversee *People and Society* and *Hope English*, two lesser-known programs on CCTV-10."

The success of *Lecture* would be hard to replicate, Wan later told me. Indeed none of the post-Yu lectures attracted much public attention, and *Lecture* was pronounced dead by the media by late 2008 amid several larger events unfolding in China during its Olympics year.

Before we wrapped up our interview, I asked him about his take on CCTV's new round of restructuring. What is his view on the revival of news programs?

Wan surprised me with his candid assessment about CCTV's new leadership and new direction. "The newly anointed president [Jiao Li] took less than an hour to summarize what he intended to do for CCTV, chiefly anchoring the network with news. After his speech, we had a meeting of all division chiefs. I was the last to speak, and my view differed from the others, who mostly endorsed Jiao's motto of 'Anchoring CCTV with News.'" Wan expressed his concerns on the grounds that, given the nature of Chinese news, which functions to serve the party, it would be wiser to have less yet more efficient news than to have big and all-encompassing coverage. "The same news delivered repeatedly and loudly might turn people off. News media elsewhere work because they provide multiple perspectives and viewpoints. Given that we have only one voice, why bother to multiply it?" Wan's assessment is in sync with his philosophy for programming, which is lean and simple. Wan thought that the leadership took his view well, but he intended to have further discussions with Jiao alone later.

Wan advocated anchoring CCTV with culture instead. "Don't compare ourselves with the West with regards to news; adopting the Western way of handling news would create confusion in China. Multiple perspectives would confuse the Chinese public, who are accustomed to only one unified voice. The success of *Lecture* spoke to the viability of anchoring a network with Chinese culture. It would be a popular direction." Wan emphasized that news would not push CCTV onto the world stage but Chinese culture would: "Chinese culture has a long sustained history and can benefit the entire world."

I don't know how many of Wan's colleagues at CCTV share his conviction. When I spoke about Wan's proposition of anchoring CCTV with Chinese culture to Bai Yansong a few days later, he rebuffed it, insisting that news has its value and that CCTV ought to assert itself onto the world stage with big-muscled news programs. Wan's and Bai's divergent views might indicate an inevitable turf war within CCTV as the new round of restructuring means adjustment in resource allocation and scheduling. The question of whether Chinese culture would "conquer" the world is an intriguing one, though. China has yet to establish itself as an authoritative voice to the world in both domestic and global affairs. On the front of popular culture, as Michael Keane elaborates, the attempt by the Chinese state to regulate a market-driven entertainment culture has made Chinese pop culture less cool than fashionable Korean and Japanese pop culture. As it stands, it is hard to imagine the world rushing to embrace Chinese culture, let alone one represented by CCTV.

"Chinese culture has a lot to offer to the world," Wan insisted. He gifted me a DVD set of signature lectures on *The Lecture Room*. Unfortunately for the world that hopes to see what Chinese culture has to offer, there are no English subtitles.

8

"GOING OUT" VIA CCTV-INTERNATIONAL

In a symbol of the new Chinese ambition, China is expanding its global media presence to match its rising ambition on the international stage.[1] Hu Jintao personally opened the inaugural World Media Summit, organized by Xinhua News Agency, in October 2009, bringing to Beijing executives from 170 media outlets from around the world. In the massive formal reception rooms of the Great Hall of the People, foreign delegates applauded as Hu offered a vision of a "true, correct, comprehensive and objective communication of information." Rupert Murdoch's News Corporation, the Associated Press, Reuters, the BBC, Russia's ITAR-TASS, Japan's Kyodo Agency, Turner Broadcasting System, and Google, still chummy with the PRC at the time, co-hosted the so-called Media Olympics.

Back in 2001, Jiang Zemin, the then Chinese president, urged the Chinese media to bring China's voice to the world; soon after, Xu Guangchun, who was then deputy head of the Propaganda Ministry and head of SARFT, launched the "going out" project to take the PRC's voice to the world. The goal was to land China's TV and radio channels overseas within five years and to provide multilanguage and regionalized broadcasting and coverage by 2011. The strategies proposed included broadcasting CCTV's international programs in important regions around the world. "Going out" was to present China's voice globally. The CCP warned Chinese media practitioners that it was unrealistic to expect the West to promote China's cause and perspective. CCTV was thus entrusted with the duty of advocating on behalf of China and Chinese culture overseas.

CCTV stepped onto the global stage with the establishment of CCTV-International, which early on broadcast programs in the Chinese language to viewers in Hong Kong, Macao, Taiwan, and major Chinese enclaves around the globe. As John Jirik notes in his research,[2] the origin of CCTV-International can be traced back to a program launched in 1986, *English*

News, a daily fifteen-minute bulletin of items translated into English from the previous evening's edition of the *National News Bulletin*. But CCTV in the 1980s focused exclusively on domestic coverage. The idea of reaching out to overseas audiences did not take real hold until the 1990s. As Yang Wei-guang recounted to me during our conversation in summer 2008, the initial outreach effort was a modest one, aimed at audiences in Taiwan and the Asia-Pacific region. In 1990, with the backing of Ai Zhisheng, the then head of the Department of Radio, TV, and Film, CCTV decided to open an international channel targeting the East Asian region. Yang Weiguang was to lead the effort, and in September 1991 he established the Production Office of Taiwan Programs, whose first program developed under Yang was *All Together*, a variety culture and entertainment show targeting audiences in Taiwan. The program was enthusiastically endorsed by Ai and was expanded from the initial thirty-minute program in the early 1990s to fifty minutes in 2002.

Riding the wave of the program's success, Yang called for a conference that brought together people from the international publicity departments of several provincial TV stations to Xiamen, a major city in Fujian Province, just across the Taiwan Strait. Yang was to announce CCTV's decision to beam satellite signals to Taiwan at the conference and apply for state funding for the planned Taiwan-targeted satellite television channel. But the Ministry of Finance had no budget for CCTV's initiative. At the time, the Ministry of Finance had an annual budget of CN¥3.6 million for international publicity efforts, and the money all went to mailing VHS tapes of CCTV programs to Chinese embassies around the world. The programs on VHS tapes were often hastily edited together, so the quality was less than satisfactory. Given that the tapes often took one week to travel to their destination, by the time CCTV programs reached North America, many of the major new stories had already been reported by local Taiwanese-controlled Chinese-language stations in the United States. So the taped CCTV programs appealed to nobody overseas. When I lived in San Francisco in the early 1990s, the Chinese-language programs on local Chinese-language channels were predominately pro-Taiwan and Hong Kong. Two of my classmates interned and later joined the local Chinese stations as anchorperson and producer. From what I heard back then, people who worked at those stations were quite condescending toward their PRC competitors.

Yang Weiguang wanted to change the situation. As soon as he was appointed the president of CCTV in 1992, Yang decided to forge ahead with establishing CCTV-4, the envisioned international channel, with or without the financial support from the state budget. As Yang put it, "If the 1980s were a golden era for CCTV's domestic development, then the 1990s should be a golden era for CCTV's global expansion." CCTV-4 debuted on October 1, 1992. Quite a few people within CCTV expressed their skepticism about the future of CCTV-4, and rumors spread that Yang was pushing for a premature "great leap forward." Fortunately, Yang had the support of the Propaganda Ministry. In 1993, Ding Guangeng and Li Tieying from the Propaganda Ministry attended a forum at CCTV and praised Yang's vision for building a global-scale network. By then the development of CCTV-4 had become part of the strategic step of the Propaganda Ministry's international outreach effort. The PRC-backed North American Oriental Satellite TV started to beam its signal on August 28, 1993, with CCTV supplying eight hours of programs each day out of the total twelve hours of content. In 1996, CCTV-4 landed in Japan under a similar arrangement.

CCTV-4 now broadcasts around the world through ten transponders on eight satellites, and in collaboration with a number of overseas TV organizations, CCTV-4 has "infiltrated" local cable networks in many countries and regions in Asia, Africa, North America, Europe, and Oceania. It can be watched in the United States on DirecTV satellite channel 454, Dish Network satellite channel 582, Verizon FIOS channel 1750, and other U.S. cable systems. It can also be watched streaming over the Internet directly from CCTV-4's website.

The primary audiences for CCTV-4 programs are heritage audiences overseas who are interested in connecting with their cultural roots and want to be informed about China's current affairs. Despite its expanded audience reach, the limited number of reporters overseas means that CCTV-4 has to rely on news from major Western organizations such as CNN and the BBC. Firsthand international news remains scarce. But it hardly matters; broadcasting twenty-four hours a day in four units rotating every six hours, CCTV-4 is a comprehensive channel with programs focusing on news and current affairs as well as documentaries, music, dramas, sports, and cartoons.

As CCTV-International's Chinese program began to take shape, CCTV began to expand its English news team in 1995. On February 8, 1996, Yang officially proposed to establish an English-language channel at an internal awards ceremony. July 1, 1996, saw the founding of CCTV-English Channel and the beginning of CCTV's experimentation with broadcasting programs in English. Jiang Heping, who was then a deputy director of the News Editorial Board at CCTV-1, was appointed director of the English News Department in 1998. By 1999, the English News had developed its own identity within CCTV's Overseas Service Center, which managed CCTV-4 and later CCTV-9, the official English-language channel. *English News* was responsible for three daily half-hour bulletins on CCTV-4, produced by an editorial team with some thirty members. CCTV-9 was eventually launched on September 25, 2000, transforming the English News Department within CCTV-4 into an independent twenty-four-hour international channel. Instead of sharing audiences among the Chinese diaspora with CCTV-4, the Mandarin-language channel, the newly established twenty-four-hour English service would later aim at the global English-speaking audience. CCTV-9 was launched on a series of satellites that provided the channel with a footprint that aimed to cover 98 percent of the world.

CCTV's "going out" ambition would further expand, driven by China's growing integration into the global world. Soon after Jiang Zemin's exhortation in 2001 for Chinese media to carry the country's voice overseas, Xu Guangchun launched the "going out" project. The strategies proposed included implementing the plan to broadcast CCTV-4 and CCTV-9 in important regions around the world, initially western Europe and North America; encouraging TV and radio stations to expand overseas and to carry out international cooperation; establishing strong overseas marketing and distribution teams and agencies; and improving research on foreign countries' laws, regulations and policies, culture, and audience tastes in order to assist with government policy making.[3]

In a meeting with SARFT in 2001, Xu Guangchun used the term "China's CNN" to describe the role of CCTV-International in the context of the "going out" project. In October 2001, CCTV expanded CCTV-9 into cable delivery and began to partner with global media firms such as AOL Time Warner and News Corporation by giving them limited access to the PRC's television market in Guangdong Province in exchange for Time Warner cable delivery in New York, Los Angeles, and Houston in the United States and for access to News Corporation's BSkyB satellite service in Europe. The following year, CCTV-4 also underwent a major overhaul in efforts to remodel itself after CNN. The channel built a twenty-four-hour information assembly line and an open platform, which resembles CNN's newsroom, where journalists, editors, producers, and news anchors share a large open space that accelerates information flow and unifies production standards.

The "going out" project continued to intensify in subsequent years. The party Politburo member in charge of publicity at the time, Li Changchun, made a number of comments "on the question of improving television's external publicity work" in 2003. Li issued written instructions to CCTV on September 16, 2003, mandating that CCTV-9 was to present a Chinese perspective on issues that interest the world and that the channel must report world news in a timely fashion.[4] Then, on September 22, 2003, Xu Guangchun led a delegation of senior leaders to CCTV for a discussion on external publicity, calling for the transformation of CCTV-9 into a real international news channel. On the backs of these two demands, CCTV-9 management set about restructuring the channel. Thus, CCTV-International was relaunched in May 2004 with the goal of helping the world to understand China and the world to understand itself: hence the channel's new slogan, "Your window on China and the world." As a result, the quantity of foreign news was increased, albeit reported from China's standpoint and with a Chinese perspective. The refocused channel implemented a rolling service for general news to strengthen the channel's identity as a serious news channel rather than a comprehensive channel. The rolling service increased the number of hours of reporting, airing bulletins at the top of the hour, every hour. With such changes, CCTV-9 successfully pivoted from its identity as a comprehensive channel similar to the four big networks in the United States toward being "China's CNN." New broadcast schedules were established to target audiences in Asia, Europe, and the Americas while it retained its traditional service for foreign expats living in the PRC.

CCTV-International further expanded its foreign-language services, introducing the Spanish Channel (CCTV-E) and the French Channel (CCTV-F) in 2004. That same year, CCTV signed a deal with EchoStar to make a Great Wall TV package that would be available to satellite subscribers of the Dish Network in the United States. Great Wall TV expanded its service to Asia in 2005 and to Europe in 2006. CCTV continues to aggressively market its international channels overseas, and there is no shortage of willing partners who hope to gain access to the PRC market by collaborating with CCTV.

As the Persian Gulf region became increasingly important, CCTV-International added the Arabic Channel (CCTV-A) on July 25, 2009, with news programs as its core and culture, service, and entertainment programs as supplementary. The channel currently consists of nine time slots that belong to four program types—news, documentary, entertainment, and education. The main programs are *Dialogue, China Story, Documentary,* and *Science & Technology Review*. The programs rebroadcast six times a day, while news is regularly updated.

Though the channel is exempt from the pressure of ratings, the budget for CCTV-International had traditionally been low. A boost in funding came during the period leading up to the 2008 Beijing Olympics, as the Chinese state launched a media offensive to protect and burnish China's image abroad. Earlier that year, while CCTV-9's Olympics preparation report focused on Olympics-related topics such as public security, air quality, food safety, transportation, good civic behavior, and so on, what cluttered Western media in their Olympics-related news reports were the issues of Tibet and human rights, which angered patriotic Chinese. The coverage by foreign media of the riots in Tibet in March 2008 was a turning point for the Chinese state's determination in launching a full-blown image-building campaign. This triggered extra funding to CCTV's international channels, allowing them to make more programming adjustments. On August 1, 2009, both CCTV-4 and CCTV-9 unveiled changes to their program structure, content, and style in an effort to make the communication more targeted, attractive, and persuasive. Meanwhile, an August 2009 essay published in *Seeking Truth* (Qiushi), an important Communist Party journal, charged that "the inequality of the international news and information order, its lack of freedom and fairness, is now impelling a number of victimized nations to strengthen their capacity for projecting information internationally."[5]

Fueled by a reported injection of up to CN¥45 billion, the latest addition to the CCTV-International global family is a Russian-service channel launched in September 2009 that targets 300 million viewers across the former Soviet Union. "There is continuous bias and misunderstanding against China in the rest of the world," Zhang Changming, the vice president of CCTV, complained as he unveiled the Russian channel, citing as evidence "biased and untrue reporting about weather and food quality problems" before the Olympics. "One of the major goals of the expansion of international channels is to present China objectively to the world," said Zhang. Currently, CCTV-9 broadcasts a mixture of informational, educational, and entertainment programs such as news, sports, music, cooking, travel, and nature shows, as well as documentaries and Chinese lessons, all with the aim of presenting a positive image of China and bringing to the world the Chinese perspective.

How has CCTV-9 fared in attracting audiences and building credentials? As noted by Limin Liang, one way of boosting its international credentials is to conform to global reporting practices.[6] With target overseas audiences who are less accustomed to naked propaganda, CCTV-9 has to adopt a news format and lexicon that caters to Western viewers. An idiom in the Chinese official media policy, "*nei wai you bie*," which means different criteria should be applied to domestic-oriented and international-oriented broadcasters, speaks volumes. CCTV-9 is thus granted more leeway in adopting news practices that are steeped in the tradition of Western journalism. In a study that looks at innovations in news-making practices during CCTV-9's coverage of the major phase of the second Iraq War, Limin Liang examined forces leading to the changes and their impact on news routine and news content at CCTV-9.[7] Liang finds that the introduction of live studio interviews in an attempt to open up room for greater diversity of opinions was the key reform measure. This diversity of opinions was also replicated at the global level, with CCTV-9 putting forth Chinese opinion as an alternative to the perspectives presented by the likes of CNN and the BBC. Meanwhile, given that the Iraq War was not close to home, control from the top was relatively relaxed, which allowed for Western-style news practices to flourish. With a journalism background from a British university, CCTV-9's former chief director Jiang Heping adopted a series of reforms to increase the channel's international influence during the war. The live broadcasting format was an important step toward reaching that influence. Jiang reportedly adopted a suggestion by John Terenzio, CCTV-International's consultant from News Corporation, to bring an English-speaking expert on board for the war coverage. An expert military analyst with fluent English was invited to join the coverage two hours after the war broke out and quickly became indispensable, appearing numerous times over the following weeks. The commonly acknowledged Western news practice helped to project the Chinese perspective.

There were more than a dozen foreign experts working as copy editors and anchorpersons at CCTV-9 when I visited the channel in July 2009. One copy editor I met there was from Los Angeles, a middle-aged woman who was obviously a second-generation Chinese. She was an English-language teacher before she was recruited by CCTV-9 to do translation. Even without formal training, she soon made her way up to be a chief copy editor. I also spoke to Edwin Maher, a New Zealand–born TV journalist who established his broadcasting career in Australia, working many minor roles, particularly as a weatherman, before beginning a twenty-five-year stint with Australian Broadcasting Corporation in 1979. He was remembered in Melbourne mostly for his creative use of various pointers to highlight items when delivering ABC's Victoria state weather forecast. In 2003, CCTV sought to expand CCTV-International to be more professional and accessible to Western audiences, and its senior executive Jiang Heping approached Maher, who was then already working with CCTV as a voice coach, to become one of the first Western anchors for the revamped network. Maher was offered the position because of his clear English diction and his experience in voice coaching. Maher started his new CCTV gig in March 2004, coaching the Chinese staff while hosting a news broadcast. During a private dinner gathering, I asked him about the charge from down south that he has become a paid mouthpiece for Chinese propaganda; he shrugged, saying, "Ah well." He looked a bit worn, so I did not further pursue our dialogue down this line. Self-censorship applies to people of Western origin as well here at CCTV. CCTV-9 regularly sends its staff to CNN for training, and foreign news networks such as CNN and the BBC are among the most frequently watched channels in the news-room. During my visit in July 2009, the offices of CCTV-9 had several TV sets tuned to CNN, which was covering nothing but the death of Michael Jackson.

Yang Rui and CCTV-9

CCTV-9's outreach effort since its Iraq War reporting did not go unnoticed by Western academia. At a conference, Anne-Marie Brady, an expert on Chinese propaganda at the University of Canterbury in New Zealand, suggested, "If Chinese journalists were allowed to do what they are capable of, I'm sure the Chinese version of events would find a global audience, just as Al-Jazeera has." [8] Brady did not miss the opportunity to throw a punch at Western practices by pointing out that "Western media outlets are just as propagandistic." A good example of a direct counterpunch to Western propaganda is CCTV-9's flag-ship program, *Dialogue*, a weekday interview show commenting on current affairs. The program has been likened to a *Larry King Live*–style talk show in which the host interviews various politicians and celebrity guests about their take on current events. The parade of known political figures passing through *Dialogue* includes Bill Clinton, Jimmy Carter, former secretary-general of the United Nations Boutros Boutros-Ghali, and various foreign ministers and am-bassadors. Bureau chiefs of overseas media organizations in Beijing, Chinese and foreign academics, entrepreneurs, and scientists have all appeared on the show. The topics covered are wide-ranging, including international relations, human rights, religious freedom, the death penalty, political reform, the rise of critical journalism in China, transformations of governmental functions, and the rise of the private sector and the faltering state-owned enterprise reforms. While issues concerning environmental protection and sustainable development allow for diverse perspectives on the show, provocative topics are introduced to chiefly underline and justify the Chinese perspective.

One of the more experienced and better-known hosts of the show is Yang Rui, who made no bones about the role of his program as the Chinese state's external publicity platform. As Yang said flatly to me in July 2009, "It is natu-ral to communicate the arguments and policies of our nation to the world." To this end, Yang was not shy about attacking guests who present views that do not conform to the Chinese state perspective. Here the nature and style of the show departs significantly from that of *Larry King Live*, to which *Dialogue* is frequently compared. Unlike Larry King, who functions as a neutral interviewer or debate facilitator, Yang takes it upon himself to defend a set position. His combative style is not unlike that of his colleague at CCTV-1 Bai Yansong. In fact, both have been called "bullies" by their detractors.

Born in 1963 in Jilin, Yang grew up in China's northernmost province, Heilongjiang. The family relocated to Nantong in Jiangsu Province, and he attended his last year of high school in Nantong. Yang had the highest English score on the national college entrance examination and was accepted into Shanghai Foreign Studies University in 1980, majoring in both English literature and international journalism. Upon graduation in 1986, he joined the World News Department of the Central People's Radio Service as a subeditor for world news. He left the Central People's Radio Service in 1988 and joined CCTV, becoming the co-host of *Focus*, CCTV's first current affairs magazine show in English. He then moved on to be the producer and reader of *English News* and producer of *China Report* and *China Today*. Yang was sent to the United Kingdom for advanced training in journalism in 1992–93. Upon returning, he worked on several other gigs, and then took over *Dialogue* on September 25, 2000.

On the steamy summer afternoon of July 7, 2009, Yang sat down with me and John Jirik for an interview. It was only a brief chat since the eruption of the Xinjiang riot two days before required Yang to delay our prescheduled interview to do a last-minute live segment about the riot. I arrived on time and so had to wait at CCTV's media center when Yang went on air to do the show. As none of the TV sets functioned at the coffee shop where I usually waited, I settled for a small TV in a hair salon inside the media center.

It was unclear what happened in Ürümqi on July 5, 2009, but the Chinese government immediately assigned blame for the rioting to overseas "terrorist" organizers, specifically Rebiya Kadeer, an exiled Uighur activist living in Washington, D.C., who was acting president of both the World Uighur Congress and the Uighur American Association. CCTV-9 energetically promoted this official account in news reports and additional programming. The *Dialogue* installment titled "Rampage in Ürümqi" that aired live on the day of my initial visit with Yang Rui was one of these additional programs.

Until shortly before that time, I rarely watched CCTV-9. It was by accident that I turned to CCTV-9 one day and saw Yang Rui's program *Dialogue*. I do not remember what the topic was, but I do recall that there were foreign guests on the show. Yang was rather smug when the foreign guests voiced opposing opinions. On another occasion, the topic of SARS was discussed. The guest, Jing Jun, a professor from Tsinghua University, stated in no uncertain terms that Beijing lied to the people and tried to cover up SARS cases and was forced to come out with the truth only when the lies became too apparent to the people. Yang Rui quickly changed the topic. I was disappointed but not surprised.

For the Xinjiang riot show, Yang had on as a guest Wu Xu, a young professor in political communication at the Cronkite School at Arizona State University, a regular guest on *Dialogue*, and a safe bet for this extremely sensitive occasion. A native of Beijing, Wu studied journalism at People's University of China from 1988 to 1992. Upon graduation, he worked as a national correspondent and domestic news editor at Xinhua News Agency before attending graduate school in the United States. With credentials as both a Chinese journalist and a U.S.-based academic, Wu beamed expertise, balance, and objectivity. Yang, meanwhile, kept up his image as an aggressive but fair-minded and authoritative host.

Credentials and appearances notwithstanding, the interview came off as feigned and choreographed. Yang asked loaded questions and Wu resisted just enough to keep his academic integrity intact. In the main, Wu followed Yang's lead, only adding detail and nuance to Yang's blunt narrative of events. Yang asked how the riot started. Wu started to answer that it was "initially a peaceful demonstration" but Yang interrupted immediately: "Do you really believe it was initially a peaceful demonstration?" Wu: "Reportedly so." Yang again: "Where did you get the reports? From the official news agency of the PRC or from Western reports?" Wu: "From some of the Western reports." Yang: "That's questionable." Wu agreed and explained that he saw the incident developing in two stages: first, a domestic "social disturbance" in reaction to stories of Uighur workers killed at a toy factory in Guangdong Province; this was followed by general unrest intensified by rumors, misinformation, and calls to action spread over the Internet by overseas organizations that seemed to want to "take over this event." He could not say for sure that the rioting was organized by overseas organizations (defending his integrity again), but he theorized that conditions changed from "social disturbance" to violent rioting so quickly that it must have been organized, and that it was, in effect, a "terrorist" incident.

Yang pointed out that the victims were mainly Han Chinese, and Wu riffed on this, criticizing the foreign media for misrepresenting the riots as a government crackdown on peaceful demonstrations, whereas if they were honest about who was being killed, then they would discover a "hidden agenda" by "another political group" behind the rioting. Yang briefly recognized that a "majority" of Uighurs "yearn for independence," but this was just an obligatory nod to journalistic objectivity, not a point for discussion. He dropped it without further comment and asked leadingly, "Who is the mastermind . . . responsible for triggering" the incident—the World Uighur Congress or the Turkestan Islamic Movement? Wu said he was not in a position to answer that question, but he thought both groups were "very likely" to use the Internet to take advantage of the toy-factory incident to advance their cause and to change the "social disturbance" into "rampage."

Adding to his earlier deduction, Wu said the fact that within two hours there were more than a hundred people dead proves that it was an organized activity "rather than some random kind of event." He had no evidence on who might have organized it, "but if you looked at the nature of the sequence of events," Yang pressed, "there's 'voluntary' use of mobile phones, and then there's use by political organizations which called for independence, controlled by an organization outside China; which one do you think is closer to the true picture?" "I think it's a mixture of these two," Wu replied, but he also believed that it was organized to a greater extent than not. He also characterized Kadeer and the World Uighur Congress as probable terrorists and suggested that if the Chinese government could establish "concrete evidence" of her participation in organizing or promoting the riots, then it should negotiate her extradition to China under international law.

Yang then steered the conversation to government policies designed to speed economic development in Xinjiang. Wu agreed that the government has been doing a lot of fine work that hadn't been publicized enough. Yang suggested that the Uighurs were ungrateful for all the government help. Wu demurred, saying they might have some legitimate concerns about "cultural erosion" in the face of a Han Chinese invasion.

It was both astonishing and amusing to see how aggressive Yang was in getting the official line across. I was told later at a private gathering with some of the CCTV-9 foreign experts that Yang frequently bullied his way through his show.

After the live show, Yang came out for our interview. The air was tense, given the gravity and the seriousness of the Xinjiang situation. An anonymous source told us that Yang was pulled aside for a quick chat about our scheduled interview today.

But Yang was an intense person even without the tense situation unfolding. "I only have thirty minutes," he said as soon as he sat down.

With a sleek tie and suit, Yang looked well tailored and tastefully groomed.

Someone told me later that Yang has a taste for society events and fancy cars: "The guy drives a Jaguar to work and wears designer suits."

The interview was conducted in English, and we started out by asking if this was the toughest show he had ever done.

"No, it's not."

"What was the toughest show?"

"The toughest show? There are many. The one I did with Margaret Thatcher. The former British prime minister was very tough because she avoided almost all of the most interesting questions deliberately. She knew very well that I would ask questions about the role she was taking in engineering the peaceful handover of Hong Kong before 1997. She kept mentioning Zhao Ziyang, and she knew very well that Zhao Ziyang had fallen disgracefully in politics. So she gave me a hard time. She was not truthful about facts, about history. That let me down."

"How do you feel today doing the show?"

"Since we are not able to enjoy firsthand access to the truth, we are confined to only two sources of information. One is Western media; the other is official reports, either CCTV News Channel or Xinhua News Agency. The *People's Daily* might also quote Xinhua News. Now, I find very big differences between the two sources, or origins of information. With the West emphasizing a lot Uighurs calling for independence and the Chinese side talking endlessly about ethnic unity and how victims of Han nationality have been beaten, killed, or discriminated against following a very tragic incident in a small city in Guangdong Province that took place on June 26. And also the Chinese side emphasized the direct link between the tragic incident in Xinjiang, Ürümqi, and the headquarters of the World Uighur Congress. I have not done independent investigation into the claims on both sides. So, based on the very different accounts of 'facts,' we are asked to make comments. We tried to bring the truth as close as possible." Yang was projecting a more journalistic position than what he appeared to take on the show, which reminded me of Chen Xiaoqing's remark about the difference between Yang's public and private personae. "We all wear two faces," another anonymous CCTV employee once told me over a beer.

"Was it your idea to do the show?"

"It's both. The management and I both realized that we have to go on there and comment on something that is very meaningful for the future of China's stability. And social stability is the top concern within Chinese leadership. That's the consensus shared by the majority of well-educated Chinese. No one wants to see any riots, chaos, because we want to enjoy the stability. It is out of a basic sense of professionalism that we did the show. What happened was huge. After the Wenchuan earthquake, everybody knows that we can't wait to let Western media take the initiative in covering the truth. It's a basic sense of professionalism. It is the consensus shared by management at different levels in CCTV that we have got to respond very quickly to the emergency." Yang finished his answer with a bit of a caveat: "But how to respond? That's another matter."

"How do you feel after ten years doing this?"

"I'm proud of being the team leader of this program and the chief anchor of this program. We achieved broad recognition from inside and outside China. There must be reasons for the broad recognition. Of course there are criticisms." Here Yang made an unexpected turn, throwing in an interesting anecdote. "For example, we allowed some American guest speakers to criticize human rights violations in Turkey, and some of the guest speakers from Europe were critical of human rights in the Gulf States. So we heard protests from the embassies of those Gulf States. I apologized many times. I had to apologize because this is the state-run media, and anything that happened on the state-run platform is viewed as the official voice. This is very stupid. Those Arabic diplomats don't care that those guest speakers are from the West. They take them as someone who represents the official views of the Chinese government. This is wrong. They say those Westerners should not be allowed to use the platform of the Chinese government to voice their criticism about what they called a 'human rights wrecker' in Arabic countries. This has embarrassed me a lot. I had to apologize to my producer; I had to apologize to the viewers; and I had to do very severe self-criticism about what went wrong. This is the dilemma of *Dialogue*."

When asked whose voice it is that he represents, Yang said, "In theory, it should be the voice of the media. You know and I know, but the viewers may not necessarily know clearly from time to time. This is the state-run media. A state-run media means you have to side with the government on critical issues. You've got to know the position; otherwise, you'll lose your job. It's not your own private company. But I think within this broad framework of state ownership, you can do a lot. Because we know the target audience is very different from the domestic audience, you have to tell the truth. You have to put forth the Chinese interpretation of the key events inside and outside China. Our perspectives are of course different, sometimes slightly different, and sometimes vastly different. We take into consideration the overseas demands for truth. Their demands are very different from domestic ones. In the age of globalization, that perception gap is narrowing. You can't make very clean or clear distinctions between the overseas demands and domestic tastes. However, this channel was deliberately built to live up to the expectation of the overseas viewers who want to know the Chinese perspectives and who want to know how the Chinese look at our homegrown events."

"What drives you? You've been doing this for ten years."

"I am here to present facts. I think previously most news coverage about China has been criticized to a degree because they ignore some important facts. Yesterday I was talking to my young colleagues in the office during our weekly meeting. The picture that the West has about China is incomplete. What we call news gathering is actually a process of selection. We have ten facts about the same truth, but for Western media, they deliberately choose the four negative ones, ignoring the six positive ones. You can't say their reports are not factual. They are factual, but it's based on prejudice, and it's highly selective. Professionals from the same media industry, Western and Chinese, agree universally that there's no absolute impartiality."

Yang rambled on, returning to the established line of "state media." "This is the state media of the PRC, so we of course would try to balance the picture from a Chinese perspective, from the government's perspective. Namely, we want to give a better picture about the livelihoods of our people, instead of being critical and negative. A good news report should be one that talks about both the nasty aspects and the good ones. But as we know at the same time, the instinct of Western theories on communications and journalism is to be critical, is to be negative and to act as a watchdog. You are not supposed to praise the ruling party. You are not supposed to give a rosy picture about whatever happened. Your mandate is to criticize, to give a hard time to whoever is in power. This is basically the bottom line of Western media practice, which is very different from the Chinese principles. From day one of my journalistic education, I knew that our mandate is very different, partly because China has been painted as dark, dictatorial, totalitarian, paying no respect to human rights. For instance, they only talk about the brutal consequences arising from the one-child family-planning policy, whereas they ignore that up to 400 million people have been lifted out of poverty because of the policy of family planning. Otherwise, far more people would rush to share the dividends of the limited outcome of the economic reform. That would be very bad for the general strategy of the country."

"Is there a particular show or particular time that is the best in the past ten years?"

"That happy moment first occurred when I was allowed to go on the air live. This is true journalism. But interestingly enough, that took place during the Iraq War. It wasn't a domestic event. Also because the U.S. doesn't care about our opinions on such matters, it was an opportunity to take liberty in criticizing as much as we liked without receiving countercriticism from them. They are confident enough. That gives rise to the next question, about how we look at those who criticize China. If you are confident enough, we should not be afraid of being criticized. Just go ahead." It's interesting that Yang thought the Chinese ought to be more receptive of criticism. Many Chinese people I spoke to continued to be rather thin-skinned about unflattering remarks about China.

When asked about the style of his show, Yang responded, "*Dialogue* is a mixture of many programs. It could be *Larry King*; it could be *Charlie Rose*; it could be Jerry Paxman of the BBC; or Tim Sebastian of *Hardtalk*. It's a combination of all of those. We cannot afford to have different-style talk shows on the same channel, as that would dry up the quite limited sources of guest speakers. So I persuaded our producer not to add more talk shows. As for my own style, to be a Charlie Rose in China is a mission impossible because of the nature of the state control. You can't maneuver freely, asking whatever questions you like. You've got to be restricted; you've got to be regulated. Having said this, as I said earlier, *Dialogue* is exceptionally good for enjoying more latitude in inviting guest speakers, in going live with guest speakers who have very different cultural and political backgrounds."

How has his program managed to convince several well-known guests to come on as commentators?

"With the growing influence of the program, more influential viewers tune in to watch our program. When they consider it a respectable-quality program that is worth their attention, they spread the word to their friends and recommend experts to be on the program. They can recommend, for instance, ex-generals from the U.S. Army who are willing to talk about the sectarian violence in Iraq and the consequences of the Bush administration's abuse of wartime policy in counterterrorism. One of our guest speakers used to be the senior VP of China National Offshore Oil Corporation, who speaks excellent English. He has an acute awareness about the national conditions of China and knows very well the rules of the game in the West. He also knows journalism. In fact, he knows everything! CNN and the BBC and Al Jazeera have interviewed him many times. So he has become the darling of CCTV-9. We want to recruit more such regular commentators so that when we go on air for issue-driven topics, they are there to provide quality comments. Good English is the most important qualification for a commentator to be on our show. Secondly, they have to be experts on relevant areas of discussion, like the Gulf affairs, human rights, education, medical care reform, whatever. But they are also aware that CCTV-9 is influential and *Dialogue* represents our influences overseas, so they want to promote their public influence as opinion leaders. So we gradually build up a network of human resources via word of mouth. We continue to broaden the base of our resources. I think the broad recognition from international society enables *Dialogue* to enjoy more qualified guest speakers from the West or from countries outside China."

Yang said that they have two broad program categories: one is guest driven, the other issue driven. "We found it easier to get hold of guest speakers for issue-driven stories."

"Do you have pet topics you would like to discuss often?"

"Of course. I want to talk about world affairs. I want to talk about social and political issues, and I want to really talk to influential people in my guest-driven show because these guys have great minds and they give you very deep analysis. They give you very thoughtful and well-formed opinions. They deserve your respect."

I wondered whether after ten years of working on the program he still had the same drive.

Yang said that being an opinion maker has been the driving force behind his pursuit, and he considers his pursuit a noble one. But noble intentions bring stress. "You have moments of depression, either because of your change of mood, or the occasional program that you're not fully prepared for, or sometimes your personal views may not be exactly the same as those that come from above, right? That kind of conflict will occur inevitably. So you have to reconcile your personal views with the official perspective, and to continue to present a balanced picture. This sort of unpleasant mood will sometimes make you wonder what's the point of sticking to the job. Are you able to enjoy sufficient freedom to tell the complete picture? But when the BBC and other Western media interviewed me, it occurred to me that they were not 100 percent free or balanced or impartial. So why should I worry too much about the impartiality? Yes, impartiality and objectivity are the ultimate goals for serious journalists, but those are never unconditionally applied by Western news organizations. Peter Arnett, who did the story about Death Valley and who interviewed Saddam Hussein, was fired by CNN under pressure by the Pentagon. So you know you have to be patriotic after 9/11; otherwise, you'll be kicked out. The same is true here in China. We are only human."

I sensed ambivalence in Yang's semicritical reflection on the constraints imposed on his program. He nevertheless managed to justify censorship and self-censorship and to ultimately endorse the practice of censorship. In the end he simply said that "this is a good platform for me and for the whole country, and for CCTV-9." As CCTV-9 grows in its influence as a result of "less state meddling," it will inevitably incur more stringent censorship. "When you are weak, you have more freedom. When you are strong, you are more restricted. Such is the paradox in China," sighed Yang.

"Have you ever done a story that had to be put on the shelf?"

Yang took a long pause. "During Jiang Heping's reign, a couple of things were killed. One was about the Vietnam War and the other I cannot remember at the moment. I killed one program by myself because I think I asked some stupid questions. I was not satisfied with my own performance, and I said forget about this shit. So it's from both sides. I've killed programs too."

"Do you have favorite CCTV shows?"

"I seldom watch CCTV. That's a very embarrassing question for me. I would think that a talk show such as *Face to Face* hosted by Wang Zhiwei could be good. I think Wang Zhiwei does a marvelous job, but he's a victim of his own vanity and egoism plus internal power struggles and office politics. I don't have any particular shows that I dislike because so many people are working like hell. We should respect their work and their dedication. If they are working for entertaining programs, it's because they want to woo the commercials. They want to increase the income for CCTV. Entertainment programs are cheap, but they are fun. That's perhaps the most important part of the nature of the media in our days. You've got to entertain people. But my program wants to make people think, which is very boring for the younger generation."

Yang conceded that his program must also be able to entertain. "So on weekends we run fun interviews. We do guest-driven programs. We interview actors and actresses, the showbiz people."

These celebrity and entertainment shows are not only more attractive to general audiences, but also more in line with the tastes of Yang's younger co-workers. "The majority of our producers and editors think *Dialogue* is boring. My young colleagues work for fun. They don't care about being opinion leaders or influencing policy makers. This is just a job to them. Media practitioners of my generation took it upon ourselves to serve the role of opinion leaders from day one. I want to foster positive or at least balanced public opinion about China. We have to update our Western viewers about present-day China. We also want to fulfill our watchdog function and keep the behavior of the government in check. We need to let the public employees know that they are the civil servants. Their behavior is subject to the code of conduct of the Chinese state. They need to project a positive image so that China can be viewed as a responsible stakeholder of a global world. But I don't think this is the principle governing the minds of my young colleagues. They work for fun and for paychecks. I don't think they're fully aware of the important position they occupy. Sometimes I don't like attending the weekly meeting with them because their focus is on trivial technical or management routines. I want to give the program a soul and a spirit. We have to give the program rich and meaningful content. But those things are regarded as too lofty and too snobbish, even foolish, according to my young colleagues. So the narrow-mindedness of the young generation of journalists, not necessarily all of them, but some of them, is quite worrisome."

The disappointment with the lack of conviction of the younger generation is a shared sentiment among CCTV veterans. Yang made clear his disapproval of his young colleagues. He recounted an instance when a young producer whined about not knowing what to do when a breaking news event happened. "What would a shark do after smelling blood?" Yang asked. "Out of my professional instinct, I pounded the table and scolded him. 'It's a shame,' I said to him. When such an event takes place, we should get excited. Disaster is the feast of journalists. You have to act very quickly to do what you can to mobilize resources and to put them together to create a story for the program."

Yang ended the interview shortly after the designated thirty-minute time frame. Perhaps he and I could talk more on a different day, I said to him before he left. "Yes, we could," he replied. Yang and I met again several days after for a more relaxed chat. Reflecting on career, philosophies, and inspirations, Yang filled our conversation with varying degrees of insight. The air was seductively casual during our private chat. His gentle demeanor and thoughtful musings on the road he had taken contrasted sharply with the public image of him on TV, certainly with what I had seen only a few days ago. Yang said that he sensed I *understood* what it meant to be practicing media in China. Ultimately, I think I was rewarded with a more forthcoming chat not only because the chemistry was right but also because he trusted that I would not distort his words. As Chen Xiaoqing later remarked to me, it's inevitable that people tense up when questions regarding censorship and political freedom were fired at them by foreigners "who are clueless about the reality of China but are all too quick to pass judgment." I too went through the same defensive phase when I first landed in the United States decades ago. Questions of this nature initially felt accusatory rather than genuine. So I understood what went through the minds of some of my Chinese interviewees. My empathy brought mutual trust, which helped break the ice. The resulting interviews were frequently revelatory. To seek connections with him, I mentioned a visit he had made to Karl Marx's graveyard that I read about online. The article described how Yang sat in awe for a full hour in front of Karl Marx's tomb at Highgate Cemetery in London, unable to get a handle on his feelings. I told him that I too paid homage to Marx's tomb during a visit to London a decade or two ago. "It was during the London tube strike, so the traffic was horrendous and I was quite frustrated with the inconveniences cased by the organized labor strike." We laughed at the irony.

Yang opened up to me in a softly pensive tone. "I bear the obvious imprint of a generation that entered college in the 1980s. Ours is a generation of lofty ideas and grand ambitions, a sense of social responsibility. The eighties was a lot more open than now. It was a time when Western thoughts were allowed to be introduced to China and critical debates were encouraged. We learned that there were different ways of looking at the world and that ours was only one of many. It was an exciting time.

"Anyhow, it is under this backdrop that I selected international news as my major. I benefited from a new policy by the administration of RTF [Ministry of Radio, Film, and Television] in the 1980s, which strived to foster the first generation of news professionals who could speak a foreign language. The goal was to be able to send journalists overseas who could speak the local language. I was lucky enough to be selected to study international journalism at the Shanghai Foreign Language University. Before that, I was contemplating being a diplomat or a scholar."

In his clean-shaven composure, his publicly assertive yet privately gentlemanly demeanor, his slightly seductive secrecy, and his ability to speak another language effectively, Yang certainly possessed the aura of a diplomat about him. "The state wanted to have a group of young talents to enter the field of foreign relations and hoped that our presence could change the Western media's outdated image of China. It was a moment when my personal ambition and the needs of our nation converged. Upon graduation, I was allocated a job at the International Division of the Central People's Broadcasting Station in July 1986. My duty was to conduct research and write reports for the 7:20 A.M. show on international news and events. I remembered writing about negotiations on military reduction between China and the Soviet Union during the cold war."

The position at the People's Radio allowed him rare access to internal memos and reclusive scholars, a privilege that brought Yang a sense of superiority, which he has held till this day. Yet the ambitious Yang was straitjacketed by regulations and censorship. After a number of his news reports were delayed or ignored by his superiors, Yang couldn't take it anymore. "I became really depressed. I found the ideological restrictions suffocating. The job was not a good match either. The lack of basic respect on how news should operate told me that the place had become a dinosaur. The place had become the symbol of death. All I wanted was to get out of there."

Yang eventually left for CCTV in September 1988. "I had options at the time and was contemplating going to the U.S. for graduate school. My wife at the time did not want to go to the States, so I gave up. I joined CCTV instead. It was not easy to enter CCTV. I got in through the 'back door,' via my connections with a renowned broadcaster at the People's Radio, Ling Ru. Ling's husband was once the president of the radio station and was later promoted to be the deputy chief of SARFT. His endorsement helped me to secure a position at the international unit of the *National News Bulletin* program. Later CCTV-International took me under its wing to do English news for them. After spending five years working there, I was promoted to be the deputy head of our division, which would later become CCTV-9. We had only a dozen or so people at the time and my boss wanted me to become a manager. I said no and expressed my desire to be on the front line and on camera. To be honest, my vanity was at work, as I enjoyed being on camera. I had several failed hosting gigs and spent a lot of time doing research about how to most efficiently promote China overseas. With the aid of graduate students from Beijing Normal University, I prepared a report entitled 'A Preliminary Analysis of the Strategic Positioning of the English Channel in Promoting China Overseas,' which was published in *TV Research*. The piece caught the eye of the then newly appointed deputy president of CCTV, who summoned me for a private talk. He was impressed and saw potential in me. I later turned the report into my thesis in the UK when I attended Cardiff College at Wales University from 1993 to 1994, studying mass communications."

Yang chatted briefly about his UK experience. "I did not study hard but managed to receive good grades. Time was spent interning at the BBC and working to earn some extra money. The UK experience was eye-opening, as I learned skills in news gathering, management, and writing. I made a qualitative leap in my understanding of news. In practice, upon my return to CCTV, I experimented with a small column called *In Depth Report*."

But Yang ran into some obstacles in putting his UK knowledge into practice. He gave me examples of how two stories he did fell short of receiving the Rainbow Award, a prestigious professional journalism award given by the Chinese government. "When I went to Guiyang to report on a local flood, I did a standup story by the riverbank. I piled up pieces of wood from damaged houses and asked why the municipal government, given the frequent flooding here in the city, took no preventive measures. I further questioned the lack of reports on the local residents' demand for action. Most of the media stories were about how the local flood refugees praised the government's relief effort. I thought mine was a serious story, so I submitted it for the Rainbow Award. But my boss was not happy. He told me that I was criticizing the government, so the story was not seriously considered. The other story I sent for the same award was about industrial pollution in Beijing. One part of the story involved a state-run steel company near the Beijing train station that had caused environmental problems. We entered the company's territory unannounced. The head of the company was well connected, and he and his son ran the factory as if it were their family business. Anyhow, to make the story dramatic, I chose to stand next to the sign 'Green Company,' with the thick smoke coming out of the factory's chimney as background. I pointed at the sign and said that the pollution here was severe and that we hoped that the company would keep its promise of providing the country with a green factory. In the midst of my standup reporting, a dozen or so thuggish-looking guys interrupted us. They wanted to confiscate our tape and my ID. After some back-and-forth, they agreed to let us go but asked us not to include footage of their attempts to stop our reporting. My boss liked the story and appreciated my effort to do watchdog journalism. But he wanted me to delete the standup part of the story. I refused, and he was not at all happy. The story won the second-place award instead of the first-place award it rightly deserved. I was vindicated later in 1999, as a story I did that year finally brought me a first-place Rainbow Award."

Yang said that the more roadblocks he ran into, the more determined he became in doing investigative journalism. "I established an English Channel report team, traveling all over China for hard-edge stories. Four or five years after leading the interview team, I realized that field reports were not the best route to fulfill my dream of being an opinion leader. So I reevaluated my options yet again. It was possible for me to go overseas as my then wife was assigned a Foreign Service job in Australia. I agreed to go with her but was not sure if I wanted to be the husband of a diplomat. It was during that period that the then host of *Sunday Topic*, the predecessor of *Dialogue*, was leaving the program. My boss asked if I wanted to step up and host the show. He gave me one night to consider the offer. I decided to do it. So I stayed behind as my then wife left for Australia. Our relationship deteriorated and we ended our marriage. But career-wise I made the right decision. *Dialogue* was an excellent platform and I was able to strike a balance between the voices of the state and the public, China and international, East and West, developed and developing countries, and positive and relatively critical. It was a weekly program when

I took over ten years ago. It gradually expanded, first twice a week, then three days, four days, five days, and eventually became a daily program. I also made the gradual transition to a live show." Yang now hosts the program three times per week but is in charge of overall program planning and broadcasting.

Would it be possible that one day he could separate his own voice from the voice of the state? I mentioned Bai Yansong's yearning and confidence that the day would come when he would be allowed to stake out his own position.

"It is a luxury to consider implementing Western principles of journalism in China under the current political system. Under the circumstances, people frequently feel passionate about independent opinions and are driven by professional ideals and principles to do something about it. This is commonly felt among our generation. I remember when commemorating the death of Walter Cronkite a few years ago, we were all in awe of his integrity as the most trusted man in America. He set the yardstick and raised the bar for the news profession. So I understand Bai from the perspective of individual desire to adopt a certain type of news practice. I understand spiritually Bai's desire to push for a breakthrough in the system and to carry forward his own individuality. Yet a strong individual flavor inevitably brings in subjectivity so I think his is a delicate role. What he wanted is no longer a simple report of facts and factors but to stake out a position. He is branching out to be a news commentator, which is different from what I consider my role to be. Sure, I too want to be a commentator, staking out my own position and voicing my own personal view. But as an interviewer, a journalist, if you want to contribute to the progress of Chinese media, I think we should focus more on how to standardize our professional practice and raise the bar to match news practices in the West." Here Yang retreated from his own description of his ambition of being an opinion leader. Like his colleagues at CCTV, Yang holds conflicting ideas about what he can or should do. Obviously he conveniently ignored the very fact that he has already been staking out positions in his program, albeit the party's positions. Meanwhile, Bai has indeed made himself a commentator on his *News 1+1*, sharing the hosting role with a young colleague.

Unprompted, Yang further compared Bai's program with his own. "The global perspective is what I have but Bai does not, and that is our difference. I think he represents the most vanguard and politically savvy newsmen of domestic orientation. He is capable of expressing personal views that balance the needs of the larger system, the individual, and the news organization he serves. I once teased him about his new program, *News 1+1*. I told him that *1+1* resembles the Chinese character 'king' in writing, so he is the King of News." Yang told me that he urged Bai to be cautious by reciting a famous

Mao quotation, the great herdsman's exhortation to the Chinese people to prepare for rainy days, "dig deep tunnels, preserve massive amounts of grain, and not seek hegemony."

"I told Bai that a lot of it has to do with the amount of independent room you are allowed in your operation, in terms of policy and censorship. Success or failure has nothing to do with your individual talent. The most important factor in any type of interview program is the space for alternative ideologies and thinking. If a guest were not allowed to speak freely and to respect facts and to represent alternative perspectives, then the impact of the program would be diminished. It would mislead the public and make you a laughing-stock. So I told him to defer crowning his program as the King of News. He would be wise to lower his expectations."

Yang next sought to discuss corporate culture and the constraints of a corporate culture on any given individual program. "A topic I discuss frequently on CCTV-9 is about the impact of culture on a channel, much like how corporate governance influences its operation and culture. The corporate governance for CCTV-1's news program is the CCP principle and hence the party culture. CCTV-9 must match the expectation of the global news operation and therefore enjoys more relaxed ideological control. Incidentally, prior to meeting with you, I was talking to a couple of my young colleagues. The younger generation is more up-to-date with the new technology, yet they are more susceptible to political pressure. They don't have the political, moral, and professional courage that come from life lessons and experiencing hardship. You gain courage and wisdom through setbacks and life lessons that will enable you to make the right judgment call at the critical moment. Courage also comes from idealism, which is what our generation has in abundance. All elements have to come together to prepare you for the mission of building a positive image of China to the world. It is about building commonality, not individuality. In today's pluralistic world we need to advance our own beliefs and interests but at the same time safeguard the collective interest based on common knowledge and common sense. The subordination of individuality to common need can be cruel but has to be done. I believe that Bai would agree with what I said.

"Bai and I share the same desire to be opinion leaders. But at a channel where the governance adheres to the party principle, news principle comes second. So the culture of CCTV-1 is the culture of the party, which conflicts with the culture of media commonly acknowledged in the West. There are many things in China that cannot be reconciled, for instance, the need of the state to obtain stability against the need of the media to report events that might or might not disrupt stability. China's progress is reflected in the media's continuous exploration, the search to balance the interests of the party and the public in terms of control with the public's right to know. I understand Bai's individual courage in pushing for societal progress and for the media to build a positive and responsible social image, but I think his individual voice is not that significant. The most important thing is to let the global society see a positive future that China is building. I am sure Bai and I share the same goal." Yang suggested nevertheless that he had been trying to provide balanced reports on his program, which allowed for diverse opinions and voices while adhering to the program's core political principles of safeguarding China's national interest. "It goes without saying that our program needs to adhere to a political and ideological bottom line. Beyond that, I do encourage debates."

I asked him whether there was any room for improvement in his own program.

He paused, appearing a bit surprised by the question. "I suppose a step forward would be to interview people that actually made the news or interview people who witness whatever major events took place. Right now, we have no original news reporting, so it's not authentic and authoritative. Our interviewees are commentators but not event makers or witnesses. If possible, I would like to expand my guest list. It would be a real pity if my program could not expand its guest pool to include people who made or witnessed the news."

I wondered whether he minds being known first and foremost for his aggressive interview style and asked how he responds to the "bully" charge.

"Well, people have different takes on my style. Different people prefer different styles. To me, as a host of a news commentary program, my subjective position certainly has an imprint on my program. It is no surprise that I elicit polarizing reactions, which helps to popularize the program. People feel strongly about me, positively or negatively, which is a testimony to my high visibility. As for the charge of bullying, I don't think I have done enough pushing and shoving. Too often our interviewees exercise self-censorship, so our interview becomes my effort to squeeze opinions out of my guests. People speak up only when they are provoked. They speak truth when they are pushed against the wall. Under the current system, given that we cannot do an investigative news show, the only choice we have to get to the bottom of the truth is to investigate and enrage my interviewees. So being aggressive and provocative helps with truth seeking. I think one's hypocrisy can be captured on TV and it is up to the host to peel off the artificial layers of the guests so as to get to the bottom of things."

Yang acknowledged that it is in his nature to be tough and sharp. "I prefer getting right to the point and letting my own intuition lead the conversation.

I can be ruthless, especially with foreign guests. It is frequently a battle of wits when interviewing foreign guests. I have to either coax or provoke or seize the right moment to ask an unexpected question so that the interviewees are cornered before they reveal what's really on their mind. They frequently ask us to delete what they perceive as politically inappropriate comments after the taping. So political self-censorship applies everywhere. Though I make them sweat, many foreigners like my edgy style and are surprised that a show like mine exists on CCTV."

The third reason for him to be aggressive on the show, as Yang puts it, has to do with ratings. "There is the imperative of making the program more exciting and palatable. It is, after all, a show." Yang said that he was torn between being a showman and being a deep thinker, but he held no illusions about the fact that he is in show business. "On topics of a nonsensitive nature, I am happy to fan the flame and instigate heated arguments, which is to make it a bit scandalous for the purpose of audience appeal. The key is to not fall in love with your interviewees; nor should the host be too narcissistic. One performs the best when one forgets one is hosting a show."

"What motivates you?"

"At a nobler lever, with the growing integration of China into the world, I feel increasingly that I have the commitment to erecting a positive image of China as a major responsible stakeholder in the world. To be a responsible stakeholder, China should actively participate in global initiatives that aim to build a better world. We should send our troops overseas to help maintain world peace. We should address environmental issues, particularly when our massive consumption of natural resources could bring a negative impact to energy preservation and environmental conservation. Due to the lack of understanding, anxieties have abounded in the West about the ramifications of China's rise—will China become a threat to the Western power? Will the rise of China benefit the rest of the world? Concerns have been expressed about China's political system and its economic developmental model. Can China sustain its growth? Well, things are still uncertain at this stage. There are many unsolved puzzles in China's development. After the recent financial meltdown, people have started to rethink the standard economic practices in the West, which might shed new light on China's developmental model. Is the Chinese model universally applicable? Is it possible to change the rules of the game as defined by the West? At least the world is willing to listen to China now. China's voice grows louder as the country becomes more powerful economically and culturally. Our voice represents not only China but also that of the developing countries. In the 1980s, the topic for the East-West relationship was peace and for the North-South relationship development. These topics continue to be relevant today, although peace has more to do with antiterrorism now and development focuses more on the impact of emerging markets. It is true that China's development has many problems and that we are not perfect. On the other hand, there have been either ignorant or willful misconceptions about China. I hope that people in the West would come and see for their own eyes many of the positive aspects of China's development. To this end, my program helps to explain China to the world. Few TV programs or newspapers could have the same impact as *Dialogue* in this regard. As a result of our persistent effort and cultivation in the past decade, *Dialogue* has accumulated international acclaim. But we are far from doing enough in fostering mutual understanding between China and the rest of the world." Yang was realistic, though, as he understood that the world would not continue to be so accommodating toward China if the country fails to maintain its status as an economic superpower.

It's interesting that Yang's answer to many questions always came back to his projected mission of "building a positive image of China to the world." Yang's feverish patriotism borders on xenophobia. His often-combative stance when encountering what he perceives as unjustified criticism of China notwithstanding, Yang took real actions in "safeguarding China's image." In preparation for the celebration of the sixtieth anniversary of the PRC in 2009, Yang discovered that, by coincidence, programs on CCTV-9 featured excessive images of military men and women. He took up the issue with CCTV's leadership, cautioning them about what kind of unintended message this might send to the world. In Yang's view, Chinese media would benefit from avoiding unnecessary symbols and signs that potentially give mistaken impressions of China's intentions.

It remains to be seen whether Chinese state-controlled media firms can attract a big international audience or earn significant revenues overseas. CCTV-International, for one, continues to lag behind in credibility and objectivity. The perception of being propaganda vehicles for the Chinese government is hard to shake off, despite the efforts of Yang Rui and his like-minded CCTV colleagues. CCTV has yet to be the international authority on China, let alone being a credible alternative to the BBC, CNN, or Al Jazeera on world affairs.

Speaking of Al Jazeera, Yang Rui came under fire recently by calling Melissa Chan, a journalist working for the Qatar-based TV network who was expelled from China, a "foreign bitch." It is speculated that the expulsion of Chan was the result of her critical reporting of China's alleged use of slave labor by prisoners. Chan's departure prompted Al Jazeera English Channel to close its Beijing bureau in May 2012. Riding a wave of ultranationalistic sentiment and displaying his typical arrogance, Yang launched a tirade against "foreign trash" on Weibo, the Chinese equivalent of Twitter. As outrage in response to Yang's remarks grew overseas, a CCTV spokeswoman had to clarify a few days later that Yang's microblog is a personal account and that "it does not represent CCTV."

As CCTV-International continues its global outreach, global TV firms have likewise tried to tap into China, with the amount of foreign TV channels in China numbering more than thirty. These outlets provide Chinese audiences access to foreign movies, TV dramas, animated films, live coverage of international sports events, and documentaries. In the early 1990s, the central government restricted the reception of foreign signals and banned the illegal installation of satellite dishes, all in the name of "protecting national cultural solvency." Since the late 1990s, the "going out" policy changed the central government's overall orientation toward foreign media flow into China, as Chinese media had to negotiate with overseas media for import and export. Broadcasting policies in turn moved from the protectionism of the early 1990s to a combination of resistance and limited liberalization, combining defensive measures for the domestic market with an offensive approach for international expansion and influence, with CCTV at the forefront of charting the foreign territory while China's local markets are forced to open for foreign competition. Thus, tension between the central authority and local stations surfaced.

In exchange for CCTV's overseas landing rights, the central government opened cable networks in the Pearl River delta region of Guangdong Province to foreign satellite channels in October 2001. In a first-of-its-kind agreement, Time Warner won the right to distribute a Chinese-language cable TV channel in China without having to give up overall control of the content. The entrance of foreign programs created direct competition between local Guangdong TV and foreign satellite television stations, causing friction between local stations and CCTV and SARFT. The deal has been criticized for undermining local media's competitive edge, as a preexisting ban from SARFT forbids all domestic TV channels from screening imported or coproduced drama during prime time. Given that the same regulation does not apply to foreign channels, similar programs can be shown on foreign channels but not on local Guangdong TV. With content autonomy as part of the deal, foreign channels can cover sensitive topics that local channels are forbidden to touch, which further undermines the appeal of programs on the local channel. Localized programming on foreign channels also makes it easier to peel away viewers from local stations. Despite protests from aggrieved stations, more foreign TV channels have gained landing rights in China since 2001, further fanning local stations' resistance to CCTV. CCTV's biggest local challenger would come not from the prosperous Pearl River delta region but from a poor inland province, Hunan.

9

CHALLENGING CCTV'S DOMESTIC DOMINANCE: HUNAN SATELLITE TELEVISION AND PHOENIX TV

As China's largest TV empire, CCTV has a near monopoly on resources for politically significant content. It has state-of-the-art facilities, and it attracts the bulk of China's television advertising revenue. The power of CCTV is therefore considerable, a legacy of its status as the official party organ. As the main source of domestic and world news, CCTV sets the national agenda for political and current affairs. The central government regularly leaks information to CCTV, enabling it to be seen as the most authoritative news medium in China. Moreover, as mandated by state policies, at least ten of CCTV's channels have automatic access to the cables that transmit television signals and link most of Chinese urban and township households. Though operated by local television authorities, the cable systems, which are capable of carrying just over thirty channels, are required to also accommodate between ten and twenty local, provincial, and municipal television channels, some of which continue to relay CCTV content, including the evening news.[1] As a result, little room is left for other signal providers.

CCTV's apparent monopoly is further reflected in its dominance of the advertising market. The sixty seconds of advertising airtime following the *National News Bulletin* is the most expensive slot in the country. The evening news program further increases the ratings of the *National Weather Forecast* and the investigative news program *Focus*. Overall, CCTV made up one-third of total TV advertising revenues, while the other thirty-one provincial-level TV stations—including four municipalities, Beijing, Shanghai, Tianjin, and Chongqing—combined made up only 40 percent of the total.[2] CCTV's dominant position is also evident in the sheer number of eyeballs its programming commands; roughly two-thirds of all television hours in China are spent watching CCTV shows.[3]

Furthermore, CCTV presides over the national professional television associations responsible for setting and policing industry standards and regulations. CCTV has maintained its domestic dominance through a series of protectionist policies granted by the state, the most significant being its "must carry" rule. Under the government's four-tier mixed-coverage policy, CCTV is the country's sole broadcaster allowed nationwide coverage; others can reach audiences only within their respective geographical jurisdictions. Each provincial TV station is allowed to operate one satellite TV channel with signal coverage capable of reaching the entire nation technologically; yet because of the administrative boundaries and local protectionism across provinces, each provincial TV station has to negotiate with other provinces to bring its satellite channel to their local cable networks. In addition, CCTV has the exclusive coverage rights to national and international sports events, including the Olympic Games and the World Cup, which bring in huge profits to the network. SARFT justified this policy by asserting the need to maintain the smooth operation of sports broadcasting so as to better serve the audience.

SARFT, and its predecessor, MRFT, has been consistently criticized for suppressing attempts by provincial TV stations to expand regionally and nationally, thereby securing CCTV's national monopoly. The conflict set off calls for rethinking the relationship between CCTV and local stations and, more important, the role of CCTV. Yet, despite the increasingly loud local protests, the central government continues to mandate policies that give CCTV preferential treatment. A case in point is the regulation pertaining to dialects. All across China, but especially in areas like Guangdong and Shanghai, audiences prefer local channels and programming at both the provincial and municipal levels. Regional sensibilities, including the usage of local dialects, account for part of the appeal of non-CCTV programming. From 2004 to 2005, SARFT issued three sets of regulations that essentially banned programs that spoke nonstandard Mandarin.[4] The ban protected CCTV from audience encroachment, as the strong local appeal of dialect programs often divides the target audience for advertising. In the end, the ban was an obvious giveaway to CCTV.[5]

With such decided built-in advantages for CCTV, one might be surprised to know that there are in fact domestic broadcasters and networks that have succeeded in carving out their own niches in recent years. Regional satellite TV stations are challenging CCTV's long-standing dominance; their program quality, name recognition, and market share continue to improve, attracting serious attention from advertisers, investors, and foreign content providers. The market, however, is dominated by a small circle of big players, with smaller, more local channels finding it difficult to reach beyond their geographic boundaries. The five major players in the regional satellite channel sector include youth-oriented Hunan Satellite Television (HSTV), TV-drama-oriented Anhui Satellite TV, family-oriented Jiangsu Satellite TV, entertainment-format-oriented Zhejiang Satellite TV, and news-dominated Shandong Satellite TV. HSTV, for instance, has boosted its viewer ratings with the popular talent show *Super Girls*, a Chinese version of *American Idol*, and *Ugly Wudi*, a Chinese version of *Ugly Betty*; both are open to product placement and tie-ins as well as auxiliary merchandizing. In recent years, CCTV lost the broadcast rights to the EPL, the world's most watched soccer league, to a consortium of regional broadcasters. In 2006, Shanghai's Dragon TV broadcast its own *Spring Comes to the East* program at the same time as CCTV's *Spring Festival Gala*, encroaching on CCTV's regional audiences. Most recently, HSTV's 2012 *Spring Festival Gala* featuring Shaquille O'Neal kung-fu fighting with children upended CCTV's deadly earnest enlightenment gala. Indeed, HSTV in particular has been adept at tapping into the needs of China's youth audience, considered the most important target of state propaganda. In 2008, HSTV topped the list for ad revenue among satellite broadcasters, raking in US$220 million (CN¥$1.38 billion). HSTV's aggressive entertainment programming won the hearts and minds of millions of Chinese youths, making it a leading competitor to CCTV on the converted youth market. The reaction of CCTV to the rise of HSTV has been frustration and anger, as viewership numbers, advertising revenue, and social influence are all at stake.

HSTV Versus CCTV

HSTV is one of the most successful provincial satellite stations. Founded in 1997, HSTV is the satellite television network of its parent broadcasting company, Hunan Broadcasting System (HBS), formerly known as Golden Eagle Broadcasting System. Founded in 1970, HBS TV became China's first provincial-level consolidated media group in 2000. Hunan TV, the TV station under HBS, established seven television channels in 2001: a satellite TV channel (HSTV), a news channel, an economics channel, a culture channel, a sports channel, an entertainment channel, and a channel devoted to urban living. HSTV enjoyed steady growth throughout the 2000s, winning landing rights in major cities in every province in China.

HSTV's innovations in programming are driven largely by necessity. It did not set out to diminish CCTV, though the end result has threatened CCTV's comfortable dominance. The quick rise of HSTV surprised and alarmed CCTV. SARFT took action to clamp down on the more boundary-pushing aspects of HSTV programming. As reported by David Barboza, in 2003, "government officials pulled the plug on a slightly erotic weather show that featured several scantily clad beauty pageant winners cooing the weather forecasts while lying on a sofa or bed."[6] In 2004, the debut of *Super Girls* sent a shock wave through CCTV leadership, who branded the show "a rogue program" produced by "the rogue broadcaster" and "a sneak attack on Pearl Harbor."[7] The language used reflected CCTV's perception that it was under a vicious attack. Gross overstatement notwithstanding, the Pearl Harbor analogy betrayed CCTV's self-image as an unchallenged media empire. CCTV launched its own "healthy" yet less successful talent-quest show, *Dream China*, in 2005, which was hosted by Li Yong, CCTV's king of pop culture, though Li told me that *Dream China* was conceived before *Super Girls*.

Feeling the heat for becoming increasingly irrelevant to the masses, especially the youths it was mandated to reach and unify, CCTV fired back with a story on *Focus* in June 2005 criticizing the prevalence of entertainment shows modeled on foreign programs and their detrimental impact on Chinese society. On July 19, 2005, CCTV sponsored a much-publicized industry summit attended by top propaganda officials and television hosts from the country's major broadcasters. Three of the anchor hosts who spoke at the summit specifically criticized *Super Girls* for being vulgar and condemned ratings as "the source of all evil." Wang Taihua, general director of SARFT, complained that there were too many low-quality and lowbrow reality shows that catered to the least common denominator and that the government had to strengthen supervision of entertainment programs and restrict the number of reality shows allowed on TV.[8] In December 2006, CCTV decided to ban reports about celebrities' private lives as part of an in-house campaign against "vulgarity on the screen" and "lowbrow programs." With rhetoric reminiscent of the anti–spiritual pollution campaigns, CCTV pledged to adhere to its vocation of "spreading advanced culture" and "actively advocate mainstream values in line with the times."

Furthermore, the network lobbied in private to the Propaganda Ministry about *Super Girls*, leading to speculation that the program might be banned. During the pre–satellite TV era, just by filing a document with the propaganda department of the central government or of the local government, CCTV would have activated an immediate ban of the program in question. The network no longer retained such sweeping powers, and in the end no ban came. However, the critical scrutiny did eventually halt HSTV's "super" momentum,[9] and CCTV took other steps to limit the *Super Girls* fever, including informally banning on its major channels the appearance of all Hunan TV stars.

In my interview with Ouyang Changling, the authority behind *Super Girls*, he reiterated that all they wanted in the beginning was to make Hunan TV profitable, and concentrating on entertainment seemed to be the only viable option. With such a strategy in mind, *Super Girls*, a singing competition show modeled on Fox's *American Idol* and ITV's *Pop Idol*, was conceived. In contrast to international media practices of buying the rights to popular formats, Hunan TV didn't bother with such conventions; rather, the company simply copied the formulas outright. For domestic audiences restricted to the dominant style of CCTV's programming for so long, these copycat programs appeared new and inventive. Unlike CCTV's *Dream China*, which was heavily scripted, from talent scouting to the actual competition, *Super Girls* accepted 150,000 entrants with very limited manipulation or intervention by HSTV staff, both in the production of the performance and in the selection of winners. The selection was based about one-third on the judges (who were representatives of the commercial music industry), another third on peer competitors, and the last third on SMS voting by fans. HSTV structured the program so that it resembled its international prototype rather than the typical Chinese television program, which was what *Dream China* did. The decidedly nonedgy *Dream China* bombed, ranking outside the top forty shows in the entertainment category during its ten days of screening in most Chinese cities.[10]

Super Girls was finally suspended after a three-year run from 2004 to 2006 amid harsh criticism. But the show's sequel, *Happy Boys' Voice*, debuted in April 2007. Prior to the new show's debut, SARFT issued a list of rules, banning star gossip, fans screaming and wailing, and unorthodox hairstyles and clothes. Hunan TV agreed to abide by the SARFT rules, which later even included the banning of talent shows during prime time, between 7:30 P.M. and 10:30 P.M., and a prohibition against offering prizes to attract contestants. The strict guidelines partly reflected the Chinese government's wariness in light of the upcoming 2008 Beijing Olympic Games. The timing of the crackdown by SARFT could also be linked to the Communist Party Congress being in session during the time, which frequently prompted tightened controls on media to enact measures to maintain the status quo.

The central government further stipulated that while TV stations could continue hosting singing shows, they had to remain regional competitions, which meant that the ratings and buzz would never reach the heights of those of their nationwide predecessor *Super Girls*. After a year siesta in 2008, when the Beijing Olympic Games preempted all other events, HSTV made an attempt to relaunch *Super Girls* at the national level, but under a different name, *Happy Girls*, in 2009. In order to air a national version again, Hunan TV had to agree to certain SARFT conditions. *Happy Girls* could last for only two months (about half the length of an *American Idol* season), each episode had to air after 10:30 P.M., and judges were required to restrain their comments. Publicity revolving around the private lives of contestants was banned to further curb the "sensationalization" of the show. Also, text-based and online voting systems—possibly one of the biggest draws of the last shows—were no longer allowed, although Hunan TV found a creative way to get around the ban: the fans were able to show their support each week by downloading MP3s of their favorite artists' performances. Finally, competitors were forbidden from hugging each other or expressing extreme emotions onstage, and no fan groups were allowed to cheer for contestants in the studio. Though never a fan of reality competition shows, I can hardly imagine a show of this nature without raw emotions from either the contestants or the fans or the judges. The draconian directives of SARFT were astonishingly amusing.

The conditional approval for *Happy Girls* came after Hunan TV's attempt to host a similar contest in 2008 was canceled due to criticism that it promoted vulgarity and overnight celebrity. To prepare for the 2009 launch, the management of HSTV liaised with the central propaganda department, pledging cooperation and moderation. Well-known revolutionary artists were invited to appear as special guests, and revolutionary and traditional songs were staged before the competitions. The network turned down all requests for interviews and reports by domestic and international media to curb the impact of the show. In short, HSTV took great pains to drive home the point that *Super Girls* was not aimed at competing with CCTV.

Nie Mei Explains *Super Girls*

On a hot summer day in July 2009, I visited the headquarters of Hunan TV. The office was located on the outskirts of Changsha, the dusty provincial capital of Hunan, known historically as home to bandits and spicy, greasy food. Hunan is also famous for producing quite a few politicians in recent Chinese history, including Mao Zedong, former Chinese premier Zhu Rongji, the late president Liu Shaoqi, and the late marshal Peng Dehuai.

Surrounded by mountains and hills in southeast China, Hunan was slower than most provinces in adopting Deng's economic reforms in the years following Mao's death in 1976. As a result, Hunan fell behind other provinces in developing a market economy. The lack of cash flow in Hunan forced Hunan TV to seek revenues elsewhere, which contributed to the bold program initiatives with popular appeal. Ouyang Changling attributed part of the success of HSTV to a cultural environment that fostered passion, determination, and creativity among the Hunanese. In other words, it is not a coincidence that Hunan gave birth to programs such as *Super Girls*, as the province's unique geography and culture naturally lead to programs of high energy and distinctive characteristics. "We Hunanese love spice and spicy women!" one Hunan TV employee told me. Though perhaps not "super girls," women in Hunan are thought to have fiery personalities, much like the red-peppery food they consume.

At HSTV, I had an interview arranged with Nie Mei, the director of the Central Office of Hunan Group. Probably in her early forties, Nie is a native of Hunan with a radiant round face and engaging eyes. She attended a local teachers college from 1987 to 1991 and later worked at the Hunan Economic Channel before moving to Hunan TV's central office. Like many young professionals of her age, she went to the United Kingdom for a training session in 2005.

I remarked at the spaciousness and relative glamour of the Hunan Group building as compared to the old CCTV building I had previously visited. The five-hundred-acre site north of downtown Changsha had a four-star hotel, luxury villas, a twenty-thousand-seat convention center, a workers' dormitory, a bulky office tower, and several studios for live music and entertainment shows on "campus." Indeed, the openness of the spaces was intentional, meant to foster creativity and open lines of communication. Nie remarked that they had moved in after a relatively successful period in the 1990s, but just as the company was looking to expand, "competition intensified and the stations' ratings soured; 2002 was HSTV's toughest year. To salvage the situation, top executives met and carved out a new direction: they decided to focus almost entirely on entertainment programming and youth audiences. The only requirement was to change all cultural programs into entertainment programs with mass audiences and high ratings. Thus, a slew of entertainment shows such as *Who's the Hero?* emerged. The station even adopted the slogan 'Happy China,' created a bright orange logo, and vowed to be a hip network, targeting viewers sixteen to twenty-four years old. Since then, revenues have gone from about US$35 million [CN¥220 million] in 2002 to US$90 million [CN¥567 million] in 2005, when *Super Girls* came around. During the second year of the show, more than 120,000 women in five provinces participated. The show succeeded, in part, because it allowed viewers to participate, which generated a great deal of interest. We even charged them a fee to vote by mobile phone—another source of revenue for the station."

Super Girls did not enjoy exceptional ratings when it first aired. It did, however, attract the attention of Sun Jun, a marketer working for Mongolian Cow, a firm that sells, among other products, Mongolian Cow yogurt. Nie said that Sun had been hired to triple the sales of the already popular yogurt from CN¥700 million to CN¥2.5 billion within a year: "He saw young women as his target and the *American Idol* format a perfect venue. He persuaded HSTV that an infusion of cash from the Mongolian Cow company would help *Super Girls* reach more nationwide audiences. Once HSTV was on board, Sun launched an integrated marketing campaign that included advertisements on television, on the Internet, and in print media, as well as posters in grocery stores and restaurants. The *Super Girls* logo was prominently displayed on Mongolian Cow yogurt packaging. Sun exceeded his sales goals and Mongolian Cow yogurt improved its standing in China's yogurt markets from the third to first place. *Super Girls* became a national sensation."

"It brought tension too," I noted, "especially from CCTV, right?"

Nie quickly clarified: "We are not CCTV's competitors. We do not use this concept. The gap between us is huge. We are far behind them in terms of ad revenue. We are number one among the STVs [satellite TV stations] but we're not one of CCTV's rivals. The market is huge in China and we aim for something different from CCTV. We don't compete with CCTV head-on."

"But CCTV does not think this way," I insisted.

"That's because they are so used to having the entire market all to themselves. What we really need to do is to build up the market together. When Bai Yansong was here a couple of days ago, he said that 80 percent of the income for CCTV-1 came from news and TV dramas. Obviously we cannot compete with CCTV on news. Thus, we have to differentiate our programs from theirs. There is no competition involved when you differentiate programs. We each go down our own path but together expand the market and bring more diverse programs to the viewers. At HSTV, we emphasize ratings and stipulate that the average rating for HSTV programs must be maintained in the top five among the over fifty STVs nationwide. We might rank third among STVs this year, but we know far too well that we will never be able to beat CCTV-1, which is to say that we never aim to come above CCTV-1."

Nie was very careful not to speak ill of CCTV. When asked if CCTV's lobbying of SARFT had created hurdles for HSTV, she said simply, "Have they done that? I don't feel that they have." However, she admitted that CCTV probably wouldn't mind seeing HSTV stumble. "Perhaps one could say that

CCTV is used to being the only child and thus is not happy to have to share with a newly emerged additional child from, well, a concubine." Nie chuckled at her own choice of words here.

"What about the various restrictions on *Happy Girls*?"

"These are not from CCTV. The rules are handed down by SARFT, although people do link CCTV with SARFT," Nie said. She couldn't help revealing a bit of frustration with the scheduling restrictions. "The rules handed down to us are the most strict. Other programs of a similar nature are allowed to be broadcast during prime time, yet ours can't be shown before 10:30 P.M. There is nothing you can do about it. Media management in China continues to be haphazard and to not abide by the rule of the market."

I then asked her about the critical charge that the titillating content of *Super Girls* appealed to the lowest common denominator.

"Bear in mind that the program was not meant for scholars or lofty-minded critics. It caters to the grass roots, especially women and young people. Entertainment programming is what we are able to do well, and this is how we take a stake in the STV market. This tells us that Chinese TV has room to expand and grow," Nie said. "The popularity of this particular program suggested that China's overall TV programming had been too monolithic—not enough diversity."

Nie spoke fast and was much in demand. Her phone rang frequently during our interview. At one point she carried on a phone conference with her colleagues about a meeting with Ouyang later during the day. I took the opportunity to ask her about Ouyang.

"Ouyang is a visionary who used to work for the international exchange division of Hunan TV, where he had proved to be an aggressive program developer. He launched Hunan Economic Channel during the period of channel expansion. This turned out to be a blessing, as channel allocations would soon become very competitive due to the scarcity of resources."

Ouyang Changling and the State of Hunan TV

As many interviewees have commented, Ouyang Changling, now the president of Hunan Group, has been instrumental in helping to transform Hunan TV into a media empire. "Our program strategy is grounded on three 'locks': locking in entertainment, locking in youth, and locking in a national market," Ouyang told me as we sat down together in Hunan TV's conference room. A medium-sized man with a serious expression, Ouyang wore an immaculate white shirt with a pair of black slacks and spotless dress shoes. Perhaps the presence of my local handler, who used to work for him at the Economic Channel, made him a bit overly formal, or perhaps this was how he always carried himself. Whatever the reason, he had a commanding presence that made it clear who the boss was in the room. Compared to this, my sit-down with Yang Weiguang was like shooting the breeze.

Ouyang began with a sort of mission statement: "Chinese television has traditionally put too much weight on news programs and programs of high culture. TV's entertainment function has been neglected as a result. It is good for Chinese TV that *Super Girls* emerged to help break the old pattern. The problem now is that people are rushing in to make cookie-cutter programs, which once again stifles innovation."

Once Hunan TV began to dominate the entertainment niche, other satellite stations in China took notice of the viability of reality competition shows and countered with shows of a similar fashion. SMG's Dragon TV, one of the few privately owned television stations in China, has been Hunan TV's biggest rival in entertainment. *My Hero*, the SMG version of *Happy Boys' Voice*, launched in 2006 and turned out to be just as popular as *Super Girls*. The runner-up winner in the *My Hero* competition in its debut year, Song Xiaobo, had a speaking and hearing disability, which sparked a nationwide wave of sign-language learning and attracted even more viewers to the show. And Jane Zhang, the most successful star to come out of *Super Girls*, did not sign with Hunan TV–based eMedia, but opted instead for the big talent agency Huayi Brothers, which is partnered with Jiangsu TV, another rival STV.

"Nobody paid attention to us when we struggled to get things off the ground; now we are the object of envy and everybody is out to destroy us." Ouyang further lamented, "One problem with Chinese culture is its lack of synergy and the excessive internal friction. Everybody wants to be in your way the moment you succeed. There is an old saying that the Chinese will bid down the price while competing to see who can sell more and bid up the price while competing to see who can purchase more. The vicious competition continues to plague Chinese media. China has no shortage of talents, but we have yet to find a way to bring out these talents and for people to work toward a shared success."

Ouyang has sought to upend these principles, though, with Hunan TV partnering with Shanda Interactive, a Shanghai-based online games and book publisher, to create a new production and distribution company. The joint venture kicked off with a remake of Hunan TV's popular 1998 drama series *Princess Huanzhu*, all of which was facilitated by Ouyang.

"Our local economy continues to stagnate. So what do we do to maintain the lead that we've built? We are pushing to develop new media, new program content, and the international market. The domestic market is now oversaturated and homogeneous. Various STVs with similar programming vie for both the local and national markets. The resulting programs are not distinguishable from one another. So the market structure is cumbersome, with too many channels broadcasting similar programs." What Ouyang said essentially was that it was a waste of resources to have so many look-alike STVs in China and that consolidation via competition to eliminate the small and weak ones would be the only logical course. However, the current system forbids such an option. "The current TV system in China defies the logic of a market economy," he said. "The biggest constraint in China is administrative approval for any new program. This is a killer. Secondly, there is no copyright protection in China, so *Super Girls* has no protection against cloning.[11] Thirdly, there are local bulwarks in the Chinese market. For instance, many local networks scramble HSTV programs to make it disappear or unwatchable so as to protect their own local market. Local protectionism and the monopoly of local market are both killers. These problems can be avoided if we do business overseas. Given that cross-provincial consolidation is not an option, expansion can only be achieved by branching out into the international market. Our first step would obviously be the Chinese-language market overseas. The benefits of going out are multifold. First of all, there would be no more administrative interference in the way of program approval. Second, copyright protection is in place. Third, operations would function according to the logic of the market.

"Yet Chinese TV programming has yet to establish itself overseas," Ouyang said. He offered a hypothesis why: "As you know, East and Southeast Asia have been receptive to Korean programs but not to Chinese programs. For the most part, Chinese programs are geared toward domestic audiences; the motivation is not yet here for the Chinese TV practitioners to make programs that would cross over because the domestic market has been big enough to absorb all of us. On the other hand, the Koreans, faced with a limited market, have no choice but to branch out. Likewise, the room for growth in Hunan is limited, so we need to look elsewhere for sustainable future growth. We perfected our entertainment-oriented programming strategy because we were literarily pushed against the wall, given that the relatively backwater Hunan did not attract big advertisers. I came up with the concept of a 'Happy China' program series as a way for us to cross over to the national market. I also pushed for TV dramas of transregional appeal. Korean TV understands the market much better than we do and is able to produce TV dramas with universal appeal, unlike in China, where a diverse culture dictates that TV dramas often emphasize regional flavors. In China, you could have a drama welcomed by northerners but dismissed by southerners, and vice versa. Some of the CCTV programs cannot even cross the Yangtze River."

Having made a strong presence domestically, Hunan TV has showed signs of its international ambition. In March 2009, Hunan TV became the first Chinese station to sell one of its show formats to a foreign television company, when Thailand bought the rights to remake *Beat the Mic*, a karaoke show. And on May 20, 2009, the network expanded its service to Hong Kong.

Together with some CCTV channels, HSTV is considered one of the first-tier channels in China in audience size. As *China E Capital* reports, HSTV was among the top six STV channels for seven consecutive years in the second half of the 2000s and as of October 2009 has been the number one provincial STV for eighty months in a row.[12]

Ouyang was nonetheless realistic about how far Hunan TV could go to branch out of its domestic market. He acknowledged that Hunan TV has yet to come up with a viable program model that would work in the overseas market. "We do not have sufficient knowledge of the overseas market. Our operational model of combining production and distribution under one media group further impedes competition. Broadcasters have no incentive to purchase programs elsewhere, as everything is already provided in house. TV drama is the only place where production and distribution have been separated, and competition among producers and between broadcasters has brought out many quality dramas. For products other than TV drama, broadcasters still hold the greatest sway, as they ultimately get to decide what is aired. Broadcasters monopolize products and therefore profits. This is unreasonable. What we should have is a system where a producer retains the ownership of a product and is free to sell products to the syndication market, the print market, and particularly the Internet market and cell phone market."

Ouyang then gave a concise economic analysis of the auxiliary market for a TV show like *Super Girls*. He elaborated, "The aftermarket for music is not good at the moment. The entire Chinese-language record-album market has collapsed. Many previously successful record-album companies have gone under or are operating in the red. There are two contributing factors here; one has to do with the lack of original songs and music, as most singers and performers only repeat each other's successful records. The rise of online downloads obviously has not been kind to the old record-producing model. The performance market fares only slightly better, as people now prefer indoor, small-scale boutique stage performances over the outdoors with mass audiences. Going to a show has become an expensive undertaking reserved for only special occasions during the year and is frequently associated with cultural status and taste. So the trend is returning to indoor theaters for classical music and spoken dramas and movie houses for blockbuster films. The pop performance scene also suffers from the lack of megastars. For tie-ins to clothing lines, people still prefer Western brands to domestic ones. So the key is that winners from our *Super Girls* have to become real megastars before the market can be tapped for chain products. Their fan base is limited to the show itself. They are not fashionable products like Disney, so there are no followers beyond the TV show."

As a result, Ouyang said that the only viable market after a show has concluded is in new media. "Sustainable contents are what matters in this day and age. This leads to the strategy that I recently mapped out at one of our internal meetings: that building a brand for content producing would be our next goal. We would own the content and circulate it for profit via multiple platforms. It's unrealistic to hinge our success on the television program alone, given that many people have opted out of TV in favor of the Internet." Ouyang lamented the loss of TV audiences to the Internet. "During the 1990s, the ratings for our popular TV dramas reached 68 percent. At its height, CCTV's *Spring Festival Gala* reached 80 to 90 percent. The era of high ratings is over. TV is no longer the only medium for people to obtain information and be entertained."

Ouyang was clearly enamored with the idea of transforming HSTV into a brand-name content provider. "The programs HSTV produces will enhance HSTV's reputation as a broadcaster. Content innovation is the only way for HSTV to maintain its edge."

It is worth noting that Liu Chun, the former CCTV employee who is now the executive president of Phoenix Chinese, the China division of Phoenix TV, introduced Ouyang Changling to me. Phoenix is another formidable CCTV challenger and has outshined CCTV on various occasions, including in its reporting during 9/11. Unlike Hunan TV, which prides itself on catering to popular tastes, Phoenix's audience includes a sizable number of elite white-collar professionals with relatively rarefied cultural tastes. The high-end adult market Phoenix garners is the opposite of the low-end youth market HSTV fancies. Yet a shared mission of having a national presence has brought the two close.

Phoenix TV and Capturing the Highbrow

A Hong Kong–based broadcaster, Phoenix TV was launched on March 31, 1996, as a joint venture between Satellite Television Asian Region (a subsidiary of STAR Group Limited, which is itself a subsidiary of Murdoch's News Corporation) and Liu Changle, a well-connected mainland Chinese businessman. Phoenix initially made its name for infotainment programs that featured a mixture of political and economic news, current affairs shows and talk shows, film and music reviews, movies, and TV dramas from all over East Asia. Phoenix TV currently operates five channels: the flagship Chinese Channel, the only one of the channels to broadcast in Mandarin; the Movie Channel; the twenty-four-hour InfoNews Channel; the Phoenix North America Chinese Channel, which broadcasts on both EchoStar and DirecTV satellite systems and shares the same programming with Phoenix Chinese News and Entertainment Channel; and Phoenix Chinese News and Entertainment Channel, which is broadcast across Europe via satellite Eurobird 1. The network has grown from around two hundred initial employees to more than a thousand today.

Over the years, Phoenix has carefully cultivated a cozy relationship with the Chinese government. In January 2003, SARFT granted landing rights to Phoenix InfoNews Channel, making it one of the few nongovernment-related television broadcasters in mainland China able to broadcast information about events not covered by the state media. "But the preferential treatment from the Chinese government has started to wane as Phoenix's rise began to challenge CCTV's monopoly," said Liu Chun, the head of the Phoenix local Chinese branch in Beijing.

We walked through Phoenix's Beijing offices, which were housed in a building rented from a middle school affiliated with the People's University. Liu, a gregarious and energetic man packed into a compact frame, gave a quick tour of the floor where his office was located before settling down for a chat. "I am only in charge of production here in this building. There are other branches of Phoenix Chinese here in Beijing. We have various branch offices all over Beijing. Our boss's office is at Diaoyutai." Diaoyutao Island is an exclusive area that houses visiting foreign dignitaries and provincial government officials.

"What's it like being in the heart of Beijing?" I asked. "It must annoy CCTV, no?"

Liu laughed. "Phoenix is not going to grow much. Rest assured that Phoenix has reached its plateau. All it has is a good reputation. We are watched carefully. Every reform issued at CCTV was targeted at us. The CCP leadership wants CCTV and other local stations to imitate Phoenix, but in public it denounces us. What assholes." I was a bit astonished by Liu's directness, which is drastically different from Hunan TV's cautious denial of CCTV's menace.

"But you worked for CCTV before."

"Yes, I was at CCTV. I know their tricks, as I was a victim there. CCTV is such a strange media entity. Neither public, nor state, nor commercial. And they monopolize. Their power of monopoly is terrifying."

"But Phoenix has been able to give them trouble, so much so that they are now consistently compared unfavorably to you."

"What we have on our side is nothing more than public opinion. Everybody is sick and tired of CCTV, yet CCTV is still all encompassing. You can go out of your wits dealing with CCTV. So when one or two little bean sprouts emerged from our side, people imagined them to be giant trees. In reality we don't have the power of a giant tree. We only stand out in news and current affairs commentary shows. CCTV has a monopoly on everything else, so you can't beat it. Let me give you a simple example: Phoenix is allowed to air in only three-star and above hotels and some selected residential areas, such as affluent apartment complexes and residential areas for government and military officials. The for-profit operations that might offer Phoenix TV as part of their attractive cable package in upscale apartments are actually illegal. Viewers in places like Shanghai and Shandong have no access to Phoenix. Beijing is a little better. You can watch us at many places in Beijing."

"I guess the restricted access further helps cultivate Phoenix's exclusivity."

"We are eager to be raped," Liu said in colorful language. "We're allowed landing rights in the Pearl delta area, but our commercials are replaced with the local commercials. We don't care, as we are happy just to be available. Yet, as a commercial network, this makes it hard for us to survive. I see no future here."

"Do you mean Phoenix TV?"

"No, I mean Chinese TV in general. I see no future in Chinese TV. TV is the weakest link in China's economic reform, though the overall reform in China is a mixed bag, as, for instance, reform on state enterprise in recent years under Wen Jiabao's reign has retreated to more state and less individual shareholders. Reform in the TV sector has lagged behind print media. You are allowed to apply for a license to publish a newspaper at a city different from where you are from. Yet television continues to be locally operated, though people do manage to bait and switch by registering with a local firm and investing in a local operation. But that's no solution."

"What do you see as the most fundamental problem in Chinese media?" I asked.

"The desire of the state establishments to keep it all to themselves. The synergy between the rich and the powerful is obscene in China. The Chinese government is investing CN¥45 billion in improving its image, and all that money had gone to *People's Daily*, Xinhua News Agency, and CCTV. Nothing is spared for NGOs and small communities that could actually benefit from the investment. The policy makers know far too well that nonstate media organizations such as Phoenix TV would have been in a better position to promote China's image overseas, but they did not give one cent to us because they wanted to keep the money for their own people. Many of the people who are heading the state-run enterprises are sons or daughters of the party leaders." After a short tirade against China's princelings and crony capitalism, he continued. "The problem with Chinese television is that it's become a dead knot—hard to untie. In fact, it will explode if you try to untie it. I have written articles about the dismal future for Chinese TV under our current system. I'm putting my bets on the new media. The death of Chinese TV has everything to do with the fact that the entire system revolves around supporting and protecting CCTV. Every policy from SARFT is to the benefit of CCTV."

Liu used to work for CCTV's *News Probe*. In his view, CCTV's monopoly extends to its hoarding of human resources. "Eighty percent of talented people are now under CCTV, but what have they accomplished?"

"Well, Zhang Jie wants to do enlightenment programs."

"Zhang Jie's problem is that he is all talk. You should do more and speak less in China. I don't usually use this term 'enlightenment.' Zhang Jie needs to learn to let go. He wants to do programs about democracy and freedom, but they don't want such programs. What's the point in agitating them? There are other things you can do. For example, I have done quite a few programs about the Sino-Japanese War in the 1930s and 1940s. My program *The Departed General*, for which I myself have produced close to seventy episodes now, tells the story of the army generals from both CCP and KMT who died during the Sino-Japanese War. It completely reversed the history told by the standard CCP textbook.

"I am no Zhang Jie. I have got no lofty ideals. I am not an idealist. I'm only in it to advance my career. I have no interest in changing the world. Zhang is much loved by overseas scholars. The talks he gave at various universities are well attended by college students. It would suffice to tell the truth in China," Liu said. He repeated again, "I never use the term 'enlightenment.' 'Enlighten-ment' sounds elitist to me. Zhang Jie equates himself with Voltaire and the like now? Why don't I associate myself with idealists? I have come into contact with many self-acclaimed idealists and have seen the hypocrisy behind their lofty appearances. Their hidden desire for power makes me fearful. Their dictatorial thinking is worse than the people currently in charge. I believe in a good system. A market economy unadulterated by the state would naturally lead to sound development. So no need for a few illuminati to enlighten people. A market economy would not lead to degrading programs on TV. Competition would eliminate programs with poor quality. The transformation of *Southern Metropolitan Weekly* from a tabloid newspaper to a highbrow one is the result of market competition that rewards quality content. Of course, the market needs a variety of programs. Audiences for Phoenix programming do not cross over with audiences for HSTV. HSTV caters to a young and less-educated population. You can see that many restaurants have their channels turned to HSTV. I find the entertainment programs on HSTV nauseating."

What about CCTV's new round of reform? I asked him.

"Well, it's all top down, which is not effective. There have been similar reforms in the past. For instance, the complaint about *National News Bulletin* led to the stipulation that the length of news reports on party meetings ought not to exceed two minutes. Limits were imposed on the length of reports on the central leader's activities. International news should be allowed to lead the news, and so on and so forth. Well, the problem is that, in practice, it would be up to the relevant people at CCTV to decide what to include and what to exclude, a delicate and indeed perilous exercise that might come back to haunt them. Which leaders' activities were to be included and at what length? Why this one but not that one?

"So the pressure was high and CCTV gave up and *National News Bulletin* resumed its traditional way of doing things. So far as the reform on *News Bulletin* is concerned, I think they should focus exclusively on news about the activities of the CCP leadership and central and local governments. These reports are valuable information that only CCTV can provide. I personally love the news about the whereabouts of Hu Jintao or Wen Jiabao. The program should be called *Zhongnanhai Frontline*. CCTV had no business in doing international news. The old-timers like Sun Yusheng did have ideas about how things should run, but the time is different now. Sun's old ideas might not apply to the current situation. Political and professional needs often trump one's desire for innovation. He was a producer years ago, but now he's the deputy president, so his perspective would have changed. He is in close contact with people in power and is therefore less free to do what he wants to do. Hard to accomplish things that are handed down from the top, as he would be watched very carefully every step of the way. During the Yang Weiguang era, nobody paid much attention when we experimented with *Oriental Horizon*, so we were able to accomplish quite a bit."

With so few positive things out of Liu's mouth, it was refreshing to hear him praise Yang Weiguang. Liu actually spoke in defense of Yang when I questioned the conflict of interest in Yang's introduction of commercial considerations into the CCTV operation. "It must have been a dilemma for him. It was a chaotic time. Regardless, Yang tried to extend CCTV's function to public relations and surveillance of government wrongdoing. During Zhao's time, CCTV relentlessly pushed for ratings, and the result was the proliferation of programs that catered to the least common denominator. *The Lecture Room* was supposed to impart knowledge and critical thinking, but it has turned into a place for voodoo history and old wives' tales—so lowbrow that it's obscene, a total disgrace."

"Well, Zhao Huayong is gone now, and the new head of CCTV comes from the Ministry of Propaganda."

"The entire media leadership is from the Ministry of Propaganda. The power is highly concentrated in the hands of these few."

I asked him why he left CCTV for Phoenix, but he ignored my question. Later it dawned on me that he thought the question was insulting: I was supposed to acknowledge that Phoenix is far better than CCTV.

After several repeated probes about his departure from CCTV, Liu snapped, "Would you ask an American why they move from one place to another? The reason is very simple for me—the pay is much better. Many people have asked me the question, and what they wanted to hear is that I chose to leave CCTV for ideological reasons and that I wanted to have freedom of expression. But I only cared about a larger paycheck. My salary at Phoenix is four times my pay at CCTV. If a different place or CCTV offers to pay me four times as much as I am paid now, then I would accept without hesitation. I now want to work for new media for the same reason: money. I'm interested in stock options and dividends. One of our hosts left for Baidu before the company went public, and now he is a billionaire. No such chance working in the TV sector. The only way you can get rich working for CCTV is to play dirty and amass a fortune via bribes and kickbacks, which have been common practices among the rich CCTV employees. People trade airtime for money. An item on *News Bulletin* is worth a lot of cash. Secondly, I like to change places every now and then. I would get bored staying at one place longer than three to five years. If I were in my twenties, I wouldn't mind working for a local station such as Chongqing TV or Shenzhen TV. I actually called it quits with CCTV before the opportunity at Phoenix came along. At the time I was contemplating going back to teaching at a university. But the pay was way too low. I have tendered my resignation three times at Phoenix now. I was lucky that I did not leave. With the current conditions, I would have no better place to go."

"Why haven't many more people in CCTV chosen to leave, then?"

"They have got no place else to go," Liu said flatly. "The system restricts mobility, and other state-run stations are even less attractive than CCTV. Also, people at CCTV have grown accustomed to a certain way of doing things, and they would be lost outside of their comfort zone. When Zhang Jie does a story, for instance, he sends his team to the location. Let's say they are doing a story about crime and punishment and need to have access to a prison. The local government would have to cooperate and make things happen for CCTV. So the local prison door would be open to CCTV. Phoenix does not have this kind of access. For one thing, only state-run TV is allowed to access prisons. CCTV's access breeds arrogance. We use a lot of people for our production, including borrowing from other stations. But never from CCTV, as they have high expectations regarding pay and production budget and treatment. They bully other people."

"But CCTV has done some interesting programs, including *The Rise of the Powerful Nations*, no?"

"It's an accident. The follow-up to *Power*, *The Great Renaissance*, is only a so-so program. All good CCTV programs are accidents. You can't do a quality program under the watchful eyes of the censor. The success of *Power* also has something to do with its title, which is misleading, as many people thought that it was about the rise of China as a great power. It's a good program nevertheless, what CCTV should be doing. Chen Xiaoqing should do something like this. I would go on and make one about how the powerful nations deal with societal conflicts and environmental issues."

"Speaking of Chen Xiaoqing, would his talent be better utilized elsewhere?" Liu was introduced to me by Chen Xiaoqing, the depression-prone producer of CCTV's documentary program *Witness*.

"To Chen, the CCTV platform is the best. He really loves documentaries. The state funding is the only way he can produce quality professional documentaries. He has his own program to screen documentaries, and local stations vie for a spot on his program. He is not aware of his own monopolistic position." Liu told me that a producer at Guangxi TV was granted CN¥1 million to produce a documentary after he promised his boss that the program would be shown on Chen's *Witness*.

Liu, however, acknowledged the benefits of having worked at CCTV.

"Everything I learned professionally came from my CCTV era. I applied the skills and unfulfilled ambitions in my Phoenix program. I regret not becoming a producer before leaving CCTV. We all wanted to be a producer, as it was such an honor at the time. But I might not have left if I were made a producer at CCTV. Leaving CCTV is the best decision I ever made in my life. I caught everybody by surprise when I resigned."

Liu finished college in 1987, the same year I did. He had brief gigs as a middle school teacher and a literary magazine editor before returning to school for a graduate degree. He joined CCTV in 1994, at the age of twenty-seven. People of his generation now take up most of the important positions in media in China. What, I asked him, does he think of generational differences?

"There are three generations at work in media now: people over fifty who hold traditional views, people of thirty-five to fifty who came of age in the eighties with lofty ambitions for change, and a younger generation who sees media as nothing more than a job for a paycheck. Though I admire our generation for our personal dedication to work and to the society at large, I think that the younger generation has it right: work is work and spare time belongs to individual enjoyment."

But what about professionalism, the responsibility and the devotion to the organization one works for?

"The sense of pride associated with working for CCTV has long gone, as the overall reputation of CCTV has gone down the drain. When I joined CCTV, I felt proud because CCTV was a place where my devotion could translate into something grand. I thought TV was a form of art at the time, and making art further enhanced my sense of pride. Also, the pay was better in comparison to print media at the time. I earned a higher-than-average monthly salary plus a housing and automobile allowance. A print journalist earned much less back then. So the most talented people all flocked to CCTV. These days CCTV's pay is nothing compared to Internet companies such as Baidu, where the younger generation gravitates."

Liu is one of very few elite Chinese media practitioners who are not shy talking about money. But has he accomplished anything in addition to monetary gains since coming to Phoenix?

"Well, since 2001, I had my footprints in all of the programs we produced, including *Yihu Talks*, which replaced CCTV's *Tell It Like It Is* as a water cooler–worthy talk show. Another program is *Life's Hardship and Reward*, which focuses on the ups and downs of people living on the margin. These are all popular programs of tremendous social value. I personally produce our prime-time daily documentary program at 7:55 P.M., *The Phoenix Perspective*.

We have done over two hundred episodes of stories on the Sino-Japanese War, completely subverting the established history of the period in the CCP-controlled history book. My program also did a forty-episode documentary on educated youth. The program is our most commercially viable one on Phoenix Chinese. Our documentary programs bring in more ad revenue than TV dramas. Ours are all quality programs, though I made them not out of some lofty ideas but because of the practical demands of my job. Even so, the programs offer food for thought. The documentaries about the Sino-Japanese War changed our audience's perceptions about history, our nation, and the KMT. The value of these programs is certainly not inferior to a story about corruption. Our next topic would be on the future relationship between North Korea and China."

"And how has Phoenix influenced CCTV?"

"Well, Phoenix TV propelled several reform measures at CCTV. Our twenty-four-hour InfoNews Channel propelled CCTV to establish its own News Channel. Our 9/11 reporting forced CCTV to start doing its own live reporting on major international events. CCTV could have done this earlier, but it did not because live reporting is prone to mistakes and CCTV was too nervous to take any risks. But the pressure from Phoenix pushed it against the wall, so it had to start regular live reports on major events. Our programs over the years have produced a few renowned commentators. CCTV followed suit and started its own interview programs with commentators. But their programs do not allow for individuality. The success of these programs has less to do with the depth of analysis or whether the opinions expressed have merit or not. It's a matter of individual style and opinion, much like newspaper columns, where the attraction of the columnist lies in his or her individual point of view. But at CCTV, freedom of expression is restricted, so theirs is not a real commentary program. In a typical grandiose CCTV way, they established an office to hire three hundred commentators from a nationwide search, which further dilutes the beauty of having a few distinctive individuals as star commentators. Despite the fact that theirs are all experts in various areas, and some of them are rather eloquent and compelling, the few colorful old farts at Phoenix still outshine them."

I interrupted Liu to relay to him Yang Weiguang's take on Phoenix's success. As Yang told me during our interview, the strength of Phoenix lies in its news commentary and current affairs programs. Yang tried to recruit experts from the Chinese Academy of Social Sciences (CASS) when he was the sitting president of CCTV, but, as he told me, "People were too afraid to accept our overture. The situation changed after comrade Li Tieying was appointed the new head of CASS and encouraged people to speak up and volunteer for providing expert opinion." Yang contended, "Phoenix's news attracts upscale viewers because they are fast and comprehensive."

"Yang is right," Liu said. "CCTV imitates us on program format as well, even down to the titles. We have *Talk All the Time* and *News Today*, they countered with *News 1+1*. We have an evening program, *Editorial Time*. They came up with *Editorial Frontline*. No matter how hard they imitate, our program still beats theirs in attracting the high-end viewers, including, ironically, CCP's high-level policy makers. The story that all TV stations at Zhongnanhai, the central government compound, are tuned to Phoenix Chinese is true. CCTV's content is too predictable for the central leadership, so they have to turn to Phoenix Chinese for alternative stories and perspectives. They're tickled by our occasional praise for them. I am not kidding that Wen Jiabao's mom records our program every day so that her son can watch it after his long day at work. As our reputation grows, the CCP leaders start to accept our request for interviews for the purpose of image building."

It sounds like he is quite optimistic about the future of Phoenix, I suggested to him.

"Not really. Phoenix will hang in there, neither dead nor alive. Chances are that media reform would not take place in the next five years, so the room for growth will remain constrained. But Phoenix Chinese's future is in China because ad revenue is generated locally—the Chinese population scattered around the world at large is not going to help us financially. We have what amounts to 23 million Chinese-speaking people around the world, the size of an average Chinese province. A local beer company in China has no incentive to have its ad seen around the globe, as people overseas are not going to buy its products. The only way for us to survive is to retain our loyal audiences in China by delivering content that is not available from domestic stations. So one principle I adhere to is that we don't do programs that CCTV is able to do, as CCTV has a bigger budget and better access for such programs. Neither do we do programs that CCTV is not allowed to do, as the censorship rule would apply to us as well—we cannot touch certain aspects of the Xinjiang story either. I only do programs that CCTV can but is reluctant to do, the same news story but from a different angle. I know what the limits are and I am not afraid of pushing the envelope—within limits, that is. CCTV is different. It has more money and better resources, but it also has a political function, so consequently it is more tightly monitored and supervised. While ample resources bring high production standards and larger teams of reporters and producers, CCTV's propaganda responsibilities make it harder to introduce more audience-friendly content or to replace dull and formulaic programs with inspiring programs, which is what I aim to do."

Liu paused and then continued, "But we are constantly warned. We put a lot of energy into cultivating our relationship with the government. Phoenix is half commercial and half state, a strange combination in its own right. This has become an obstacle in our future development. The leadership at Phoenix wears confusing hats. Are they government officials or media entrepreneurs? Is it a family business or a state-controlled business? There is no long-term strategy, as the top-level management at Phoenix is near retirement and therefore not motivated in making long-term strategic planning. Our attitude is wait and see. I'm quite pessimistic personally. I think I'll leave the TV industry altogether. I'm sick and tired of the existing structure of Chinese TV. State capitalism breeds monopoly, which stifles innovation and sucks the vitality out of talented people. Further reform is hard because it would destabilize the existing power structure."

Indeed, the local challenge provided by Phoenix to CCTV does not necessarily generate program diversity, as regional broadcasters often produce and screen content with similar formats, subject matters, genres, and production styles, and even scheduling that follows that of CCTV. Many of the local broadcasters emulate CCTV's structure of multiple specialty channels by setting up their own economics channel, sports channel, legal channel, education channel, and so on. In this "arms race" CCTV is thus pushed to further excel in its own programming rather than innovating or changing its orientation and mandate in any substantial way. The more potent challenge in terms of ad revenue might come from new media, as advertisers have been turning to new media platforms, which are seen as more effective and cost-efficient.

Liu and I wrapped up our conversation and I was invited to grab a quick bite at Phoenix Chinese's canteen in the same building downstairs. The canteen provided complimentary food to all employees. Most of the employees I saw there were in their early twenties. They chitchatted over a simple and quick lunch. I felt more at home there than I had in CCTV's pompous media center.

10

HALF THE SKY AND WOMEN'S PROGRAMMING

Half the Sky is the only program on CCTV that explicitly uses the window of gender to comment on social change. The program's name comes from Chairman Mao's revolutionary slogan "Women hold up half the sky." While this is now adopted as a universal maxim for progressive gender politics and social equality, its lofty ideals point to a lack of equality in gender issues in contemporary China. There has been little room for women in the Politburo's fraternity, and the glass ceiling for women in Chinese corporate life is distressingly low. Meanwhile, women have contributed greatly to China's export-led economy, often being exploited in sweatshops and export-processing zones. *Half the Sky* seeks to address these imbalances and inequalities. The program began on CCTV-1 on New Year's Day 1995 and eventually relocated to CCTV-10 in 2009. During its early days, the program was more of a vehicle for stories about successful female role models than a platform for social empowerment. Over time gender-awareness training seminars for writers and producers changed the style of the program and, subsequently, its perception by viewers. Today, *Half the Sky* consciously positions itself as a champion for women's rights. Much of the initiative for reform has been precipitated by Zhang Yue, one of the program's most visible hosts and producers.

A plump and stylish woman, the outspoken Zhang took over the program as a producer in 1995. "The program evolved in anticipation of the Fourth World Women's Conference in Beijing in 1995," Zhang said. "It is customary for Chinese media to initiate special-topics programs and reports in advance of any scheduled major event. So CCTV-10 put together a women's program at the end of 1994. At the time, many TV stations across China also initiated women's programs, but *Half the Sky* is the only one that survived after the women's conference. Many such programs are contingent upon the special events, so the programs usually disappear once the event is over."

Interest in the 1995 women's conference in Beijing was intense. Hillary

Clinton, the honorary chair of the U.S. delegation, descended on Beijing under tight security. The Chinese government was ambivalent about hosting the
conference in Beijing. At the same time, the Clinton administration, which
prioritized maintaining good relations with China, was exceedingly nervous
that Hillary might be too outspoken, which they correctly predicted.

Hillary was scheduled to speak in an auditorium provided by the Chinese
that could hold a few thousand people at best. Delegates queued up early in
the morning on a rainy day to enter the auditorium. When Clinton arrived
and entered the auditorium, she walked up to the middle of the stage, threw
out her arms in exasperation, and said, "This is humiliating. This is all they
offered the women of the world? I am disgusted." She then proceeded to talk
about the major issues affecting women globally, speaking more forcefully
than any American dignitary had done on Chinese soil about human rights.
She catalogued a litany of abuses that afflicted women around the world and
criticized China for seeking to limit free and open discussion of women's issues. As a number of delegates, including exiles from Tibet and leaders from
Taiwan, were denied visas to attend the meeting and were forced to hold a
parallel gathering of private women's organizations, Hillary's frustration over
China's intolerance for dissenting views was keenly felt in the auditorium. The
foreign delegates applauded, some cheered, and others pounded the tables.
However, Chen Muhua, the former president and party group director of the
Sixth National Committee of the All-China Women's Federation, was not
amused and refused to take questions as she departed from the conference
after the speech. Most ordinary Chinese citizens did not see or hear Clinton's
speech, which was blacked out on radio and television. The official Chinese
press was instructed to ignore her remarks until an official response could be
plotted out. A *New York Times* article reported that "a senior Administration
official traveling with Mrs. Clinton was at pains after the address to explain
that it did not mark a return to a more vocal confrontation with China over
its poor human rights record."[1]

Officially, five thousand Chinese delegates selected by the party were able
to attend the conference, though thousands more interested Chinese women
had no opportunity to apply or gain access to the gathering. For the women
who were able to participate, the conference was for the most part a successful gender-consciousness-raising exercise. "We learned many new ideas,
concepts, and perspectives on gender equality," Zhang said. Obviously none
of this was covered by the nascent women's program on CCTV.

The program underwent an identity crisis after the conference. The largest section of the program had been about stories of outstanding women,

including devoted mothers, hardworking factory workers, teachers, and state officials. "Would merely reporting stories of accomplished women sustain the program? The answer was no, and the program needed to delve into reporting lives of ordinary women and promoting gender equality," Zhang recounted.

Yet shows from that inchoate period were naive and even alarmingly uninformed. While spotlighting women who were mostly sidekicks or accessories on other programs, it lacked a progressive gender consciousness. "Concepts from traditional culture created gender blind spots," Zhang explained, "and the show unwittingly broadcast episodes from the perspective of China's male-dominated culture. Nobody in the production team understood what counted as women's perspectives and issues. Women's studies was nonexistent in Chinese academia."

Zhang admitted being naive at the time about women's issues as well. She shared an anecdote about a story she produced regarding the arrival of a male teacher at a Beijing preschool. Traditionally all preschool teachers are women; hence, teachers are uniformly called *ayi* (auntie). The story suggested that it was great to have a male presence in preschool education, as a man would bring humor, bravery, and decisiveness, traits the program producers claimed were missing from young students, especially boys, who became sissies under the exclusive tutelage of female teachers. As my jaw dropped, Zhang let out a hearty laugh. "The producers of the programs were influenced by a traditional male chauvinist perspective and thus viewed women from the perspective of gender stereotyping. We obviously failed to represent the full spectrum of modern women's roles and identities." Zhang told me that during the taping, the featured male teacher basically asked the girls to play with dolls when he played army with the boys.

"Only our executive producer was enlightened about the issue at the time, and she was furious about the story. Others saw nothing wrong," Zhang recounted. The executive producer at the time, CCTV's senior editor and artistic director Sun Suping, rebuked the producers. Zhang felt her criticism was a bit harsh at the time. "I'd have made the program with the same angle back then," she admitted.

Another anecdote involved stories on female prostitution. On June 30, 1995, a report aired under the title "Women, Please Respect Yourselves!" The title reflected the program's stand on female prostitution, laying the blame squarely on the prostitutes rather than discussing social conditions such as poverty, lack of female support networks, male predatory sexual practices, and so forth, that had led to female prostitution. Remarkably, the program castigated women for "not respecting themselves" and swiftly turned a "women's problem" into "problem women." It attributed the lack of gender equality in society to a woman's inferior character traits and encouraged women to respect and strengthen themselves on their own. The episode is an example of how a women's program unwittingly became a vehicle for sexual oppression.

Even with such inherent flaws, at the time the program attracted buzz for being the first women's program on CCTV. But the real excitement came from the fact that it was one of two programs (the other being the news show *Oriental Horizon*) that allowed producers and hosts a free rein in talent recruitment, financial management, and editorial content. The autonomy meant that program producers had the authority to make most day-to-day decisions—except on particularly sensitive topics, which had to be submitted to higher-ups for final approval. Even with such a restriction, the program had a relatively free hand, especially compared to its fellow shows, and the freedom proved conducive. Despite early trials and errors, the diversity of topics was enviable.

But first of all, more gender-awareness training was in order to ensure the quality of the program, especially after several early misguided stories. Shou Yuanjun, who became editor in chief of the program in October 1996, organized training for the entire staff in November 1997, September 1998, and December 2000. At the first session, in November 1997, two female scholars reported on their research examining images of women in advertising. The two scholars' militant argument about the exploitative nature of female images in advertising met resistance among the producers, writers, and directors, as they refused to accept the conclusion that advertisements deliberately exploited female sexuality for male pleasure. The heavy-handed lecture did not sit well with the seasoned producers and writers at the program. Another gender-training session took place one year later, utilizing a more participatory and interactive style. This time employees were more receptive. The tone of discussion was moderate and enthusiastic throughout. Zhang told me, "The first time they just forced ideas down our throats, and even I couldn't accept it. The second time my gender consciousness began to awaken." She told me that a male colleague confessed tearfully to the group that he was a wife beater. He explained that he lived in a small city in northern China where men considered wife beating their natural right. The gender training raised his consciousness about spousal abuse and domestic violence and he became ashamed about his behavior. "He later apologized to his wife," Zhang reported.

"Even nowadays, many people still consider beating their wives an honorable thing to do," Zhang said. "I was in northeast China the other day, and a group of men came to me, telling me that our program was misguided and that there was nothing wrong with beating up one's wife because that was the only way to train a good wife. Domestic violence is an age-old problem, and we are up against deep-rooted traditions in rural China. Furthermore, many consider this a domestic matter that the state has no business interfering in."

"That's news to me," I said. "Mao's regulation was all encompassing, with no boundaries between public and private. He even regulated sex."

Zhang explained, "Domestic violence was made illegal in China a long time ago, but traditions die hard. The state stipulates that both men and women must share domestic chores, but men simply do not attend to domestic chores in many rural households. Hard to regulate that."

Regardless, the gender-training sessions were eye-openers. "It helped the production team to recognize their biases in their own approach as well as the gender-discriminatory nature of many of the CCTV shows," Zhang said. "The quality of programming improved significantly as a result of the training sessions. *Half the Sky* has since established close connections with scholars in women's studies and with other colleagues who are sensitive to gender issues. We hold biweekly meetings with producers, hosts, and writer-directors chaired by the editor in chief to select topics appropriate for the program. Scholars and colleagues in the media who are knowledgeable about gender issues and who are capable of coming up with new story ideas are also invited. The process frequently uncovered outmoded concepts the writer-directors had considered normal. In early 1999, the program added a 'gender consultant' to the credits of *Half the Sky*. The establishment of this position was a first not only for Chinese television but also for other fields."

In 2000, as a complete reversal to one of the original stories, the program investigated media reports that blamed female kindergarten teachers for bringing up a generation of boys who were too weak to lead. The program looked at an upscale school that employed a male kindergarten teacher and found that this teacher encouraged the boys to learn martial arts, but allowed the girls to participate in only "suitable" games. The program then interviewed two male students who were about to graduate from a professional teacher's training center in Beijing and a female kindergarten student from a city-run school. The two male educators believed in gender segregation in education so that boys would be taught science and computers and girls sewing and embroidery. By the end of the program a female kindergarten teacher spoke out against gender stereotyping. In her opinion, boys and girls were the same, and there should be no distinctions between them in the curriculum. She did not agree that boys would develop a weak character because of female teachers. She said that female teachers were also brave and tough, and she went further, posing the question: "If boys are the future pillars of the society, then what are the girls?"

"This certainly sounds like progress, although the feminist turn in the end feels a bit forced, not very convincing," I remarked. Zhang shrugged. "Obviously it takes time and experience to perfect our craft.

"Our program also shifted its focus from model workers and celebrities to women living on the margins. We did stories about laid-off workers, rural women, migrant workers, young women kidnapped and sold for marriage, girls deprived of education, women with AIDS, the disabled, the pregnant, and so on. We wanted to broaden our scope and raise audience awareness of people living in hardship," Zhang said.

As the show expanded its focus to the real rather than the ideal woman, it uncovered serious social issues lurking underneath superficial progress in gender equality. Zhang gave me an example that involved the traditional way that employers have allocated housing to new employees. It has been the ritual since the founding of the PRC that work units provide housing in the form of apartments for employees. The apartments are allocated only to men who are ready to marry, so a woman must marry a man and request an apartment through his work. Single women are thus shut out of the housing allocation entirely. *Half the Sky* did stories about this practice, pointing out the gender discrimination. The program has done many such "rights protection" stories, which reveal gender bias.

Zhang and I discussed the misguided notions of equality during Mao's era, which promoted genderless women devoid of femininity. "We were made aware of the trap of the erasure of differences between male and female by the Women's Conference in 1995," Zhang said. "The program has since tried to overcome the artificial equality that Mao prescribed decades ago. The call for equality under the basis of difference is a big leap in the evolution of China's indigenous feminist thinking."

Are her target audiences exclusively women? I ask Zhang.

"We define our program as a women's program, that is, a program for women. But the funny thing is that research suggests we actually have more male viewers than female viewers."

I told her that prior to our interview, Xu Jiansheng, the editor in chief of the highbrow *World Cinema* journal, asked whom I was going to talk to next at CCTV. I said I was researching a program that he probably didn't know. "Try me," he said. "*Half the Sky*," I told him. He not only knew the show but was also a fan of the host, and when I relayed his compliment and admission to Zhang, she and I had a good laugh about the surprising number of curious and inquisitive male viewers.

Our conversation turned to the issue of ratings. "Huge pressure," she said. They were issued warnings several times. "It is extremely difficult to keep up with other shows while on CCTV-1, which is the most competitive of all CCTV channels."

"Your program has nevertheless lasted. I am aware that many women's programs on local stations come and go."

"Two things made our program last. One, we have a solid foundation. We made the crucial transition from just featuring accomplished women to actually tackling everyday issues facing real women. Ours is not a lifestyle program that focuses on fashion and consumption, nor is it a domestic program dealing with familial relationships. None of these would have lasted this long. We're successful already, if you compare the limited numbers of programs on CCTV that have lasted this long. Over the last decade, our program has, for the most part, functioned as a watchdog for gender equality. We are actively engaged in media surveillance, reporting instances of gender bias and abuse in official and popular culture. Though we do not want all stories to be about the battle of genders, we are clear in our mission to be the guardian of Chinese women."

Even with such ideals, ratings pressure has forced the program to add the occasional hard-edged and practical-skill-oriented stories in addition to purely enlightening stories. So the program started to do stories about criminal investigations of rape, murder, and other forms of extreme violence, as well as practical stories that teach life skills like cooking and sewing, both of which are popular with the audiences.

"I used to refuse to look at the rating charts, as I was afraid that I'd let the chart dictate the types of stories I do. I insisted on pursuing stories of ordinary instead of extraordinary women. Yes on life and no on hyperdrama. Moving but not stirring. I had to modify my personal program philosophy the moment I was put in charge of a production team. As a producer, I have to worry about ratings and commercial returns, as there are over forty people working for me and their livelihoods are dependent upon me. I have no choice but to pay attention to ratings. I have to read, you could even say 'study,' the weekly ratings chart, though I continue to be apprehensive of stories of a sensational nature. Rousing topics would further worsen our living conditions, which are quite violent as it is. I make compromises by selecting popular topics that I don't fancy but can tolerate. Stories about relationships, however melodramatic at times, could work. Celebrity interviews are fine too."

Responding to ratings pressures, the show started to bring back celebrities.

In fact, most of the shows featured celebrities in the few months prior to our interview. "There is nothing wrong with devoting episodes to stars and celebrities, as they are human beings as well. The problem is that it is difficult to have a real quality conversation with people in the spotlight, as they tend to be guarded and the program can seem insincere and shallow. If a dialogue cannot be frank, then I'd prefer not having it," Zhang said. "What I like to avoid are crime stories, especially stories of rape, which frequently amplify and in turn glorify the crime itself. Featuring a rape victim and asking her to discuss her experience of being violated is a terrible thing to do. It is like pouring salt on the wound. We try to maintain balance by not betraying what we believe and what we set out to achieve."

Half the Sky has not been helped by what appear to be CCTV's perplexing scheduling decisions. From 1995 to 1997, the program was forty-five minutes long and aired midmornings from Thursday to Sunday. Between 1997 and 2003, the program was reduced to the now standard thirty minutes, but it retained the same schedule. Starting in 2003, the program was moved to a late-afternoon slot that ran every weekday. At the time of our conversation, the program continued to run on weekday afternoons, paradoxically, when professional women are all at work and only the retired and the unemployed are around to catch the program.

"The scheduling does not make much sense to me," I said. "Do you complain?"

"No, media practitioners in China do not whine about our environment, as we can only work with the cards that we are dealt." She explained that when they were advocating on behalf of the program, all prime-time slots were taken. Zhang said that from CCTV's perspective, *Half the Sky*, like children's programs and programs for minorities or workers, are narrow niche programs, while prime-time slots are reserved for programs with broader appeal. Zhang felt the need to clarify her position on scheduling: "I want to add one more point, which is that we failed to make our program as influential as *Oriental Horizon*, which initially had the same lousy time slot at 7 A.M. but was later moved to prime time, as it demonstrated its ability to reach a wide range of audiences. *Oriental Horizon* gained the right to be on prime time, but we failed to match up. So it is our own responsibility."

For a month or two in summer 2006, the program was moved to the 4 A.M. time slot, which caused an outcry from its loyal audience. It was quickly moved back to its late-afternoon slot.

"I've never dreamed about grabbing a prime-time slot but a midnight slot would be a coup." Zhang speculated that people who watch TV at midnight might be the audiences more suitable for the program. "Hard to tackle complex issues for a daytime program with daytime audiences."

"Why not establish a women's channel, then?"

"The concern might be with how to fill the time if you do open an entire channel catering to women," she said.

However, she told me that it was an honor to be on CCTV-1, no matter how bad the time slot is. "Being kept on CCTV-1 means that CCTV values the program. It is to CCTV's leadership's credit that the program stayed on CCTV-1 for all these years." At the time of our interview, though, Zhang was not at all aware of what was yet to come: in fall of 2009, the program was canned from CCTV-1, a casualty of CCTV's restructuring. But perhaps this is all for the better, as leaving CCTV-1 means that the show is subjected to less ratings pressure.

Even before the cancellation of *Half the Sky* from CCTV-1 and its shift to mornings on CCTV-10, Zhang was already considering what the show might be like without having to compete so desperately for eyeballs. "What's your ideal program without the ratings pressure?" I asked.

Zhang paused to think. "Well, I am not sure about the ideal program. But I certainly know aspects of the program I do not like. The format of our program varies from in-studio interviews to field shooting, and there is also the talk format with audience participation. Three years after I began to work for *Half the Sky*, I became bored, tired of talking nonsense on a daily basis. I wanted to quit but did not know what I wanted to do. Talk shows were all the rage, and our program was adopting the same talk-show format, with me chatting away with guests on issues ranging from what's better for a woman, obtaining financial independence or catching a good husband, to how to deal with your in-laws. Basically what you do is to bring to the studio two groups of people with opposing opinions and let them fight it out. The format created a lively atmosphere for audience participation, but I personally did not find much inspiration or meaning in this type of program. No definitive conclusion would come out of these 'debates' anyway, as many of the issues are within domestic and personal confines and no yardstick could be established. To me, this type of program was a waste of media resources, though I became a well-known figure by doing this same type of program." Zhang chuckled. "I was pretty good at chatting away and instigating debates."

In fact, she was excellent, a natural. Zhang was granted her own talk segment on the show *Who Is Coming to Visit* in 1998. The first guest was the well-known female host from *Oriental Horizon*, Fang Hongjin, discussing the topic of whether it was better for a woman to work or be a housewife. During the show's first year, celebrities including news anchor Bai Yansong and film director Feng Xiaogang appeared as guests.

As Zhang reminisced about her program experiences, she told me that she started out doing the weekend program. As the weekend schedule phased out, she took over one weekday program. Eventually CCTV settled on her being the sole host of the thirty-minute program in 2007. She is in charge of her own production unit. "Before I started working at CCTV, hostesses were all professionally trained broadcasters with pretty faces and beautiful voices delivered in a standard and formal manner. They functioned merely as readers and were not accustomed to expressing their personal views. They stuck to their prepared script. They were not spontaneous and colloquial. Starting in the 1990s, CCTV wanted to break the monotonous pattern and brought in new talents that defied conventions. I, among others such as Bai Yansong, who came earlier, and Cui Yongyuan, who came later, emerged as a new face with an alternative delivery style. No longer made by a cookie cutter, each of us had our own style and our own way of thinking. There was room for us to throw some of our own views into the stories we did. Audience responses were mixed, especially to my appearance. Given that I was not your usual beauty-pageant type, letters were written to the CCTV president, asking if all beautiful women in China had died and they had to put such an ugly and fat woman on to insult the audience. Some speculated that I must have gotten this job through some high-level connection. But others enthusiastically heralded my arrival, calling it the beginning of an era of Western-style broadcasting."

A graduate in Chinese literature from Beijing Normal University in 1988, she initially was a teacher at Beijing Finance and Economy College, where she became known for her eloquence and quick wit. Zhang started to write comic skits and became involved with various programs on CCTV through her classmates who went to work for CCTV. "Weight Loss," one of her comedy skits based on her own experience, was performed on CCTV, featuring well-known actors. "I notified the entire world to watch my masterpiece on TV, as I thought mine was far superior to all others. As I settled down to watch the comedy skit myself, I almost committed suicide, as it was *not at all funny.*" Zhang chuckled. "The experience was so traumatic and humbling that I no longer have the nerve to ask people to watch my programs."

Her comedy-writing career flourished nonetheless, and she was soon recruited by Ying Da, the mastermind behind many sitcoms on Chinese television, to work on what would become China's first domestic comedy series, *I Love My Family*, a show so popular that it continues to have reruns.

As Zhang made inroads in project planning and writing, she befriended the people at *Half the Sky*. At the time, *Half the Sky* was considering a new segment for the program that would be modeled on reality shows in the United States and the United Kingdom. The segment would be called "Good Dreams Come True." The creative team of *Half the Sky* was frustrated, as most of the women they screened as potential candidates for the show wanted to be either models or pop stars. After several episodes featuring young women with similar dreams, the segment ran out of steam. During a casual conversation, Zhang told her friends at *Half the Sky* that the dreams on the new segment had become boring. "If it were me, I'd want to be a chef. I have always wanted to be a chef, but opportunity never knocked," she said to her friends. Little did she anticipate that a few days later, the program would approach her about appearing as a fan of cooking whose dream of becoming a chef would come true.

"They knew that I preferred southern cuisine, so they arranged for me to go and visit with a renowned chef of Suzhou cuisine to learn a couple of recipes." Zhang agreed right away, as she could not possibly pass up an opportunity of enjoying good food and cooking while being on TV at the same time. Zhang put this fun episode behind her once the show had aired. Yet one of the producers of *Half the Sky*, Xie Qing, took notice of Zhang's witty and eloquent remarks as well as her relaxed demeanor. The program was searching for a host for the new segment, someone with broad interests, a quick mind, and a casual demeanor. Zhang's teaching background, literary knowledge, intellectual upbringing, and experience in expressing her opinion in a witty manner were a perfect combination for the segment.

Yet placing Zhang as a host at CCTV would not be easy. Zhang's looks and manner were way out of the usual comfort zone for CCTV management and audiences. "The audiences might have a general strike against CCTV if they put me on without forewarning," Zhang joked. "The normal procedure for recruitment was for CCTV to request my dossier and then invite me over for test screenings. The producer would bring both the written and audiovisual material to CCTV's leadership for evaluation and approval. Once approved, a new hiring would be notified to start working at CCTV." In Zhang's case, knowing that a simple glimpse of her photo would turn off the HR people at CCTV, the producer of *Half the Sky* had to find a way to get around this.

Zhang was invited to be a guest co-host on the show as a writer of TV comedies. "At the time, the network was airing one of the comedies I had helped write. I was the least significant writer among the group. But I was too full of myself to notice that my being a co-host had little to do with my achievement in writing. I sincerely believed that I was this great female screenwriter and went on the show with a sense of entitlement," Zhang said, in her characteristically self-deprecating manner. "And they called me back for another episode the following week. I thought that whatever star guest they had booked for the week must have bailed at the last minute and they needed me to save the show, so I went. Then another call came for yet a third guest-hosting gig the week after. I started to feel odd. They then told me that I should be prepared to return for a fourth show." After the fourth taping as a guest host, the producer revealed to her that the intention all along was for her to be the regular host. "Given my unusual look and résumé, they had to be strategic in broaching the conversation with CCTV's management. Now that they had run several episodes of the program and the audience seemed to have reacted calmly, they could officially make the case for hiring me to their divisional boss. I knew none of this as it unfolded. I had hosted the show for a month without recognizing that I was hosting the show. This was how it all started, me opening my mouth and giving my take on current events, which became the trademark of my show. At the time I was delighted to get a position hosting one episode of the show per week. I was a teacher, and doing the show brought me extra income and made me a minor celebrity, which suited my vanity."

After a successful three-year run, Zhang went through a professional identity crisis, feeling fatigued about the talk-show format of her segment, which predominantly featured celebrities and model (which usually meant traditional) women. "I don't like to argue with people on the show, especially about trivial matters, which was frequently the case." She no longer looked forward to showing up for tapings and refused to watch her own show afterward. "I was ashamed about doing the show and was convinced that I was wasting both the audience's time and the platform provided by CCTV."

She finally went to her producer, calling it quits. They tried to persuade her to stay, promising whatever they could to accommodate her ideas. No, she told them, new ideas wouldn't do, as nothing excited her anymore. Okay, then, they said to her, she could take a break. They would be ready to embrace her anytime she decided to come back.

Few contract employees had ever had the nerve to walk away from CCTV before; Zhang did. She left for two years during the height of her career. "I did nothing during the two years. I shopped, cooked, read, and hung out with friends."

She still maintained a close relationship with her colleagues at CCTV, and they occasionally discussed potential projects together. One day she went to a neighborhood massage parlor and struck up a conversation with a talkative masseuse. She later related the incident to her CCTV colleagues, who agreed that a story featuring working-class women like the masseuse might breathe new life into *Half the Sky*. To Zhang, it seemed she ran into ordinary women of colorful or inspiring life stories all the time during her leave. Would it work to turn their stories into a TV program? For years, *Half the Sky* had sustained itself by mostly featuring accomplished women or women with recognizable faces. Could the program feature nobodies? She and her former colleagues at *Half the Sky* toyed with the idea. She wanted to feature ordinary people and to check the pulse of China through the lives of these women. "The ups and downs of ordinary lives are tightly linked to the changes in Chinese society in the past two decades," Zhang said. Finally, after a two-year sabbatical, Zhang was successfully wooed back to the show with the assurance that she would be able to produce her common-women segments—plus she needed the paycheck.

Zhang started out by doing a story about someone she already knew, a Shenzhen radio announcer, Hu Xiaomei. Growing up in a dirt-poor mining village in Jiangxi Province, Hu had the burning desire to get out, leaving the town where death was omnipresent, as mining accidents were a routine occurrence. She headed south toward the bustling city of Shenzhen, at the time a newly designated Special Economic Zone just across the border from Hong Kong. She landed a job in a sweatshop in a village outside the city, but limited free time and meager pay prevented her from venturing to Shenzhen. She became disillusioned and contemplated returning to her hometown. But home meant that she would follow in her mother's footsteps: getting married, having kids, and spending the rest of her life being a miner's wife. Before making her final decision on whether to return, she booked a cheap tour bus and treated herself to a trip to Shenzhen. During her evening bus ride, she listened to a radio program, a live talk show with listeners calling in to discuss their lives. She was moved by the random stories of successes and failures and wanted to share her own story with listeners. She dialed the call-in show's number upon her return to the factory. She was on the show immediately and poured her heart out. Her story took up the entire show that night, attracting a record number of listeners to the radio station. The station manager was listening that night and was impressed by her spontaneous expression, logical thinking, and mesmerizing voice. She was soon invited to the station for a chat, and there they offered her the job of hosting the show.

By the time Zhang and her *Half the Sky* crew came to interview Hu, she was already an established star in the radio industry. She was one of the earliest announcers to receive the highest honor in the broadcasting industry, the

Golden Microphone Award. Hu's dramatic change of fortune in Shenzhen, a symbol of Chinese hopes and opportunity, made for an inspiring story.

"Since I knew Hu Xiaomei's story inside out, nothing in particular stirred up emotions during our interview and in-studio shooting. Before we wrapped up our taping, we had to shoot some outdoor segments, and I thought that the Shenzhen train station would be a good spot." The crew went to the Shenzhen train station to do the taping and found themselves overwhelmed by the chaotic scene of the arrival of a massive migrant population. "Some might find success here, but many others would languish," Zhang said. The scene from the Shenzhen train station became the opening shot of the program, setting a much-needed emotional tone for Zhang's new debut.

What further solidified Zhang's idea of turning her lens to ordinary folks was a random trip to the public bathroom she made while at the Shenzhen train station. "As the crew did the shooting, I wandered around the station and at one point entered the public bathroom there. I was shocked to discover so much graffiti in the bathroom. I had never seen anything like this before," Zhang said, "Normally, ladies' bathrooms in China are relatively free of graffiti, as Chinese women are more reserved in public. You can only find graffiti at unisex public bathrooms, where the perpetrators are most likely guys. But there at the ladies' bathroom at the Shenzhen train station, the walls and doors were filled with writings." I thought she meant sexually explicit writings and images. "No. Nothing sexual. They were poems about longing and disappointment, simple statements such as 'I love you, Shenzhen. You granted me my wish,' or 'I hate you, Shenzhen, you took away my soul.' One note in particular hit a nerve. It read, 'I have nowhere to go tonight. What should I do, Mom?' While browsing the anonymous writings, I had this strong urge to get to know these people and their lives. Who are they? Where are they from? Why are they writing these? What happened to them? Did she find a safe place to stay that night? Their individual stories are the reflection of China at the time. So many lives were at stake, and I was completely humbled. These are the stories I wanted to do." The emotional encounter cemented her desire to use her time slot to tell the struggles of ordinary people.

Reenergized, Zhang felt good about the segment on Hu Xiaomei. Yet the first rough cut of the segment did not come out as Zhang had expected. The emotional charge was not there in the story. She was disappointed and ordered a recut. When this was done, the anticipated energy was still missing. So the editor went back for yet a third cut. Still she was not satisfied and lost her patience with her editor. "Well, all the raw footage is here; be my guest," the editor told her, equally frustrated. She went over all the footage and realized that her editor was right. The segment was not as exciting as she had hoped. She apologized to her editor. "I was confused. I somehow equated my emotionally charged experience at the public bathroom at the train station with the Hu Xiaomei story we actually shot. These were two different stories with different experiences." She realized that she was more touched by the less fortunate stories. However disappointing, Hu's story was the debut feature of *A Chat with Zhang Yue*, a full-fledged program in 2001.

I told her that the story of Hu reminded me of a recent story on Chen Xiaoqing's *Witness* about the struggle and courtship between two young migrants to Shenzhen, their successful joint-business venture, and the eventual dissolution of their marriage and joint company. Zhang said that people had commented about how her programs are actually documentaries. "They call it oral history. The topic might be similar, but the way I approach the subjects is different and is distinctively mine." Zhang considered her interview program to be the culmination of her television career and the best representation of what she hoped to contribute. The episodes of her program she felt authentically hers were the ones where she chatted with people on location, not the structured live studio shows. Over time, as she turned her attention to the less fortunate, her interview style changed from an aggressive debater to a sympathetic listener.

Zhang said that the difference between her interview show and the standard ones on TV is that hers are about the shared life experiences of individuals. "The individual stories reflect common themes of our generation and nation. I did stories on the rise and fall of tycoons, on peasant women who lost their zest for life after striking it rich, on the transformation of nouveau riche from accumulating material goods to desiring spiritual fulfillment, on the disillusioned second generation of the rich and powerful who yearned for simple joys and a quiet life in the countryside, on a drug addict's dying wishes. I let people tell their stories without judging them. One story featured a former CEO of a bank who realized that his knowledge and old way of doing things could no longer keep up with the rapidly changing new reality and resigned on the day China joined the WTO. He enrolled in a university, seeking to reinvigorate himself. All in all, I feel that my program is finally in touch, and in sync with the pulse of China."

I told her that I watched a recent episode of her program, which told a story about the breakup of a marriage over the purchase of an apartment. The story involved a man, his former wife, and his current girlfriend, but only he appears on camera and the story is told solely from his perspective. "How could you tell a story about the relationship only from one person's perspective? Shouldn't the program have taken a more balanced approach by bringing in the perspectives of the ex-wife and the current girlfriend?"

"We tried, but neither one of them was willing to talk to us, as they did not want to be seen on camera. The Chinese tradition associates divorce with losing face. The current girlfriend had to deal with resistance from her parents, who objected to their daughter dating a divorced man many years her senior. Thus, we had to approach the story from the experience of the man. His ordeal with earning and saving enough money to purchase an apartment is a daunting task that every middle-class couple can relate to. It's not about who bears the blame for the messy affair of his domestic life but about how the burden of saving for housing crushed him and his marriage."

I pointed out that he came across as very sympathetic, which inevitably put his ex-wife and current girlfriend in an unflattering light. Zhang was a bit uncomfortable: "The bottom line is that no harm was done."

But Zhang's sympathy was clearly with the man who was crushed by the burden of owning an apartment. Zhang told me that many parents now demanded that their future sons-in-law purchase housing before getting married. Bank loans are not permitted. Parents do not want their daughters to suffer the hardship of monthly mortgage payments, which frequently devour most, if not all, of a young couple's salaries. I thought of the new Chinese phrase *yueguang zhu*, which has the romantic English translation "the moonlight group." Playing on the pun, the literary meaning of *yueguang zhu* is "empty-handed by the end of each month," an apt description of many young couples.

"All our featured guests came to our program voluntarily. We take into consideration the potential impact on our interviewees of being on our program and make it clear to them the potential harm it might cause to share their private stories in a very public manner. For instance, when we did the story about 'three companions,' we suggested to the featured woman that we ought to conceal her face and use a pseudonym."

"Three companions?" I did not understand her.

"Nightclub dancers who keep patrons company by drinking, chatting, and dancing with clients," Zhang explained. "But the woman refused to conceal her identity, insisting that there was nothing wrong with her profession. Obviously a program works better without concealment of one's face and identity. So we honored her wish. But she was fired at work after the program was aired. No explanation was offered. People began to shun her. She eventually moved away, disappearing off our radar altogether. I tried to locate her, but to no avail. We finally reconnected on the Internet two years later. She told me that she was still haunted by the experience and that she would need to change her name in order to have a fresh start. This episode taught me a lesson. I had done nothing wrong legally. But I did not feel right ethically and morally. The experience made me realize that human life and dignity should absolutely outweigh all other concerns. When sharing their stories, people might not fully comprehend the risks involved. They thought it would be fun to be on TV but could not foresee what TV might do to them. We started to discourage topics or details of a story that might come back to haunt them. We would make an effort to screen the program for them, making sure that nothing would cause regret and pain."

At the time of our conversation, Zhang was doing her program once a week. While the segment she is in charge of had branched out to include a diverse range of topics, other segments on different days mostly adhered to the issue of the gender gap. "I seldom touch the issue of gender equality these days, as my focus has shifted to the issues of generational gap and the evolving relationship between individual and society."

"Has anyone objected to your shifting focus?"

"Sure, from colleagues to management. They questioned my program's legitimacy, as at least half of my programs are about men now."

"Well, how do you justify that?"

Zhang argued that, in showcasing people of both genders and from all walks of life, her program benefited women more by broadening their horizon. "The issue of gender is embodied in many of my stories."

"Has much progress been made on women's rights in China in the past decade or so?"

"The question is too broad to answer. The situation in China is complicated. The wants and needs are very different between people in urban areas and farmers living in rural areas. No single yardstick exists to measure progress, and there are differences among various interest groups. All in all, people are better off in terms of material gain. But spiritually there is an increasing sense of insecurity and confusion." It was curious that Zhang did not address at all the issues of gender in her answer. It was as if gender was no longer at the core of her program or even in her vision. For instance, within CCTV, did she not see the scarcity of women in top management positions? Perhaps she thought that too much discussion on sexism in society would divert Chinese women from self-improvement. At one point, she suggested that gender-driven stories tended to be dismissed by male colleagues and viewers as "whiny." As one female employee at CCTV told me, "The most effective way of advancing the women's cause is to avoid whining about it." Many Chinese women I spoke to over the years share this view: affirmative action on the ba-sis of gender only serves to reinforce gender inequality. One renowned female TV practitioner insisted on being judged not on the basis of her gender but on the quality of her work. Admirable, perhaps, but certainly not an easy stance to imitate when faced with such overwhelming discrimination.

Zhang continued, "I was chatting with some friends the other day, and the discussion turned to what ought to be the core values of our program. I suggested that promoting social justice should be one of the core values, although we don't have much power in practice to uphold justice. Yet we can still strive to bring out the goodness and integrity in us and call attention to the value of spiritual enrichment by producing programs that deliver hope and assurance to people, programs that can enrich people's spiritual lives."

I asked her how her program has fared in this regard.

"How should I put it? Some problems are beyond our reach. Obviously we can't talk about all issues freely. We can't always do whatever we intend to do in the program. This is a state-run entity, not mine personally. I work here and I play by the rules. But our program can still bring warmth to people and empower them."

I brought up another recent episode of her program, a lukewarm in-terview she did with a popular female screenwriter who wrote the hit serial drama *Golden Marriage*. Though the interview itself was rather staid, Zhang did relay an interesting behind-the-scenes anecdote. Zhang told me that she knew the screenwriter did not want to discuss her divorce. "Obviously we had no right in bringing up the question. It is none of our business whether there is a connection between her divorce and her drafting of a TV drama about a decades-long relationship that survived tumultuous eras, including the hus-band's long-term affair. I would not want to ambush her with questions about criticisms of her work. I did not wish to put her on the spot and force her to defend herself. Our media love to stir up things these days, and everybody hates everybody else. In this damn age, everybody is angry. So I made it very clear to my young colleagues not to expect me to stir up things in my interview. The world is ugly as it is, and I will not add more mud to the already muddy water. I want to talk about aspects of her life and her TV drama that might elicit kindness and a bright spot in humanity. I personally cannot accept the message of her drama, which exalted traditional marriage at the expense of personal fulfillment and love. I am not encouraging divorce, but I do not want to entertain living together like enemies for decades. So I asked her the question of what motivated her in writing such a drama. What's her personal take on the marriage depicted in her drama? I asked similar questions to other featured writers in the series. My conversation with her did not go deep. She did not really articulate her motivation. The drama did not bare her creative soul. The plot line, the main characters, and the final outcome of the drama were predetermined by the production company. She had no choice other than to draft the story that the sponsor wanted. The pay was good. Of course she was not going to discuss all this in public. So the program revealed little about the real her. In real life, I learned later that she is a dreamer, a hopeless romantic who fantasized about love in its most pure form. We actually talked about this in our interview, yet much of our two-hour-long interview was trimmed by my young editors to make way for stirring scenes from the drama. The total chat sequence probably added up to no longer than ten minutes. I did not watch the interview myself."

"The show feels like a promo for the TV drama," I told her.

"I am no longer the producer now, so I am not involved in the final decision about the story. Not that they wouldn't listen to me or respect my view, but I no longer wish to be actively involved in deciding final cuts. So long as the program is on the right track overall, I tried to relinquish my control and not let my thinking dictate the group direction. My values and personal taste are out of sync with the reality of the younger generation as the audience. After many years working at CCTV, I feel like an old fart now. Obviously their way of doing programs caters to contemporary tastes and brings ratings. They are not at fault, as they have to face the reality. As for me, I just need to learn to let go. I try not to watch every program, as I know I'd react and request edits. It is not fair to have my personal view overshadow the direction of the program."

Zhang told me that she frequently felt fatigued. However, the best moment of her CCTV career so far was *A Chat with Zhang Yue*. "I don't need a good time slot or a prominent channel. Give me a midnight time slot and a less significant channel and let me have time to leisurely converse with my interviewee about life and society. I don't mind working hard while earning little. Just don't straitjacket me with ratings and markets and drag me into fast-paced programming. Being marginal is fine so long as I get to do my program in a more thorough and less rushed fashion." Zhang wanted the quality weekly interview program she was doing a few years ago, not the daily program oversaturated with pleasing images and fast-paced gossip.

"TV is still the most influential medium in China, although young people have turned to the Internet for news and entertainment. I must say that the Internet is more like a reader's digest in that it does not provide much independent content and relies instead on whatever is out there reported by radio and TV. Internet does provide broader perspectives and multiple voices. But the loudest voice is still from the mainstream media, so people like me must be mindful of our social responsibilities. I was less aware of the impact of my program on people during my first few years of hosting the show. At the time, my job meant glamour and a big paycheck. I was young and careless then. I have learned to be cautious over the years about what I put out there, as I realized that what I do has an impact on our viewers."

I wanted to know what her take is on the *Super Girls* and *Happy Boys' Voice* reality shows that came out of Hunan TV.

"I have no comments. They should have the show if those are what they want to do. These are not my forte, so I do not do them. I benefited from the era of openness and the can-do spirit when the commercial pressure was not as pronounced. We were all lucky coming out of that era. Now it is difficult because you now have more competition. People like us no longer have a place." Zhang told me that she went to a best-host competition show with Bai Yansong. After the competition Bai and she looked at each other and wondered how the two of them ever managed to get to the positions they occupied at CCTV. "We would never have a chance today," Zhang said, laughing, "as they are all superbly qualified."

I told her that she was being too modest and that her success had everything to do with her unique hosting ability, which is casual, witty, and empathetic, unlike that of some of the hostesses I saw on CCTV, who could be unbearably narcissistic and artificial.

"Not sure if I still have the fire in me," she said. "Can't beat the market, nor the state."

Zhang seemed to be suggesting that CCTV had become a victim of its own aspirations. A generation of producers, writers, and editors who learned on the job about making content was inevitably overtaken by a new wave of graduates educated in the commercial logic of the global media industry. The commercial imperative now tipped the balance toward lightness, toward reality shows, talk shows, and entertainment news. The goal was ratings success, leaving little room for sentimentality and gravitas. In the 1990s, commercialization was initially a revelation, a creative license managed with proficiency by Yang Weiguang. The 1990s was a period in which new formats and programming ideas rejuvenated CCTV's image. But with the increasing imposition of commercial metrics and professional routines, and with the growth of competition from provincial channels, the brand itself became the taskmaster: this was personified in Zhao Huayong. Meanwhile, the state never relinquished its political demands. Now the industry, and CCTV in particular, has two taskmasters, and a growing number feel increasingly oppressed and careworn. But at the same time, most people at CCTV possess a sense of special responsibility, both as media professionals in general and as CCTV personnel in particular. With Zhang, I feel the same sense of responsibility, however jaded.

11

THE NEW NATIONALISM:
COVERING THE 2008 BEIJING OLYMPICS

Anyone who followed China—and even those who didn't—knew that 2008 was a monumental year for China. For CCTV, the opportunity to broadcast the Olympics also proved to be a golden chance to showcase the country's as well as its own rise. The Chinese made huge investments in infrastructure, facilities, and cultural training to ensure that spectators saw China's best side. CCTV was flush with resources to increase its capacity and handle the complex task of broadcasting thousands of hours of both live and taped coverage of the dozens of Olympic events. But these capital improvements were not a onetime infusion; the groundwork for the moment had been decades in the making. By 2008 CCTV had already come a long way in live sports broadcasting. In 1984, the network could afford to send only five broadcasters to Los Angeles, including Ma Guoli, who in 2008, as the chief operating officer of Beijing Olympic Broadcasting Ltd., would produce and provide the video feed of the Beijing Olympics for stations worldwide. By the time the Athens Olympics rolled around in 2004, CCTV had 160 employees in Europe and 300 at home, producing twelve hundred hours of programming. By 2008, CCTV used seven channels to cover the events: CCTV-1, CCTV-2, CCTV-5, CCTV-7, a new high-definition channel, and two dedicated pay channels for soccer and tennis.

Pierre de Coubertin, the founder of the modern Olympic games, advanced a vision to revive "the ancient Olympics as a form of diplomacy through culture" with a view to peaceful resolution of differences and conflicts. For China, which began campaigning to host the Olympics in the early 1990s, hosting the Olympic games was imagined primarily as a symbol of the revival of China's historical greatness and a confirmation of China's emerging status as a major power on the contemporary world stage. Media coverage of the bidding process riveted public attention in the run-up to the host-city announcement.

Preparation for the summer Olympics was in hyperdrive when I arrived in Beijing in late January 2008. CCTV-5, the network's sports channel, had already launched new programs devoted to the Olympics and had just been renamed the Olympics Channel for the duration of the Games. CCTV-5 is China's premier sports broadcaster, with extensive coverage of European football leagues and exclusive rights in China to broadcast the World Cup, the Olympic Games, and the Asian Games. During the Olympics, the channel could even be viewed for free—albeit unsanctioned by CCTV—on the Internet through TVU, a peer-to-peer video-streaming application.

Overseeing the Olympics broadcast was Jiang Heping, the former head of CCTV-International and now the director of CCTV-5. During an interview, Jiang revealed that though CCTV's sports channel was founded only in 1995, sports programs at CCTV date back to the early years, when there was only one channel, and CCTV had even formed a partnership with the U.S. National Basketball Association in 1986. A picture in Jiang's office shows him with Shaquille O'Neal in 2006 when they met in Las Vegas during the twentieth-anniversary celebration of the CCTV-NBA relationship.

CCTV-5 has been a cash cow for the network, ranking fifth or sixth in terms of viewership within the network and pulling in ad revenues second only to those of CCTV-1. Jiang headed CCTV-9, the international (English) channel, before he was asked by Zhao Huayong to head the sports channel and its Olympics coverage. The move from CCTV-9, where he oversaw Iraq War coverage, to Channel 5 in anticipation of the historic Olympics moment, suggests a "Jiang of all trades" reputation within the network.

Jiang initially worked at CCTV-1's News Division as an international news editor in 1987. He was promoted to the head of international news and deputy director of the editorial department in 1996. After a one-year leave to get his master's degree, he was transferred to the overseas service as editorial director of the English News Department before becoming deputy director of CCTV-9, then director from 2003 until his reassignment in 2005. Though working in sports now, he continues to pay attention to news. He said that he watches news for entertainment: "I listen to the radio when I'm on the way to CCTV. I turn to Phoenix TV, CNN, the BBC."

Jiang was twenty-three when he joined CCTV. His excellent college entrance exam score allowed him to escape rural Anhui, his home province, and enter the Shanghai Foreign Language Institute in 1981. A member of the "Anhui gang" at CCTV, Jiang was born in 1963, one of many people of that generation who have ascended to the middle-management ranks within the network. A typical day for Jiang and his colleagues at CCTV includes endless meetings. "From Monday to Friday, every day we have a set schedule normally. Monday morning is the planning section for the week, and Monday afternoon is the regular meeting for all the executives of CCTV, and then the directors' meeting for this channel." The executive meeting Monday afternoon brings department heads together with the president and vice president of CCTV.

As head of CCTV-5, Jiang's main job is to secure the rights to significant sporting events and to approve the broadcast schedule for this channel. Jiang has total control over scheduling. "Every Monday morning, we decide the schedule for two weeks at a time, and we put all the resources on the table, and we discuss all the sports and we give every sport a time slot. Sometimes we have to coordinate with the organizer for the sport." Some sports organizers, Jiang said, lobby him for favorable slots in the broadcast schedule, but he keeps them at bay by not taking bribes.

Jiang said that three priorities determine sports programming. "Our first priority is live broadcast. Live sports are number one. Second are events that have crossover with other programs, such as news and feature programs. Our third priority is the popularity of the sport. The popular live sports are the main content of this channel." The most popular sports in China are soccer and basketball. Table tennis, badminton, and volleyball also get good ratings.

Jiang's patriotism showed when asked about the Beijing Olympics. "A fabulous time for the whole nation," Jiang said. "In my opinion, a successful Olympic Games is the best publicity for the whole nation." Jiang thinks hosting the Olympics has boosted sports in China, and "people are now more emotional for sports. More people are involved in sports. That's the good result for the country." Going forward, though, he expresses a desire to do more for what he calls "elite minority" sports, or less popular sports with niche audiences. The aim seems to be to develop and diversify new revenue sources. "On the one hand is the popular majority; on the other hand is the elite minority. The elite minorities are now also growing. I can give you one example. Years ago snooker was not that popular. But now snooker is quite popular, and the ratings are above average. It's just in the past several years that we promoted this sort of sport. Now the rating is there, the sponsors are coming, and broadcast slots are dedicated to this sort of sport."

Jiang felt proud of the Olympics but downplayed his impact. "I'm simply playing a role, a professional role at CCTV," he said modestly. Asked what the future holds for him, Jiang said, "No one can tell. I never prepare for the so-called future; rather I prepare for the present. I'm not foresighted." This opinion concerning future prospects was repeated almost unanimously by everyone I spoke to in China for this book, and not just the people at

CCTV—academics and ordinary viewers said the same thing. One doctoral student from the Communication University of China explained that planning for the future could hardly keep up with policy changes in China, so it is of no use to think about anything but the present. Or as Jiang put it, "To work on today, rather than on the future," is most important.

On another subject, Jiang lamented that some of the programs his team produced were less than professional compared to similar programs in the West. As an example, he noted that CCTV-5 failed to anticipate bumps along the way to the Olympics, such as the protests and counterprotests that dogged the torch relay. In fact, CCTV-5's inauguration as the Olympics Channel had kicked off on a markedly unprofessional note in an incident that Jiang seemed happy to forget.

The launch of the Olympics Channel on December 31, 2007, began with a personal scandal. Zhang Bin, sports news director and CCTV-5's lead anchorman, held a grand press conference to announce CCTV-5's renaming in honor of the 2008 Beijing Games. As the event proceeded, Zhang was interrupted by the sudden appearance of his wife, Hu Ziwei, a well-known sports anchor on Beijing TV. Hu walked to the podium, grabbed the microphone, and announced to the shocked crowd that just two hours before she had discovered that her husband was having "an improper relationship with another woman." As Zhang dithered, clearly uncertain what to do, his wife appealed to the country's sense of honor before ending her tirade with an apology: "Sorry, Director Jiang." Jiang's mood darkened when he was asked about it. There is nothing he could have done to prevent this from happening, he said.

Interestingly, Hu had precipitated another media fiasco just months before, in July 2007. In the "cardboard baozi" incident, Hu apparently fabricated a sensational story about steamed buns sold by street vendors in Beijing being filled with softened cardboard in place of pork. The report was aired on Beijing Television and even picked up and rebroadcast by CCTV before the hoax was uncovered and apologies issued. Luckily, the CCTV-5 renaming event was being recorded for future broadcast, a common precaution in a country eager to hide embarrassing and politically sensitive incidents, and the scene was edited out of the final broadcast. Inevitably, though, a video of the scene made its way to the Internet. Hundreds of thousands of Chinese Internet users watched the online video of Hu hijacking the news conference to denounce her husband for infidelity. As a couple of graduate students from Beijing relayed to me shortly afterward, "it was all the rage on the Internet."

The renaming incident presaged how the high-profile Olympics would be vulnerable to unexpected events and activists who wanted to draw attention

to their own causes. Sure enough, live coverage of the torch relay was interrupted with protests, which were censored out of later reruns. During the 1997
Hong Kong handover coverage, when asked whether CCTV had any plans
to cover protests, a senior producer retorted, "[We] are here to cover Hong
Kong's return to the motherland, an event significant to more than 6 million
people in Hong Kong and more than 1 billion people in China. How could a
couple hundred protesters have anything to do with this momentous event?"[1]

Things would be different by early 2008. Authorities seemed confident
that they would be able to handle the closer scrutiny from foreign media that
the Olympics would bring. Eager for China to be accepted as a responsible
member of the international community, the state lifted restrictions on foreign journalists traveling within the country and interviewing locals. Meanwhile, potential interviewees were being trained to deal with reporters from
abroad, including how to handle thorny issues such as censorship, and a live
broadcast portion of the Games was supposed to be routine sports coverage.
Of course, it was not.

Just months ahead of the Olympics, China's national image overseas was
tarnished by a series of revelations about contaminated consumer products,
including pet food, infant formula, and painted toys. As the government
struggled to contain the damage, anti-Chinese riots in Tibet made things
worse. On March 14, 2008, violent demonstrations erupted in Lhasa, the capital of the Tibet Autonomous Region, followed immediately by sympathetic
reactions and demonstrations around the globe. Pro-Tibet demonstrators
followed the Olympic torch relay everywhere except in China over the next
two months. French president Sarkozy threatened to boycott the Olympics
unless China toned down its response to Tibetan independence protesters
and opened a dialogue with the Dalai Lama. On April 6, 2008, although the
torch relay ran successfully through London, it was reported that protesters
attempted to snatch the torch, extinguish the flame, and stop the relay. On
April 7, on its way through Paris, the torch had to ride on a bus much of the
time to avoid protesters.

Counterprotests and the Angry Youth

Popular sentiment in China was appalled by the Tibetan rioters and their
global sympathizers' disruptions of the torch relay. While the patriotic pag-
eantry of the Olympics did not excite many of the Beijingers I met, the fracas
around the torch relay and Sarkozy's boycott threat infuriated them. The
Chinese government implicitly encouraged counterprotests, demonstrations,

and boycotts of French products by both domestic and overseas Chinese. Angry nationalism briefly reigned in Beijing. An outraged cabdriver gave me an earful one night about the malicious intentions of the Western media. "Why are the foreigners so agitated about Tibet? The place is an impoverished backwater that our government has tried for decades to civilize," he said, waving his free hand. "Our government has thrown millions of dollars at Tibet, which I could surely use if the Tibetans are so ungrateful," he said. The Chinese Internet, meanwhile, blazed with patriotic heat. A six-minute video produced by a Fudan University graduate student, "2008 China Stand Up!" railed against perceived Western imperialism. The video received millions of hits, capturing the nationalist mood that surged through China.[2] Making matters worse, on April 21, 2008, the Paris City Council made the Dalai Lama an honorary citizen. The next day, the spokeswoman of the Chinese Ministry of Foreign Affairs, Jiang Yu, condemned the Paris City Council's resolution as gross interference in China's domestic affairs and accused it of damaging Sino-French relations. Thousands of Chinese demonstrated in front of Chinese outlets of Carrefour, a French supermarket chain, in retaliation for France's pronouncements. Charles Zhang, who holds a PhD from MIT and is the founder and CEO of Sohu, a leading Chinese Web portal along the lines of Yahoo, called online for a boycott of French products "to make the thoroughly biased French media and public feel losses and pain." My cell phone was bombarded with text messages about boycotting Carrefour, reminding me of the American nationalists who campaigned to boycott French wine and rename French fries "freedom fries" when France vocally opposed the U.S. war in Iraq. Even CCTV anchor Bai Yansong became the target of the nationalist community online when he dared to speak out against the Carrefour boycott.

Adding still more fuel to the nationalist fire, some Chinese criticism of Western media bias was revealed to be wholly justified. Some images and video of the rioting in Tibet used by Western media outlets turned out not to be from Tibet at all (they were from Nepal), and others were cropped and captioned in ways that suggested an intent to mislead. One image on CNN.com that appeared to show Chinese soldiers using force against peaceful demonstrators turned out to be cropped from a larger image that showed other demonstrators hurling something at the soldiers. The cropped image was picked up and circulated by other media outlets before it was debunked. To many Chinese, the cropping incident looked like a deliberate distortion. Adding salt to the wound, CNN commentator Jack Cafferty called Chinese authorities "the same bunch of goons and thugs they've been for the last fifty years," a quote that was splashed across the front pages of many newspapers in

China. Several angry graduate students in Beijing grilled me about Cafferty's comments and how prevalent his thoughts were among Americans.

Reacting to CNN's gaffes, a group of graduate students in Beijing set up Anti-CNN, a website dedicated to documenting Western bias. It instantly attracted a massive following, with netizens pressuring Western media to apologize to their Chinese audience. Soon people added more examples from the *Times of London*, Fox News, German television, and French radio. The foreign media were accused of trying to infiltrate and sabotage the Chinese Olympics effort, making things especially tense for the many foreign journalists on assignment in Beijing for the Olympics.

Though the global debut of Anti-CNN in 2008 caught the world off guard, as Xu Wu reminded us, Chinese cybernationalism actually started during the 1996 Atlanta Olympics as the result of comments made by NBC announcer Bob Costas, who had discussed on air China's "problems with human rights, property right disputes, the threat posed to Taiwan."[3] This was the same moment that an impassioned anti-Western book titled *China Can Say No* had come out to overwhelming popular acclaim. Outraged by Costas's comments, several online groups claiming to represent more than seventy thousand overseas Chinese wrote to NBC asking for an apology. They collected donations online and bought an ad in the *Washington Post* accusing Costas and the network of "ignominious prejudice and inhospitality." NBC apologized. China's patriotic angry youths grew in number and intensity as their online activism brought results.

Fast-forward to spring 2008, when the perceived Western distortion of the Tibetan riots again enraged the angry youths, inciting another onslaught of cybernationalist activism, which again seemed to get results. Several Western media, including CNN, the German-based RTL TV, and N-TV, made corrections to their websites and apologized.

A year later in New York, a Chinese student questioned CNN's Christiane Amanpour about the Tibet controversy during the "Time Warner Presents— Media and Politics 2008" conference at CNN's New York headquarters in the Time Warner building. Together with the *Newsweek* international editor Fareed Zakaria and *Time* deputy managing editor Romesh Ratnesar, Amanpour was part of a panel titled "Defining the American Experience—the State of the Global Superpower—How the World Sees Us—How We See the World," moderated by Wolf Blitzer. Befitting the panel's theme, the Chinese student passionately charged CNN with distorting the Tibet riots in March. The floor went quiet. In answer, Amanpour blamed the Chinese authorities for blocking Western journalists' access to the area. "The blackout does not help," Amanpour charged back. Amanpour later repeated the same line to me while talking about reporting China stories. Amanpour's view is shared by most of the Western journalists who were in China at the time. As one *China Beat* editor wrote at the time,

> In the absence of information, the mind races even as the fingers type, and western journalists are generally trained in such a way that when a government appears to be hiding something, it must be something worth hiding, and so they begin to suspect the worst. On the day the violence erupted, only *The Christian Science Monitor* and *The Economist* had people on the ground filing stories as Beijing Street in Lhasa burned. Everybody else was in Beijing (the city) desperately trying to get as close as they could to the action but to little avail: the government was not letting any more foreign journalists into Tibet. Facing the demands of a 24-hour news cycle, and working with rumors, recycled information, and a limited pool of images and footage from Lhasa, too many journalists relied on preconceived notions and faulty assumptions with predictable results.[4]

While the sloppiness and arrogance of some Western reporting on the riots in Tibet was indeed appalling, it was also shocking to witness the vitriol on the streets in Beijing during those heated moments, even if it didn't itself turn to rioting.

It was fascinating to see how nineteen years after the crackdown on student-led protests in Tiananmen Square, China's young elite rose again in the spring of 2008, this time not to denounce China's authoritarian state but to defend China's national image. And it was not just in China that angry Chinese cybernationalists took on the West. Chinese students overseas emerged as some of the most vocal defenders of China. At the University of Southern California, for one, Chinese students marshaled statistics and photographs to challenge a visiting Tibetan monk during a lecture. A young man threw a plastic water bottle in the monk's direction, and campus security removed him. Right after the incident, I flew to USC for a conference. A Chinese doctoral student who was sent to drive me from the hotel to the conference told me that she was just interviewed by the *New York Times* about the incident. "What did you say?" I asked. She gave me the same quote she gave to the *Times*, "I believe in democracy but I can't stand for someone to criticize my country using biased ways. You are wearing Chinese clothes and you are using Chinese goods."

Back in New York in the fall of 2008, I screened Chinese independent filmmaker Li Yang's *Blind Shaft*, a strikingly realistic film about the inhumanity that pervades the Chinese coal-mining industry, for a graduate seminar at the City University of New York. After the screening, an exchange doctoral student from Beijing expressed her dismay that films like *Blind Shaft* unjustly perpetuate a false image of China as backward and inferior. Her classmates, all of them non-Chinese, tried to explain that they understood that the film reveals only one aspect of China. The exchange student was mild tempered, not an angry-youth type, but her frustration was keenly felt. Growing up in the 1980s, her generation experienced a China that was prospering and full of opportunities. She was frustrated by what she considered a skewed image of China held by the rest of the world and demanded an updated understanding.

In April 2008, during breaks at the USC conference, I chatted about the "angry-youth" phenomenon with fellow Chinese cinema scholars and Chinese expatriates who came to the United States in the 1980s. Together we lamented that the idealism and cosmopolitan outlook of our generation, the "June 4 generation" (referring to the Tiananmen Square protest), had apparently been superseded by Sino-centrism in the new generation. As "angry youths" ourselves in the 1980s, we had decried social injustices, especially the political and legal corruption that plagued China in the 1980s. Now the youths rose again, not in pursuit of liberal democracy but rather in defense of national unity and prosperity. In contrast to the previous generation, which soured on the nationalism that was forced on them by an omnipotent state, the new generation of educated youth seems captivated by an updated nationalist doctrine, a marriage between "wounded nationalism" and "confident nationalism."

Of course, there are others who reject the angry attitude. Changing the intonation of Chinese words changes their meaning. A common re-pronunciation of the words for "angry youth" changes their meaning to "shit youth." Offended by cybernationalism and the angry-youth phenomenon, Han Han, one of China's most popular bloggers, asks, "How can our national self-respect be so fragile and shallow?" And in an email exchange with me, a Chinese scholar with a fresh doctoral degree who now resides in Canada expressed his alarm at the new breed of nationalism. "Their global experiences, either in terms of studying abroad or in the form of voracious reading of world philosophies, has failed to translate into an understanding of the fluidity and artificiality of nation and/or state." Even the party-state understands that nationalism is a two-edged sword—great for the state's popular legitimacy, but also impulsive and ugly at times, with potential to damage China's public image. China's leaders ultimately reined in the angry youths of the spring and summer of 2008 with a call for "rational patriotism." Wu Jianmin, a former ambassador to France, also denounced the boycott of French goods, urging that ultrapatriotism guided by emotion rather than reason would damage China's own interests. The grassroots effort to boycott Carrefour soon fizzled.

Throughout the rocky pre-Olympics news season, CCTV duly followed state directives in its reporting. When the state tacitly supported the early protestations of China's angry youth, CCTV news programs unleashed shrill diatribes against Western media bias. One CCTV reporter posted an entry on the *Spirit of the Night* blog, asking, "Who is really behind the Tibet riots?" and answering that the CIA was responsible.[5] Jin Jing, the disabled athlete who famously struggled to protect the torch with her body when a pro-Tibet protester attempted to snatch it from her in Paris, was depicted on CCTV as a "smiling angel in a wheelchair." CCTV also featured Jin Jing on its popular *News Livingroom*. Li Huan, an overseas Chinese student in France, gave a speech at a demonstration held by overseas Chinese in Paris on April 19, 2008, condemning the French media for their distorted reports of the demonstration in Lhasa. CCTV-9 interviewed him on its flagship program, *Dialogue*. CCTV-9 also reported extensively on the efforts made by overseas Chinese students in collecting and exposing the various inaccuracies in Western media reports on the Lhasa riots. An assortment of foreign witnesses including Tony Gleason, field director of Tibet Poverty Alleviation Fund, Ursula Rechbach, of the Lhasa-based Project for Strengthening Tibetan Traditional Medicine, and Guzman Escardo, of the Association for International Solidarity in Asia, were seen on CCTV-9 confirming that the Western reports were false.

CCTV's tone changed when the state shifted to contain the nationalist outrage. On April 21, 2008, CCTV reported in its prime-time *National News Bulletin* that the chief executive of Carrefour Group had affirmed that Carrefour had never sponsored Tibetan separatists. On April 22, the same program reported a Chinese Ministry of Commerce statement saying that "Carrefour entered the Chinese market in 1995. It currently employs 40,000 people in China, which account for 99 percent of all its employees in China. . . . Ninety-five percent of the products sold by it are made in China. . . . Recently the French government and French enterprises have taken measures to improve bilateral relations. Enterprises such as Carrefour have declared their objection to Tibetan separatism and support for the Beijing Olympic Games. We welcome this." Between the orchestrated efforts of the Chinese government and the state media, the tide of angry nationalism gradually ebbed.

The 2008 Summer Olympics was to be a "coming-out party" for Beijing, establishing the PRC as a global player. Instead, the Chinese state and its tightly controlled media battled with overseas media for framing news about Tibet, Darfur, Burma, human rights, environmental protection, and food safety. By dismissing, instead of facing, the challenge from the West to the legitimacy of its governance in Tibet, the Chinese state failed to make a case for itself in the arena of foreign public opinion. Clearly caught off guard, the government left the task of "making China's voice heard" to angry nationalists, failing the geopolitical public relations war.

The Opening of the Games

Beneath a canopy of haze with occasional sunlight, the summer air in Beijing was stagnant and thick. Both my daughter, Frances, and I were getting restless. After the chaotic spring, the popular sentiment seemed to be "Let's get it over with already." A friend of Frances from her elite public school near the embassy district was selected as one of the children who would participate in the opening ceremony helmed by Zhang Yimou. A couple of years older than Frances, the girl rode the same school bus as Frances every day. Her parents were Iranian expats living in Beijing; her father, who speaks fluent Chinese, is working as an on-camera journalist for Iranian TV. We were invited to their place a couple of times, and the anti-American sentiment ran high in their household. I suspected she had been chosen to perform at the opening ceremony because of her nationality. At any rate, her family too wished that the grueling rehearsal schedule the mother and daughter had to endure would soon come to an end. Eight hundred and forty-two million people tuned in to CCTV to watch the opening ceremony on August 8, 2008.

I had been working hard editing a documentary film, another purpose of my stay in Beijing, during the month leading up to the opening. August 8 was a Friday, my last day putting final touches on the film. I ventured out to the production company early in the morning, hoping to wrap up and make it home by early evening to watch the show with Frances. As the clock approached 5:30 P.M., I ordered some takeout Chinese food and then called to get a cab.

The apartment I rented was on the east edge of the so-called commercial business district in Beijing, on Chaoyang Road. The apartment complex, called Ocean Paradise, is an upper-middle-class residential complex. The film studio was located on the west side of Beijing, normally about an hour and half away by subway and taxi. The subway was always unbearably crowded and taxis inched forward during rush hours, but on the eve of the Olympics opening, I thought that the street would be empty, as everyone would already be home with friends and family, and that a cab would get me home in a jiff. What I hadn't considered was that most taxi drivers would be at home for the momentous occasion as well, and it was nearly impossible to get a cab. After several failed attempts, I pleaded with the cab switchboard clerk to send me a cab so I could get home in time for the opening ceremony, promising to pay double or triple for a cab if necessary. The taxi operator sounded sympathetic, and when my ride finally arrived, I hopped in with gratitude. The ride was pleasant, as there was indeed little traffic.

Reinforcing a cliché about foreign journalists and academics taking the pulse of the local scene, I had grown fond of talking with cabdrivers. They would ask me about life overseas and my views on politically contentious issues such as Tibet and human rights and Falun Gong. We'd get into some interesting debates, which usually ended with me getting lectured about Chinese history and reality as well as China's *uniqueness*. China, state, society, and media workers alike, regards itself as a special case, but also one that could become a model for other developing countries eager to advance in the world but uncertain that everything should be trusted to the vagaries of voting publics and invisible hands on the economy—the Western liberal democratic model. The Chinese public is largely happy with the national narrative of Chinese political and economic exceptionalism driving China's exceptional rise to new wealth and renewed prominence in the world. That is why cabdrivers who don't shrink from sensitive political topics almost always also tell you that China is different and that it has good reasons for its policies that grate against Western sensibilities.

As much as I "enjoyed" being lectured by the Beijing cabbies, I was puzzled initially as to how the cabdrivers could tell that I was not local. I thought I blended in with my Chinese face and authentic Mandarin (though I was missing a Beijing accent). My outfits hardly stood out in comparison with the fashion-conscious urban women of my age. I finally asked one friendly driver, "How do you know I'm not a local?" He motioned toward my seat belt, which was diligently fastened over my shoulder. My habit of putting on the seat belt the moment I sat down betrayed me, as the restraints were considered decorative by most natives.

After giving my miraculous cabbie an extra tip for extending his workday into the Olympic evening, I rushed upstairs to my twelfth-floor apartment.

My little girl was not really alone, of course; she was with a graduate student who had kindly offered her assistance. They'd had some leftovers for supper, she said. The graduate student decided to stay put and we settled in to watch the show together.

The official numbers that came out after showed the opening ceremony attracting more than 83 percent of television viewers in China, breaking CCTV's viewership records. CSM Media Research reported that 10 percent of the audience tuned in for the entire four-hour-long ceremony and 43 percent watched for two hours or more. CTR Market Research reported that 90 percent of the audience was pleased with the artistic performances, with an astounding 98.5 percent thinking that it displayed the highlights of Chinese history and culture. The most popular and most eagerly anticipated moment of the ceremony was the lighting of the torch, to which 93.6 percent of viewers in that time slot tuned in. Of this vast audience, 75.3 percent were pleased with the lighting, and 63.6 percent reflected that they felt very proud to be Chinese after watching the ceremony. The total audience of CCTV-1, CCTV-2, CCTV-Olympics, and CCTV-7 was up more than 45 percent during the Games as compared to before the event started (August 5).

Frances and I left Beijing a few days after the opening ceremony. During that time, we soaked in the round-the-clock Chinese patriotism displayed on TV and in the streets. In the moments we spent outdoors getting around, I was amazed by the sea of foreign faces in Beijing, a scene I could never have imagined two decades earlier when I visited Beijing. As Russell Moses, a political analyst in Beijing, remarked, "Beijing made it plain. This wasn't China coming out to the world. This was the world coming around to China."[6]

Indeed, it would be the rest of the world that would have to adjust to China and not vice versa. Almost as soon as the Olympics was over it was back to business as usual, especially after ethnic rioting flared up in Ürümqi, the capital city of Xinjiang Province, during the following summer. Observing that the Internet and media appeared to play a critical role in setting things off, the state shut down Internet and text messaging services across the province for months afterward. As in Tibet the year before, foreign journalists were again banned from traveling to the scene, and Chinese media were ordered to adhere to the official line dictated by Xinhua and CCTV. Reporting on the 2010 Nobel Peace Prize award to imprisoned Chinese dissident Liu Xiaobo was negative, and the popular protests that overthrew authoritarian governments in Tunisia and Egypt were only lightly covered in the state media, mainly as "antigovernment riots."

The Internet and social media have made it much more difficult for Chinese authorities to simply shut out undesirable news, or even keep it out of the traditional media. Keeping the news of collapsing schools in Sichuan or collapsing governments in the Middle East out of the state media when millions of people are talking about them online would completely undermine the traditional media and drive people to depend entirely on the Internet for news. That is another card that journalists can play in their negotiation with the state, but again, it is not as important as one might think. If news blackouts have become impractical, neither are they really necessary. It is enough to manage the volume and tone of mainstream media reporting on significant events and to dictate the official version of events. The Internet and social media themselves, meanwhile, are subjected to what must be the world's most sophisticated monitoring, filtering, and tab-keeping regime of digital deterrence. As social network media keep piling up points for "people power" movements around the world, and playing host to the world's largest community of frequently irreverent and formidably adaptive netizens at home in China, the party is virtually at war with notions of "Internet freedom" and "netizen" activism and journalism. It still believes much more in "guidance *of* public opinion" than in "supervision *by* public opinion," though both catchphrases are in common use, both conversationally and in the official lexicon of the state's endless directives on the media.[7]

To all appearances, the state's grip on media and information in China remains tight, so despite the social, economic, and technological changes that have given rise to inklings of civil society among the Chinese public; despite the state's own initiative to cultivate China's soft power, including credible and competitive global news organizations; and despite lessons from breaking-news events like the SARS epidemic and the Sichuan earthquake that suggest there is more to gain from trusting the media and the public with information than from overzealous social nannying and ideological management, professional aspirations to greater press freedom still mostly elude Chinese journalists. Of course, this is putting things in stark, simplified terms. As I discovered in my interviews with CCTV personnel, Chinese media professionals, journalists included, generally are not interested in simply transplanting Western notions of a free press and commercial media to China. Many struggle just as much with the tyranny of ratings as with the tyranny of the state, and *like* the state, they feel that media responsibilities extend beyond entertaining and informing to include some form or other of what they call "enlightenment." Although the state is used to dealing with the media in brusque, preemptive terms, the substance of the relationship between the state and the media in the reform era is more accurately characterized as an ongoing negotiation than as a contest between mutual antagonists. The trial and error of CCTV's experimentation with live coverage of major events reflects that pattern of negotiation.

CONCLUSION

CHINA CENTRAL TELEVISION
AND THE CHINESE MODEL

*After a career of more than ten years in the news, I hope that I can lose my
fear, conquer my greed, maintain my rebelliousness, and not curry any favors.
The wise are not puzzled, and the brave are not afraid, but the benevolent
will always be worried.*

—Hu Yong, former CCTV practitioner[1]

In 2001, the Chinese state designated December 4 as Legal Publicity Day,
a one-day-a-year chance for the public to hold demonstrations against ill-
functioning state and private agencies. Eight years later, in November 2009,
a memo to news outlets from the Chinese propaganda chief directed official media to not shy away from broadcasting protests, disasters, and other
unfortunate events. On the morning of December 4, 2009, a few hundred
people from around the country gathered outside the CCTV building to air
their varied grievances. The CCTV building rests on an enclosed twenty-
two-acre plot near the Military Museum. With a tall antenna rising from its
center, the building of thirty rectangular floors of concrete and glass is the
symbol of Chinese state media in all its glory and menace. The assembled
crowd in front of the CCTV building complained about issues ranging from
corruption to police brutality. They were there because, to them, CCTV
remains one of the few major means disenfranchised populations imagine they can lean upon to capture the attention of the party-state. Indeed,
to them, CCTV is the state, a symbol of power even in today's fragmented
media market. Though Legal Publicity Day was spotlighted in a report,
CCTV made no mention of the demonstration that had occurred right on
its front porch. Perhaps it did not want to show images of police vehicles
arriving at the scene, carting away hundreds of demonstrators—ironic since

some of the demonstrators had come to protest the unlawful detention of petitioners.

There were simply too many protests to pay attention to, a CCTV insider who wished to remain anonymous explained to me later over a cup of coffee near the Chinese consulate building on Forty-second Street and the West Side Highway in Manhattan. "CCTV headquarters is a popular spot for such gatherings," he said. "Demonstrators congregate there in hope of attracting the attention of CCTV news teams and in turn attracting the attention of state policy makers, much like these ongoing Falun Gong people outside the Chinese consulate." He pointed to the demonstrators with their pro–Falun Gong signs outside the Chinese consulate. "Though they mostly aim for attention from the Western media. We have enough real mass incidents that small-scale demonstrations no longer hold people's attention, much like the Falun Gong demonstration here," he said.

When I was handed the topic of China Central TV, I made a deliberate choice to link CCTV with China's overall transformation during the post-Tiananmen era. The goal of this book was to examine the role of CCTV in China's evolving state-society relationship since the 1990s. To achieve this, I mainly left it to the media practitioners themselves to walk me through the enigma that is CCTV. Three interesting threads have emerged as a result: CCTV is a microcosm of a Chinese-style state capitalism, a combination of market economy and authoritarian state control; there is a commonly held belief that China's unique history and culture make it exceptional; the employees at CCTV believe ever so strongly in the traditional Chinese concept of sage leadership, which means that powerful individuals are capable of radically shaping the course of CCTV, and for that matter China in general.

A Model of State Capitalism

With ever-expanding multiple channels (currently twenty-four) and an array of cable stations, CCTV is the very model of China's post–command economy, a media conglomerate that is financially profitable, operationally autonomous, and yet ideologically dependent. Operationally, CCTV is given free rein to implement modern organizational practices modeled on major Western media structures. Ideologically, it remains a tool for the Chinese state to facilitate domestic harmony and to project soft power globally. Financially, CCTV continues to grow and to be profitable, despite challenges from regional stations, who themselves are often commercial enterprises under the control of the party-state. The very functioning of the hybrid CCTV and its domestic competitors invites speculation over the vitality of a China model. The end of the cold war might have settled the ideological dispute over whether capitalism was the best economic system. Yet the capitalist system that is taking shape in China is not the liberal democratic one so celebrated in the West as the supreme political-social-economic system.

In his 1989 essay "The End of History?" Francis Fukuyama declared that the end of the cold war marked the arrival of the universalization of Western liberal democracy as the final form of human government and thus "the end of history." Fukuyama has since revised his claim. His recent book, *The Origins of Political Order*, though affirmative of the supremacy of democratic capitalism, seeks to delineate varied paths toward nation building and the subsequent varied forms of political structure. Indeed as China managed to transform itself from a command economy to a state-controlled market economy with efficiency, resolve, and a spectacular accumulation of wealth, the democratic capitalism in the United States and Europe has in recent years been reduced to chaos, bubbles, and crashes. For a while the Chinese-style state capitalism seems to have triumphed, creating a viable alternative for a world caught in an economic meltdown and political turmoil, never mind that Chinese-style capitalism is especially prone to corruption, with the ruling class enriching itself while also ensuring continued dominance.

Is state capitalism a viable system for development? Specifically, is the hybrid model of CCTV sustainable? Though state capitalism taps into segments of the Chinese society's nationalistic sentiment, the CCTV practitioners I spoke to expressed varied opinions about the functioning of an authoritarian state capitalism and its very model of CCTV as a state-owned commercial enterprise. From the perspective of economic development, while opponents cited monopoly and cronyism as evidence of a malfunctioning system, proponents championed the power of an authoritarian state in mobilizing resources and executing grand projects of nation building. Democratic capitalism, as they point out, seems prone to disruption and polarization, which frequently immobilizes governments even in the face of crises. The producer of special-topics programming at CCTV's Finance and Economics Channel, Ren Xuean, and several of his like-minded CCTV colleagues argue that openness, not ownership and control, is the key to a functioning market, and transparency and receptiveness to new ideas are not limited to liberal capitalism only. As they reminded me, while big corporations make money for shareholders in a democratic capitalist society, their counterparts in a state capitalist society create wealth for the political cliques. Despite the differences, the two camps have something in common—both are at the service of their powerful constituencies. Opponents argue that the benefits of "rational and long-term planning" are frequently overrun by constraints imposed on creativity and entrepreneurship. Xia Jun, the producer of the iconic documentary *River Elegy*, and a number of others assert that well-functioning markets must be protected by reliable legal systems and that only transparent and open capital markets coupled with a reliable legal system can unleash China's creativity. But even on this front, Zhang Jie, a producer at *News Probe*, reminded me that progress was being made. Though falling short of coming out to champion free elections, he told me how one of his programs covered elections at the local level, an indication that the CCP might be less rigid than before.

Regardless, the CCTV model has worked so far and the network has been asked to "go out" and test its model on a global scale. In November 2009, President Hu Jintao signaled that his administration would play a bigger role in global affairs by releasing a foreign policy plan that advocated the building of a harmonious world through joint development, shared responsibilities, and enthusiastic participation in global affairs.[2] As Beijing primes itself for a more prominent presence on the world stage, CCTV is tasked with carrying the torch for the party-state on a global scale. Yet as CCTV's most visible news host, Bai Yansong, puts it, "going out" works for CCTV only to the extent that China is powerful enough to command attention, if not admiration, from the rest of the world. At the core of a powerful China is the model of state capitalism that China is perfecting.

Chinese Exceptionalism

While announcing China's intention to be an active and responsible global shareholder, Hu Jintao emphasized that China would "explore and perfect a road [map] of development that is suitable to China's national conditions," which put to rest any illusions that China might cheerfully join a liberal democratic world order.[3] Hu made it clear that the party-state has no use for liberal democratic norms ranging from freedom of expression to multiparty politics. Instead, Hu championed a developmental path specific to China, bringing us back to the century-old China-specificity scenario, which insists upon the supremacy of Chinese civilization and the uniqueness of its developmental path.

The China-specificity theory finds almost unanimous adherence among CCTV practitioners. Ren Xuean, the producer of *The Rise of the Powerful Nations*, was emphatic about evaluating China's evolution from the concrete

Chinese situation and not from the Western perspective. When asked how CCTV fared in coverage and influence in comparison with global media firms such as the BBC, Ren gave me a lecture about not using Western conventions to judge China: "China has been changing and continues to change, but not necessarily moving toward either an American-style democracy or the same kind of authoritarian state that it was two or three decades ago. Stop referring to universal standards or making comparisons with the U.S. and start taking as a starting point China's own history and politics. Chinese media must be examined within the context of China, not the U.S. There is a value to comparative research, but too frequently it boils down to mechanical listing of similarities and differences that provides no real insights."

Ren's emphasis that the starting point for analyzing China must be China is shared by many of his Chinese compatriots. The prevailing wisdom seems to be that the roots for historic change stem from Chinese society's internal dynamics and that China's contemporary transformation can be productively discussed only within the Chinese context. Many at CCTV agreed with him. Ren and his like-minded fellow CCTV practitioners might find an unlikely ally in Fukuyama, whose recent book emphasizes historical contingencies in societies' different developmental patterns, retreating from his earlier claim that all roads lead to a democratic political order, a reversal that has caught the attention of certain segments of Chinese intellectuals and policy makers.[4]

On June 27, 2011, Fukuyama gave a keynote speech at the Equinox (Chunqiu) Institute, a conservative think tank in Shanghai, commenting on, among other things, the China model. Fukuyama essentially recapped his tracing of the origin, path, and characteristics of the Chinese political order while piling praise on the economic miracle the China model has produced so far, before arriving at the conclusion that the stability and prosperity might not last without an independent judicial system and free elections. After the talk, Zhang Weiwei, a Chinese-born scholar of international relations from the Geneva School of Diplomacy, who is also a research fellow at the Equinox Institute, conducted a dialogue with Fukuyama, challenging Fukuyama's criticism of aspects of the Chinese model. In a rather smug tone, with short and punchy sentences aiming perhaps equally at Fukuyama and the Chinese audiences assembled by the Equinox Institute, Zhang derided the U.S. model upheld by Fukuyama and refuted aspects of Fukuyama's talk. I suspect that the nationalistic temperature was high among the audience, as Zhang's militant "rebuttal" to Fukuyama's mild and at times apologetic criticism has "China Can Say No" written all over it. Zhang was clearly relishing the opportunity to score easy points and preach to the hometown choir, and his frequent punch lines at the expense of Fukuyama and the United States verged on heckling.*

Zhang's is the continuation of the neo-authoritarianism that grew out of discussions in Shanghai in the late 1980s, with Wang Huning and Xiao Gongqin emerging as two important thinkers. When discussion of political reform by means of decentralization was gaining momentum during the high-culture fever of the late 1980s, Wang wrote a series of essays that advocated a stable and efficient central government that would make reasonable decisions based on consultation with elite intellectuals. Wang further cautioned that political reform is part of a complex process of change and that a given political structure must fit the given historical, social, and cultural conditions. For China this meant a strong central government at the service of gradual economic and political reform. Though arriving at the same conclusion regarding the path China has taken, Fukuyama and his Chinese counterparts have different prescriptions for a political order. Incidentally, Leo Strauss and his concept of the gentleman ruler, that is, the ideal ruler, with virtue, who is better suited to rule over others, has become familiar to Chinese intellectuals since the 1990s. For the Chinese Strauss followers, his idea of an elite class educated to serve the public shares a kindred spirit with the Chinese political tradition that values sage leadership. The need for a new gentry class to direct China's affairs, to strengthen the state by making it wiser and more just, is seen as evident. Naturally, a leader ought to be selected by knowledgeable elites instead of being elected by the feebleminded public. Zhang nonetheless proposed a combination of election and selection to accommodate the popular opinion while weeding out the incompetents.

In the end, Zhang urged Fukuyama and the Chinese audiences to move beyond using the Western model as a reference point. He suggested that China in the reform decades essentially functioned as an open lab for experimentations on political, economic, social, and legal reform in its search for a sustainable universal model beyond the narrow confines of the United States or China. In other words, the Chinese have moved beyond emulating the U.S. model, which is itself in shambles. "The Chinese model might currently be the worst possible model, except for all the others," as Zhang puts it.

---

* It is worth mentioning that the person who called my attention to the exchange between Fukuyama and Zhang Weiwei was Ding Yun, a professor of Western philosophy and director of the Center for the Study of Intellectual History at Fudan University in Shanghai. A translator of Leo Strauss's work, Ding was also the faculty adviser to Tang Jie, the Fudan philosophy student who became an overnight hero to many patriotic youths when the anti-CNN video he made, "2008 China Stand Up," went viral on YouTube in April 2008.

He predicts that Western-style liberal democracy might actually be a brief phase instead of a final destination in human history.

Yet predictions have time and again proved futile in a rapidly evolving China. In March 2012, a spectacular corruption case involving murder and a potential cover-up in the party's highest echelons shook the very foundation of the party-state and laid bare the political struggle between the left/conservative and the right/liberal wings of the CCP. At the center of the scandal is Bo Xilai, a champion of the Chinese New Left who, until his dismissal in March, was party secretary of the southwestern city of Chongqing and had been predicted to ascend further in the once-a-decade leadership transition in the fall of 2012. A charismatic populist politician, Bo had garnered significant grassroots support for his reputation for having zero tolerance for inequality, corruption, and crime. The exposure of Bo's corruption was a huge blow to the Chinese New Left, which has advocated recentralization and a return to a more egalitarian socialist policy. The liberal camp of the Chinese intelligentsia and policy makers soon rallied behind Bo's rival, the premier Wen Jiabao, seizing the opportunity to push for what they saw as long-overdue political reform that would put the party in check under the rule of law and elections. Minxin Pei observes that a consensus among China's intelligentsia has emerged, calling for political reform that would reduce the power of the state and make the government accountable to its people.[5] The ultimate goal of this political reform is to breathe new air into economic reform, which has been stalled for quite some time. So Pei cheerfully predicts the arrival of liberal democracy in China.

Pei's prediction might prove too hasty. While it is the case that the left and the right have converged on the unsustainability of the status quo of authoritarian crony capitalism—which seems to have cast shadows on the existing China model—it is true also that both the Bo and the Hu-Wen administrations placed their bets on a strong central party-state in properly managing and distributing wealth and resources. The two political factions within the party are not that far apart in this regard. As the principle of state capitalism remains unchanged, the fundamentals of a Chinese model remain intact.

Meanwhile, there is a third ideological camp that has distanced itself from both the extreme left and the extreme right for their perceived irrelevance to Chinese culture and society and their alleged "blind" allegiance to Western models, the Marxist model on the left and the liberal democratic model on the right. As one doctoral student of Chinese philosophy (who was featured in the TV documentary on a Chinese classics book club I coproduced) told me, the third camp, which she comfortably inhabits, seeks wisdom and remedies from traditional Chinese culture, chiefly Confucianism. "Many disillusioned young intellectuals have turned to the Confucian thoughts for solutions. But, holding on to its official ideology of Marxist communism, the state is reluctant to endorse the grassroots conservative moment," she told me, referring to herself and her like-minded intellectuals as "conservative," for conserving Chinese cultural values as a counterforce to an onslaught of "Western cultural erosion." As I wrote in a piece on China's cultural war against the Western influence,[6] the effort to revive Confucianism and classical Chinese learning is nothing new among traditionalist Chinese scholars and cultural commentators. Over the past decade or two, they have actively participated in the ritual recitation of the classics, compelling Chinese youth to soak up traditional Chinese virtues and values. Responding to the demand for learning the classics in elementary education, Chinese universities have begun to train scholars of the Confucian classics. The first College of Chinese Classics was inaugurated in 2005 at the People's University in Beijing. Topics on CCTV's *The Lecture Room* mirror this trend. The turn to Chinese cultural tradition reflects an organic, bottom-up response to Chinese society's loss of moral grounding. As I commented in my piece, "Historically, the infiltration of the market and its profit logic into every fabric of a society has triggered society's protective mechanism in preserving its social and cultural integrity, through means of state legislation and other forms of societal intervention. What we witness in China is a spontaneous moral response to the shocks of a free market that threatens to tear apart China's moral fabric."[7]

Underlying Zhang's rhetoric and the rhetoric of China's left, right, and conservatives is the most important dynamic driving China's political discourse today—a confident nationalism that extols Chinese exceptionalism. Chinese exceptionalism lends domestic legitimacy to the Chinese state while also shaping its actions internationally. Historically, Chinese nationalism has driven transformative social movements from the May Fourth Movement to the Communist Revolution. As China tries to finesse its growing prominence on the world stage, the ardent nationalism of post-socialist China has periodically erupted on the streets of China, especially in reaction to perceived insults from Western media and governments. These seemingly contradictory forms of nationalism—one steeped in victimization and the other in confidence—fuel a Chinese exceptionalism as China's economy soars, providing legitimacy to the one-party rule that seems immured to change. China's furious development in the reform era has established it as arguably the world's most consequential nation. As China defines a new approach—a hybrid state capitalism that challenges the Western conviction linking a free market with democracy—the nouveau superpower is nevertheless not immune to the global economic crisis. Coupled with the Bo Xilai scandal, the country is showing signs of economic stagnation, which adds fuel to already widespread social distress. As Edward Wong of the *New York Times* put it, "It appears that the sense of triumphalism was, at best, premature, and perhaps seriously misguided."[8]

From Sage Leaders to the Desperadoes of CCTV

The Chinese tradition has always placed its bets on wise and dynamic rulers whose singular vision and devotion are trusted to be able to transcend any system, never mind the letdowns by Mao or Bo alike. In the case of CCTV, much credit has been given to Yang Weiguang, who presided over the expansion and commercialization of CCTV from the late 1980s to the 1990s. Yang initiated several watchdog newsmagazine programs that have had a profound impact on news reporting in China. Live broadcasting took hold under his reign, as did CCTV's international broadcasting. It is hard to match Yang's legacy, and his immediate successor, Zhao Huayong, received little recognition, though he capably led CCTV during its victorious Olympics reporting and oversaw several heavyweight programs, including *Rise of the Powerful Nations*, which emerged with his blessing. I do not suppose Zhao would be unanimously considered a wise ruler, which suggests that the Chinese appointment-based leadership selection can miss its target too, much like the election debacles in the United States. The tenure of Zhao's successor, Jiao Li, proved to be short-lived. As Zhao's legacy of anchoring CCTV with news awaits further assessment, a new CCTV president, Hu Zhanfan, came onboard in November 2011, entrusted with leading a new round of cultural cleansing of Western pollution. So CCTV soldiers on as both an extension and a result of China's media regulation at the service of the state and the market.

From the perspective of political control, media policy in China has been interventionist for several decades. The subservience of culture to politics, as well as the faith that media teach moral lessons rather than testing boundaries, has served as a fundamental tenet of the CCTV-China model. When it comes to law and regulation, spoken and written speeches by party leaders and senior government officials and internal documents issued by the Propaganda Department have more impact on media operations and development than statutes, rules, and normative documents. This rule-by-directive practice is built into the Chinese system of governance. The state government establishes laws, but the party apparatus ranks above the state government, and thus party directives trump everything else. For the media, this amounts to an ad hoc and informal regulatory practice that results in frequent, disruptive, and oftentimes contradictory regulatory fiddling. And for media professionals, it creates a climate of constant uncertainty and self-censorship.

The hybrid nature of CCTV as a state-controlled commercial enterprise grants the network certain leverage in content negotiation. CCTV is expected to be commercially successful while fostering political and social stability by constructing positive images of the party-state to harness popular endorsement for the government. Internationally, the network is urged to compete with transnational media corporations for the global flow of information and perspectives. These multiple functions put CCTV in a flexible position to negotiate and bargain with the state over control and regulation. Media censorship in China is both reactive and proactive, a process of negotiation among various interests and interest groups. Needless to say, issues that are politically tolerable and that resonate with citizens, such as popular nationalism, citizens' rights defense, corruption and abuse of power, environment, cultural contention, muckraking, and the like, can easily enter the public sphere. As revealed by the interviews recounted in this book, in areas that CCTV practitioners consider negotiable, they utilize various strategies and piece together strands of discourse that are receptive to the government so as to garner state support in advancing their own commercial and professional aspirations.

This complex and at times delicate "envelope-pushing" dance with the central authority performed by various CCTV practitioners is one component of CCTV that people tend to overlook. Yet CCTV is not an abstract entity. It is operated and shaped by the people who work there. Media professionals at CCTV have contributed to China's evolving state-society relationship even as censorship and political surveillance continue to rein in dissenting voices. While emphasizing state control and censorship, we frequently give little credit to either the real extent of information available or what media professionals do with it. The fluidity and complexity of the supposedly draconian CCTV reflect the complexity and fluidity of Chinese society at large. Yet celebrating subtle resistances does not suggest that one condones the selective honoring of public opinion by CCTV under the state directives. It is a consolation therefore that while sensitive topics are banned on state-controlled media, they do manage to find surreptitious and guerrilla-style existence through various transgressive tactics on the Chinese Internet. To this end, CCTV in its current configuration has largely become irrelevant to the young and educated population, which has opted for the more open cyberspace.

Rural people and lower- to middle-income urbanites continue to be CCTV's staple audiences, though the network has tried to attract young professionals by adding, since 2008, a slew of U.S. programs, such as *Desperate Housewives*, *24*, and *Lost*, to one of its high-definition cable channels. Unfortunately, the disgruntled youth paid scant attention to the network's extra effort on their behalf, as many of them have already given up on CCTV.

Meanwhile, CCTV's practitioners, veteran and young alike, are soldiering on. Depression seems rampant among the brightest and most ambitious CCTV practitioners, an occupational hazard for working under constant restrictions. As Hu Yong, an associate professor of journalism and communication at Peking University who used to work for CCTV, put it in his interview with an online publication: "The most depressing time during my career as a journalist was the few years when I worked at CCTV. We frequently took challenging tasks; they came thick and fast, but restrictions and limitations for reporting were present everywhere. Sometimes we had to race to make news before the order came down [to censor the news], and sometimes difficult things we had experienced in faraway locations were immediately made void by one order, or in the process of broadcasting the news the provincial 'public relations' people would stop it. The feelings of hardness and pain this caused are difficult to imagine for outsiders."[9]

Hu promptly left CCTV to work in new media and is now one of the best-known Chinese scholars on the topic. I interviewed him on camera while co-producing a TV documentary, *Google Versus China*, in January 2011. Hu expressed his dismay over Google's pulling out of the PRC search-engine market and is forthcoming in his displeasure with censorship and control. But he was optimistic about what the future holds for the Chinese Internet—though not for CCTV. Elsewhere, Hu paid tribute to the courage of his former fellow newspersons who continue to struggle to uphold the core values of journalism as they carry on for the mainstream media. He called his old comrades at CCTV "news desperadoes" of mainstream media and reminded us that *News Probe* did do a program about the collapsed schools after the Wenchuan earthquake, though it was eventually censored. Hu's former CCTV colleagues urged me to make sure the book recognized and was appreciative of the struggles people at CCTV had to endure day in and day out. In an interview, Hu quoted what CCTV host Zhang Quanling once said to him: "I hope you realize [that] we are struggling for survival in a highly pressured environment. Any old comrade who shakes his head at a program that's up for screening means that it won't go on air. The programs we send for approval, one in three are censored, or taken off."

In the end, this book is not about CCTV as an abstract state propaganda machine, but about the various individuals who toil at CCTV on a daily basis and who graciously shared with me their take on CCTV, China, and the world. Perhaps a bit of Stockholm syndrome is at work here, but I daresay I came away with a refreshing sense of awe and amazement at their Sisyphean tasks and with less cynicism than I'd started with. It is tempting to be critical from afar, but people who work within the system have nowhere to retreat to, aside from plowing ahead with as much dignity intact as possible, often coming away bruised. The movers and shakers at CCTV and their fellow Chinese media professionals are the ones who will ultimately determine the final shape of a Chinese model.

NOTES

Introduction

Bruce Robinson contributed significantly to some of the themes explored here in the introduction.

1. See Zhang Xiaoling, "Control, Resistance, and Negotiation: How the Chinese Media Carve Out Greater Space for Autonomy?" (paper presented at the International Forum for Contemporary Chinese Studies Inaugural Conference at Nottingham, November 19–21, 2008), http://www.nottingham.ac.uk/cpi/documents/discussion -papers/discussion-paper-47-media-control-resistance.pdf.

2. Shi Tongyu, "The Historical Significance and Communication Value of CCTV's Live Broadcast on Earthquake Rescue Efforts," *Journal of Chinese Radio and Television*, November 2008.

3. See Robert W. McChesney, *The Political Economy of Media: Enduring Issues, Emerging Dilemmas* (New York: Monthly Review Press, 2008); and *Rich Media, Poor Democracy: Communication Politics in Dubious Times* (New York: The New Press, 2000).

4. Meredith Jessup, "Soros: Communist China Has 'Better Functioning Government' than the U.S.," The Blaze, November 16, 2010, http://www.theblaze.com/stories/ soros-communist-china-has-better-functioning-government-than-the-u-s/.

5. Ron Arnold, "Why Did Big Green Follow George Soros to China?" *Washington Examiner*, January 6, 2011, http://washingtonexaminer.com/opinion/op-eds/2011/01/ why-did-big-green-follow-george-soros-china.

6. Mark Leonard, *What Does China Think?* (New York: PublicAffairs, 2008), 94.

7. Cristian Segura, "Beijing Hires a Media Guru," *Asia Times*, October 10, 2009, http://www.atimes.com/atimes/China/KJ10Ad02.html.

8. Lingjie Wang. "China Cable Television Market Assessment and Forecast to 2012," *Industry Report*, 2008, http://www.screendigest.com/reports/08chinacabletv/ 08chinacable-pdf/view.html.

9. See "China Consumer: China Multi-faceted Stage: Television," China Knowledge, 2006, http://www.chinaknowledge.com/Market/Book-ChinaConsumer.aspx? subchap=4&content=13.

1. Television as Cultural Control in China

1. Liu Shiying, *Yang Weiguang's CCTV Era* (Beijing: China Citic Press), 2007.

2. Journalism studies was first offered in the Chinese Department at Peking University in 1952. In 1955 this program was merged with a new Journalism Department

at Remin University. Yang began his studies at Peking University in 1957 and graduated from the Remin program in 1961.

3. Junhao Hong, *The Internationalization of Television in China: The Evolution of Ideology, Society, and Media since the Reform* (Westport, CT: Praeger, 1998).

4. Tony Rayns, *King of Children and the New Chinese Cinema* (London: Faber and Faber, 1989), 30.

5. Richard Curt Kraus, *The Party and the Arty: The New Politics of Culture* (Lanham, MD: Rowman & Littlefield, 2004), 11.

6. George Semsel, ed., *Chinese Film Theory: A Guide to the New Era* (New York: Praeger, 1990), xiv.

7. Anne-Marie Brady, *Marketing Dictatorship: Propaganda and Thought Work in Contemporary China* (Lanham, MD: Rowman & Littlefield, 2009), 72.

8. Ibid., 71.

9. "Three Represents," from the English website of the Seventeenth National Congress of the Communist Party of China (emphasis added), http://english.people.com.cn/90002/92169/92211/6274616.html.

10. Ying Zhu, *Television in Post-Reform China: Serial Dramas, Confucian Leadership and Global Television Market* (London: Routledge, 2008).

11. See "Chinese Communist Party Calls on Media to Toe the Party Line," *Taipei Times*, October 26, 2006, accessed April 22, 2006, www.taipeitimes.com/News/world/archives/2006/10/26/2003333450.

12. As David Shambaugh reported in his piece "China Flexes Its Soft Power," *New York Times*, June 7, 2010, http://www.nytimes.com/2010/06/08/opinion/08iht-edshambaugh.html, though China's image in Africa and Pakistan is consistently positive, its image in Asia, North America, and Latin America is neutral to poor and across Europe strongly negative.

13. Ibid.

14. Ibid.

15. Quoted in Zhang Xiaoling, "Control, Resistance, and Negotiation: How the Chinese Media Carve Out a Greater Space for Antonomy?" (paper presented at the International Forum for Contemporary Chinese Studies Inaugural Conference at Nottingham, November 19–21, 2008), http://www.nottingham.ac.uk/cpi/documents/discussion-papers/discussion-paper-47-media-control-resistance.pdf.

16. Zhang Xiaoling, "Breaking News, Media Coverage and 'Citizen's Right to Know' in China," *Journal of Contemporary China* 16 (2007): 538.

17. Ibid.

18. Ibid.

19. Cristian Segura, "Beijing Hires a Media Guru," *AsianTimes*, October 10, 2009, http://www.atimes.com/atimes/China/KJ10Ad02.html.

20. Quoted in Zhang Xiaoling, "From Totalitarianism to Hegemony: The Reconfiguration of the Party-State and the Transformation of Chinese Communication," *Journal of Contemporary China* 20, no. 68 (2011): 103–15.

21. See Michael Keane, *China's New Creative Clusters: Governance, Human Capital, and Investment* (London: Routledge, 2011).

22. Yuezhi Zhao, *Media, Market and Democracy in China: Between the Party Line and the Bottom Line* (Urbana: University of Illinois Press, 1998), 2.

23. Ibid.

24. Guo Zhenzhi, *The History of China Television* (Beijing: Culture and Art Publication House, 1997), 55.

25. Wei Qian, *Politics, Market and Media: Research on the Institutional Transformation of China's Television* (Zhengzhou: Henan People's Publish House, 2002), 80.

26. Yuezhi Zhao, *Communication in China: Political Economy, Power, and Conflict* (Lanham, MD: Rowman & Littlefield, 2008), 26.

27. For a detailed discussion, see Yik Chan Chin, *Television Regulation and Media Policy in China* (MS reviewed for Routledge).

28. Li Tieying, "Speech Given in the Meeting with the CCTV's Staffs" (1995), in General Office of SARFT, ed., *The Important Documents of Broadcasting and Film Work 1995, Beijing: The State Administration of Radio, Film and Television* (in Chinese) (Beijing: SARFT, 2000), 254–59; Chin, *Television Regulation and Media Policy in China*.

29. Li, "Speech Given in the Meeting with the CCTV's Staffs," 255.

30. Ibid.

31. Ibid., 257.

32. Sun Jiazheng, report given at the national broadcasting and film working conference (1995), in General Office of SARFT, *The Important Documents of Broadcasting and Film Work 1995*, 273–74.

33. Ibid., 277.

34. Guo Zhenzhi, "WTO, Media Industrialization and Chinese Television" (paper presented at the Transnational Media Corporations and National Media Systems: China after Entry into the World Trade Organization Conference, Bellagio Study and Conference Center, Rockefeller Foundation, Italy, May 17–21, 2004).

35. MRFT, "Several Important Problems and Opinions about our Country's Present Broadcasting Development," in *Guidebook for Decision Making* (Beijing: MRFT, 1996), 21–24.

36. Ibid.

37. State Council Decree No. 228, "Regulations Governing the Administrations of Radio and Television," November 8, 1997, cited in Yik Chan Chin, "The Nation-State in a Globalising Media Environment: China's Regulatory Policies on Transnational Television Drama Flow," World Association for Christian Communications, http://www.waccglobal.org/en/20033-china-media-industries-and-the-market/630-The-nation-state-in-a-globalising-media-environment-Chinas-regulatory-policies-on-transnational-television-drama-flow-.html.

38. MRFT, "To Protect the Systemic Development of the Broadcasting Sector by Law: The MRFT's Official Answers Journalists' Questions Regarding to the Release of Regulations Governing the Administration of Radio and Television," in *Guidebook for Decision Making* (Beijing: MRFT, 1997), 6–7.

39. Xu Guangchun, "Speech Given in the National Meeting of the Chiefs of Provincial TV and Radio Stations" (1998), in General Office of SARFT, ed., *The Important Documents of Broadcasting and Film Work 1998* (Beijing: SARFT, 2000), 262.

2. A View from the Top: Managing the Commercial Revolution at CCTV

1. David M. Lampton, *The Three Faces of Chinese Power: Might, Money, and Minds* (Berkeley: University of California Press, 2008), 138.

2. See encyclopedia entry on Zhao on Baidu, accessed April 22, 2010, http://baike .baidu.com/view/934165.htm (in Chinese).

3. Xu Guangchun, "Speech Given at the National Radio and Television Propaganda and Chiefs of Two Stations Meetings" (2000), in General Office of SARFT, ed., *The Important Documents of Broadcasting and Film Work 2000* (Beijing: SARFT, 2001), 439–54.

4. SARFT no. 585, "Notice on Problems of Approving Broadcasting and Film Conglomerates," September 18, 1998, cited in Yik Chan Chin, "From the Local to the Global: China's Television Policy in Transition," 221–40, in *Internationalization of the Chinese TV Sector*, ed. Manfred Kops and Stefan Ollig (Berlin: Lit Verlag, 2007).

5. Xu Guangchun, "Speech Given at the National Meeting of the Chiefs of Broadcasting and Film Bureaus" (2000), in General Office of SARFT, *The Important Documents of Broadcasting and Film Work 2000*, 459–78. For detailed discussions, see Yik Chan Chin's fascinating manuscript *Television Regulation and Media Policy in China*, which I reviewed for Routledge.

6. Xu Guangchun, "Concluding Speech Given at the National Meeting of the Chiefs of Broadcasting and Film Bureaus," *Guidebook for Decision Making* 9 (2002): 1–7.

7. Guo Zhenzhi, "Playing the Game by the Rules? Television Regulation around China's Entry into WTO," *Javnost/The Public* 10, no. 4 (2003): 5–18.

8. SARFT, "Opinions on Improving the Broadcasting and Film Industry Development," 2003, http://www.sarft.gov.cn/manage/publishfile/21/1568.html.

9. Zhu Hong, "To Strengthen China's Broadcasting and Film Industries through Reform: Answering the Journalist Questions of the American *Wall Street Journal* by SARFT Spokesman Zhu Hong," 2004, access no longer available, http://www.sarft.gov .cn/publishfile/35/1582.html.

10. Junhao Hong, "CCTV in the Reform Years: A New Model for China's Television?" in Ying Zhu and Chris Berry, eds., *TV China* (Bloomington: Indiana University Press, 2009).

11. Information from *China Media Intelligence* 1, no. 11 (2001).

12. Bo Xilai's removal from the party post was seen as the defeat of the anti-market New Left in its intense fight against the pro-market liberal faction within the CCP leading up to the Eighteenth Party Congress in fall 2012, with an anticipated leadership transition.

13. Description on Chinese embassy's website, accessed June 22, 2011, http:// np.china-embassy.org/eng/Culture/wh/t167618.htm.

14. Wanning Sun, "Dancing with Chains: Significant Moments on China Central Television," *International Journal of Cultural Studies* 10, no. 2 (2007): 198.

15. Hui Zhang, "The Internet in China: A Force for Democracy or Oppression?" UCLA Asia Institute, April 6, 2007, http://www.international.ucla.edu/asia/article .asp?parentid=67152.

16. Ibid.

17. Janice Xu, "Morality Discourse in the Marketplace: Narratives in the Chinese Television News Magazine *Oriental Horizon*," *Journalism Studies* 1, no. 4 (2000): 637–47.

18. Ibid.

19. For a detailed discussion, see Zhang, Xiaoling, "Reading Between the Headlines: SARS, Focus and TV Current Affairs Programs in China," *Media, Culture, and Society* 28, no. 5 (2006): 715–37.

20. Zhengmin Yuan and Xudong Wang, "The Development of Focus," in Guo Zhenzhi and Zhao Lifang, eds., *Focus on the Focus*, 4–8 (Beijing: Tsinghua University Press, 2004).

21. Sun Jiazhen, "Make Efforts to Run Well the News Commentary Program, Enhance the Level of the Guidance of Public Opinion," *TV Research* 10 (1995): 4–10.

22. Yang Weiguang, "Be Worthy of the Great Trust from the Party and the People, Offer More and Better Programs," *TV Research* 10 (1996): 4–7. Yang's remarks in Chinese were translated and quoted in Zhang's Xiaoling article "Reading Between the Headlines"; Zhang's translation is modified here.

23. Quoted in Zhang, "Reading Between the Headlines," 731.

24. Ibid.

25. Ibid.

26. Ibid.

27. Yuezhi Zhao, *Communication in China: Political Economy, Power, and Conflict* (Lanham, MD: Rowman & Littlefield, 2008), 328.

28. Zhang, "Reading Between the Headlines," 733.

29. Ibid.

30. Liu Haibei, "How Will Focus Come out of Plateau?" *TV Research* 4 (2002): 32–34.

31. Lampton, *Three Faces of Chinese Power*, 144.

32. Zhongdang Pan, Chin-Chuan Lee, Joseph Man Chan, and Clement K. Y. So, "Hyping and Repairing the News Paradigm in the Age of Global Media Spectacles," *China Media Research* 1, no. 1 (2005).

3. Making the News

1. Haiqing Yu, "Mediation Journalism in Chinese Television Double-Time Narrations of SARS," in Ying Zhu and Chris Berry, eds., *TV China* (Bloomington: Indiana University Press, 2009), 142.

2. For a detailed discussion, see Yu, "Mediation Journalism in Chinese Television Double-Time Narrations of SARS."

3. Haiqing Yu, *Media and Cultural Transformation in China* (London: Routledge, 2011), 96.

4. Ibid.

5. See David Bandurski, "Jousting with China's Monsters," March 6, 2009, accessed April 6, 2009, http://www.feer.com/essays/2009/march/media-censorship -escalates-in-asia.

6. For a detailed discussion, see Yu, "Mediation Journalism in Chinese Television Double-Time Narrations of SARS."

7. Stanley Rosen, "Seeking Appropriate Behavior under a Socialist Market Economy: An Analysis of Debates and Controversies Reported in the Beijing Youth Daily," in Chin-Chuan Lee, ed., *Power, Money, and Media: Communication Patterns and Bureaucratic Control in Cultural China* (Evanston, IL: Northwestern University Press, 2000), 152–78.

8. Chin-Chuan Lee, "China's Journalism: The Emancipatory Potential of Social Theory," *Journalism Studies* 1, no. 4 (2000): 572.

9. Yu, "Meditation Journalism in Chinese Television Double-Time Narrations of SARS," 130.

10. "China's Journalism: The Emancipatory Potential of Social Theory," 572.

11. Zhang gave a similar interview to Li Mu, who reported it on *China, National, Society* (blog): "China's Top Muckraker Wants to Tell It Like It Is," http://webcache .googleusercontent.com/search?q=cache:0PifTF0V2DYJ:josephbosco.com/wow2004/ archive/2005_11_01_wowarchive.html+CHINA,+NATIONAL,+SOCIETY:+China's +Top+Muckraker+Wants+To+Tell+It+Like+It+Is+By+Li+Mu+(Lianne)&cd=1&hl =en&ct=clnk&gl=us&client=safari.

12. Zhang's term—using a common Chinese translation of "the fourth estate," what we commonly refer to as news media.

13. The Central Party School in Beijing educates medium- and high-ranking party officials.

14. David M. Lampton, *The Three Faces of Chinese Power: Might, Money, and Minds* (Berkeley: University of California Press, 2008), 216.

15. Jingrong Tong and Colin Sparks, "Investigative Journalism in China," *Journalism Studies* 10, no. 3 (2009): 337–52.

4. Delivering the News: Profiles of Three News Anchors

1. Not surprisingly, other media organizations have followed CCTV's lead in "anchoring" their operations with news. Notably, China Central Radio and selected regional cable stations such as Zhejiang Satellite adopted the same approach in the summer of 2009. Shanghai-based Dragon TV pushed forward a similar but more enumerated series of reforms aimed at "anchoring with news programs, prospering with culture programs, and popularizing with cinema and TV dramas."

2. Wang Qian, "CCTV to Revamp Flagship Program," *China Daily*, June 10, 2009, http://www.chinadaily.com.cn/cndy/2009-06/10/content_8265952.htm.

3. Sky Canaves, "CCTV News Broadcast to Be 'Less CCTV,'" *Wall Street Journal*, June 10, 2009, http://blogs.wsj.com/chinarealtime/2009/06/10/cctv-news-broadcast -to-be-less-cctv/.

4. Peter C. Pugsley and Jia Gao, "Emerging Powers of Influence: The Rise of the Anchor in Chinese Television," *International Communication Gazette* 69, no. 5 (2007): 451–66.

5. In June 2008, rioters torched a police building and vehicles in Weng'an, a small town in southwest China, in unrest triggered by allegations of a cover-up over a girl's

death. The Shishou incident refers to a riot in the city of Shishou in Hubei Province in central China, which happened on June 19–21, 2009. The riot was the result of dubious circumstances surrounding the death of a young chef of a hotel owned by a local official rumored to be linked to illegal drug trafficking. Although police ruled the chef's death a suicide, accounts differed on what really occurred. Angered by what they saw as cronyism and lack of transparency in how the city's top officials handled the tragedy, crowds started gathering outside the hotel and soon clashed with the police, triggering a mass riot involving more than forty thousand people and ten thousand police officers. Six police vans and fire trucks were smashed and the hotel was burned down. Allegations were widespread on the Internet that the co-owners of the hotel are family members of the mayor and head of the local police, the hotel was used as an illegal center for drug trafficking, and the victim was murdered when he threatened to expose the illicit activities there. The local authorities cut off Internet connections in the area, but many users bypassed censorship and were able to relay messages through services such as Twitter. In the end, the state-run Ministry of Public Security and Tongji Medical Institute carried out an autopsy of the body, confirming that the young man committed suicide. In covering the story, Bai took the view that the failure of the government and mainstream media in providing timely and transparent information led to widespread rumors via the Internet, which escalated the tension, causing unnecessary violence. Bai broached the topic in his evening news program.

6. Pugsley and Gao have more descriptive impressions of Jing in their piece "Emerging Powers of Influence: The Rise of the Anchor in Chinese Television."

7. Wanning Sun, "The Politics of Compassion: Journalism, Class Formation, and Social Change in China," *WACC: Media Development* 3 (2001), accessed October 1, 2009, www.wacc.org.uk/wacc/publications/media_development/archive/2001_3/the_politics_of_compassion_journalism_class_formation_and_social_change_in_china.

8. Shenzhen is the Special Economic Zone city bordering Hong Kong in Guangdong Province.

9. Joel Martinsen, "CCTV Cancels a Talk Show and Shifts Its Focus Toward Entertainment," *Danwei*, September 25, 2009, http://www.danwei.org/tv/shihua_shishuo_gets_cancelled.php.

10. Yu Shi, "The Rise of China's Media Supermarket: An Appraisal of Cultural Imperialism's Relevance to the Chinese TV Industry," *International Journal of Communication* 2 (2008):1199–1225.

11. Quoted in a report, "Cui Yongyuan and His Long March," CRIEnglish.com, August 6, 2007, accessed August 9, 2009, http://english1.cri.cn/4406/2007/08/06/1581@258136.htm.

12. From a post, "Han Han on Google's Withdrawal from China," http://www.thatwrong.com/497.html (post no longer available).

13. Tom Downey, "China's Cyberposse," *New York Times*, March 3, 2010, http://www.nytimes.com/2010/03/07/magazine/07Human-t.html?pagewanted=all.

14. "Cui Yongyuan and His Long March."

15. Even during this relatively open period of news coverage, self-censorship was still instinctively practiced.

16. Xiangling Zhang, "Breaking News, Media Coverage and 'Citizen's Right to Know' in China," *Journal of Contemporary China* 16, no. 53 (November 2007): 535–45.

5. *Rise of the Powerful Nations* and the Finance and Economics Channel

1. Quoted in Edward Wang, "Rise of the Great Powers—Rise of China? Challenges of the Advancement of Global History in the People's Republic of China," *Journal of Contemporary China* 19, no. 64 (2010): 273–89.

2. Ibid.

3. Ibid.

4. Ibid.

5. Ibid.

6. See "The Rise of the Great Nations—A Chinese Documentary," November 28, 2006, Sun Bin's blog, accessed November 11, 2010, http://sun-bin.blogspot.com/2006/11/rise-of-great-nations-chinese.html.

7. See "TV Docu Stimulates More Open Attitude to History, China, the World," *People's Daily Online*, November 26, 2006, http://english.people.com.cn/200611/26/eng20061126_325264.html.

8. KNJYG, "Strongly Recommending *Rise of the Great Powers*," Tianya Club, November 17, 2006, http://www.tianya.cn/publicforum/content/no01/1/285328.shtml.

9. See "The Rise of Nations," *EastWestNorthSouth* blog, http://www.zonaeuropa.com/20061128_1.htm.

10. Tom Plate, "Tom Plate and Jeffrey Cole Interview Lee Kuan Yew," *AsiaMedia*, October 9, 2009, http://www.asiamedia.ucla.edu/article.asp?parentid=79541.

11. Joseph Kahn, "China, Shy Giant, Shows Signs of Shedding Its False Modesty," *New York Times*, December 9, 2006, http://www.nytimes.com/2006/12/09/world/asia/09china.html. Kahn writes, "President Hu Jintao set off an internal squabble two years ago when he began using the term 'peaceful rise' to describe his foreign policy goals. He soon dropped the term in favor of the tamer sounding 'peaceful development.' Yet this tradition of modesty has begun to fade, replaced by a growing confidence that China's rise is not fleeting and that the country needs to do more to define its objectives."

12. Bin Zhao, "Mouthpiece or Money-Spinner? The Double Life of Chinese Television in the Late 1990s," *International Journal of Cultural Studies* 2, no. 3 (December 1999): 291–305.

13. Quoted in Michael Keane, "Television's New Engines," *Television New Media* March 9, no. 2 (2008): 155–69.

14. Beijing TV's weekly lifestyle program *Jojo Good Living*, which debuted in 2002 and later became available nationwide on cable television's Tourism Channel, has been active in promoting Western household items. The show has tie-ins with McCormick spices, Fissler pots and pans, Fanini cabinets, Starbucks, and Toto toilets, among others. Provincial and local television stations are more willing than CCTV to allow such commercial practices.

6. Xia Jun and Chen Xiaoqing: Documentarians and Critics Alike

1. William A Callahan, *China: The Pessoptimist Nation* (Oxford: Oxford University Press, 2010).

2. Jing Wang, "He Shang and the Paradoxes of Chinese Enlightenment," *Bulletin of Concerned Asian Scholars* 23 (1991).

3. Ibid.

4. Miles Menander Dawson, ed., *The Ethics of Confucius* (Honolulu: University Press of the Pacific, 2002).

5. Limin Liang, "Going Live: News Innovation amid Constraints in the Chinese Coverage of the Iraq War" (paper presented at the annual meeting of the Association for Education in Journalism and Mass Communication, the Renaissance, Washington, DC, August 8, 2007).

6. Ibid.

7. The Cultivated and the Vulgar: Game Shows and Lectures

1. Jim Yardley, "A King Pushes the Limits, Flashily but Gently," *New York Times*, January 21, 2006, http://www.nytimes.com/2006/01/21/international/asia/21li.html?ex=1295499600&en=fe7d16f8f7c2a431&ei=5090&partner=rssuserland&emc=rss.

2. "Li Yong vs. Shaanxi," Danwei, January 17, 2007, accessed April 10, 2011, http://www.danwei.org/tv/li_yong_vs_shaanxi_1.php.

3. Yardley, "A King Pushes the Limits."

4. Ibid.

5. The other three classics are *Journey to the West, The Water Margin*, and *The Three Kingdoms*.

6. It is hinted that Qin Keqing hung herself.

7. Zhang Rui, "Betting on the Red Mansions," China.org.cn, December 4, 2005, http://www.china.org.cn/english/culture/151884.htm.

8. Mei Xinlin and Ge Yonghai, "Cultural Deficiencies in 'Second-Hand Reading' of the Classics and the Reconstruction of the Public Intellectual Sphere," *Social Sciences in China* 29, no. 3 (2008): 68–82.

9. See the post about Yi on Xiamen University's website, May 9, 2009, http://ice.xmu.edu.cn/english/showletter.aspx?news_id=1874.

10. Joel Martinsen, "Yu Dan: Defender of Traditional Culture, Force for Harmony," Danwei, May 8, 2007, http://www.danwei.org/scholarship_and_education/yu_dan_defender_of_traditional.php.

11. Ibid.

12. Zhu Linyong, "Words of Wisdom," *China Daily*, November 27, 2006, http://www.chinadaily.com.cn/cndy/2006-11/27/content_743344.htm.

13. Ibid.

8. "Going Out" Via CCTV-International

1. For a detailed report on the plan, see Pascale Trouillud, "China Unveils Its Global Media Ambitions," *Brisbane Times*, October 11, 2009, http://news.brisbane times.com.au/breaking-news-world/china-unveils-its-global-media-ambitions-2009 1011-gs41.html.

2. See John Jirik, "Making News in the People's Republic of China: The Case of CCTV-9" (PhD diss., University of Texas at Austin, 2008) http://repositories.lib .utexas.edu/handle/2152/3907?show=full.

3. For a detailed discussion, see Yik Chan Chin's MS *Television Regulation and Media Policy in China*.

4. Jirik, "Making News in the People's Republic of China," 103.

5. Guo Ji, "Freedom of Speech and the Media's Responsibility," *Qiushi*, August 16, 2009. Translation by David Bandurski of the China Media Project, http://www .uschina.usc.edu/w_usct/showarticle.aspx?articleID=10412&AspxAutoDetectCookie Support=1.

6. Limin Liang, "Going Live: News Innovation amid Constraints in the Chinese Coverage of the Iraq War" (paper presented at the annual meeting of the Association for Education in Journalism and Mass Communication, the Renaissance, Washington, DC, August 8, 2007, http://www.allacademic.com/meta/p204177_index.html.

7. Ibid.

8. Tania Branigan, "Chinese State TV Targets 300m Russian Viewers: Engagement with Wider World Aimed at Countering 'Western Bias,' " *The Guardian*, September 11, 2009, http://www.guardian.co.uk/world/2009/sep/11/china-tv-targets-russia.

9. Challenging CCTV's Domestic Dominance: Hunan Satellite Television and Phoenix TV

1. Yong Zhong, "Competition Is Getting Real in Chinese TV: A Moment of Confrontation between CCTV and HSTV," *Media International Australia*, no. 124 (August 2007): 68–82.

2. Yik-Chan Chin, *Television Regulation and Media Policy in China* (MS).

3. Ibid.

4. Wu Mei and Guo Zhenzhi, "Globalization, National Culture and the Search for Identity: A Chinese Dilemma," World Association for Christian Communication, http://waccglobal.org/en/20061-celebrating-cultural-diversity/564-Globalization -national-culture-and-the-search-for-identity-A-Chinese-dilem ma.html.

5. On the other hand, as local players move to compete with CCTV at the national level, it must use Mandarin.

6. David Barboza, "Hunan TV Cancels the Bland to Bring the Offbeat to China," *New York Times*, November 27, 2005, http://www.nytimes.com/2005/11/27/business/ worldbusiness/27iht-hunan.html.

7. Yong, "Competition Is Getting Real in Chinese TV."

8. Peter Feuilherade, "China Threatens Reality TV Crackdown," BBC Monitoring, January 16, 2007, http://news.bbc.co.uk/2/hi/asia-pacific/6263285.stm.

9. Ibid.

10. Yong, "Competition Is Getting Real in Chinese TV."

11. When I gave him a sneak preview of this yet-to-be-published interview, a fellow academic and TV scholar, Michael Keane, was enraged by Ouyang's complaint about cloning: "This is an incredible statement which needs to be commented on: they ripped everything off from international companies: I was approached by a copyright lawyer in 2007 in Beijing to assist in trying to bring action against Hunan."

12. See "Shanda Forms a RMB600 Million Joint Venture with Hunan Broadcasting and Television Group, China eCapital Advised the Transaction," press release posted on China E Capital, November 13, 2009, http://www.china-ecapital.com/content/2010/12-23/152943240.html.

10. *Half the Sky* and Women's Programming

1. Patrick E. Tyler, "Hillary Clinton, in China, Details Abuse of Women," *New York Times*, September 6, 1995, http://www.nytimes.com/1995/09/06/world/hillary-clinton-in-china-details-abuse-of-women.html?pagewanted=all.

11. The New Nationalism: Covering the 2008 Beijing Olympics

1. Quoted in Zhongdang Pan, Chin-Chuan Lee, Joseph Man Chan, and Clement K.Y. So, "Hyping and Repairing the News Paradigm in the Age of Global Media Spectacles," *China Media Research* 1, no. 1 (2005).

2. The video can be viewed on YouTube: http://www.youtube.com/watch?v=MSTYhYkASsA.

3. Xu Wu, *Chinese Cyber Nationalism: Evolution, Characteristics, and Implications* (Lanham, MD: Lexington Books, 2007).

4. "The Tailspin on Tibet: The Chinese Response to Foreign Media Coverage of the 3.14 Unrest," *China Beat*, March 27, 2008, http://www.thechinabeat.org/?p=78.

5. See "Who Is Really Behind the Tibet Riots?" *China Digital Times*, March 29, 2008, http://chinadigitaltimes.net/2008/03/who-is-really-behind-the-tibet-riots/.

6. Quoted in Simon Montlake, "China Relishes Olympics Legacy," *Christian Science Monitor*, August 9, 2009, http://www.csmonitor.com/layout/set/print/content/view/print/250378.

7. See Qian Gang, "Guidance, Supervision, Reform, Freedom: Plotting the Direction of Chinese Media through an Analysis of the All-Important Buzzword," translated by David Bandurski, July 13, 2005, *China Media Project*, http//cmp.hku.hk/2005/07/13/33/.

Conclusion: China Central Television and the Chinese Model

1. From Alice Xin Liu, "Hu Yong Interview: The Digital Age, Orwell's 'Newspeak' and Chinese Media," Danwei, April 16, 2009, http://www.danwei.org/media/hu_yong_interview.php.

2. For a detailed report, see Willy Lam, "China Unveils Its New Worldview," *Asia Times*, December 11, 2009, http://www.atimes.com/atimes/China/KL11Ad01.html.

3. Ibid.

4. Cai Yiqun, "Francis Fukuyama: Japan Needs to Face a China Century," January 19, 2010, http://218.87.136.37/szb/blog/u/9/archives/2010/48.html (in Chinese).

5. Minxin Pei, "Intellectual Renaissance: Signs of a New Tiananmen in China," *The Diplomat*, April 4, 2012, http://the-diplomat.com/2012/04/04/signs-of-a-new -tiananmen-in-china/.

6. Ying Zhu, "The Cultivated and the Vulgar: China's Culture War," *Asian Creative Transformations*, April 2, 2012, http://www.creativetransformations.asia/2012/04/the -cultivated-and-the-vulgar-chinas-cultural-war/.

7. Ibid.

8. Edward Wong, "China's Growth Slows, and Its Political Model Shows Limits," *New York Times*, May 10, 2012, http://www.nytimes.com/2012/05/11/world/asia/ chinas-unique-economic-model-gets-new-scrutiny.html.

9. From Liu, "Hu Yong Interview."

INDEX

advertising, 146, 203, 217, 218, 222. *See also* commercials
"advocate" stories, 42
Ai Zhisheng, 29, 170
Al Jazeera, 2, 4, 16, 55, 194
All Together, 170
Amanpour, Christiane, 246–47
American Idol, 149, 150, 198, 200
anchorpersons. *See* news anchors
Anhui, 129, 241
Anhui Satellite TV, 37, 129, 198
Analects of Confucius, 162–66
Annales School, 132
Anti-CNN, 246
AOL Time Warner, 172, 195
The Apprentice, 110
Arabic Channel (CCTV-A), 173
architecture, 8
Arnett, Peter, 184
art, 14, 215
Arts Channel. *See* CCTV-3 (Comprehensive Arts Channel)
Asia Today, 75
Asia TV, 39, 40
Australia, 175

Bai Yansong, 59, 78–87, 148, 167–68, 190, 228, 238
  called "bully," 86, 177
  on CCTV-1 income, 203
  on "going out," 82, 83, 258
  recruiting and hiring of, 34, 41
  on Shishou riot, 84, 273n5
  target of nationalists, 245
  Yang Rui on, 190–92
Baidu, 213, 215
bankruptcy law, 56–57
bans, 141, 264
  of commercial activities, 98
  of Dong Qian, 86
  of foreign journalists, 252
  of nonstandard Mandarin programs, 197
  of *River Elegy,* 119
  of satellite dishes, 195
  talent-show related, 199, 200, 201

BBC, 4, 16, 19, 55, 169, 171, 175, 176
  credibility, 140
  Hong Kong handover coverage, 50
  Yang Rui opinion/experience, 184, 188
Beat the Mic, 207
Beijing TV, 13, 120, 124, 127, 274
Beijing Youth Record, 61
bias. *See* media bias
Blind Shaft, 248
Bo Xilai, 39, 86, 87, 96, 123, 261, 263, 270n12
Bo Yibo, 39
book publishing, 159, 161, 164, 166, 205
bootlegging (copyright). *See* piracy (copyright)
Bourdieu, Pierre, 54
boycotts, 86, 245, 249
Brady, Anne-Marie, 15, 176
Britain. *See* Great Britain
Broken Ice, 70
bullying by interviewers, 86, 177, 179, 192, 214
Business Bridge, 110
Business Television, 110

Cafferty, Jack, 245–46
Cai Jing, 93, 99
Carrefour, 86, 245, 249
cartoons and cartoon channels, 37, 40
CCP. *See* Communist Party of China (CCP)
CCTV-1, 22, 55, 59, 69, 75, 96, 219
  income, 203
  Olympics coverage, 240, 252
  Yang Rui on, 191
  Zhang Yue on, 225, 227
CCTV-2 (Finance and Economics Channel), 37, 109–13, 118, 119, 240, 252
  Jing Yidan role, 87, 88–89
  Li Yong role, 145
CCTV-3 (Comprehensive Arts Channel), 111, 143, 149
CCTV-4 (International Channel), 32, 75, 138, 140, 143, 144, 170–72, 174

CELEBRATING 20 YEARS OF
INDEPENDENT PUBLISHING

Thank you for reading this book published by The New Press. The New Press is a nonprofit, public interest publisher celebrating its twentieth anniversary in 2012. New Press books and authors play a crucial role in sparking conversations about the key political and social issues of our day.

We hope you enjoyed this book and that you will stay in touch with The New Press. Here are a few ways to stay up to date with our books, events, and the issues we cover:

- Sign up at www.thenewpress.com/subscribe to receive updates on New Press authors and issues and to be notified about local events
- Like us on Facebook: www.facebook.com/newpressbooks
- Follow us on Twitter: www.twitter.com/thenewpress

Please consider buying New Press books for yourself; for friends and family; or to donate to schools, libraries, community centers, prison libraries, and other organizations involved with the issues our authors write about.

The New Press is a 501(c)(3) nonprofit organization. You can also support our work with a tax-deductible gift by visiting www.thenewpress.com/donate.